Walter

GW00493667

CHRISTIAN LIVING TODAY

Bill Cosgrave

Christian Living Today

ESSAYS IN MORAL AND PASTORAL THEOLOGY

the columba press

First published in 2001 by
the columba press
55A Spruce Avenue, Stillorgan Industrial Park,
Blackrock, Co Dublin

Cover by Bill Bolger
Origination by The Columba Press
Printed in Ireland by Colour Books Ltd, Dublin
ISBN 1 85607 323 8

The publisher gratefully acknowledges the use of the following material: Chapter 1, 'Models of the Christian Moral Life' is an expanded version of my article of the same title in *The Furrow*, September1983, pp 560-573; Chapter 3, 'Our Emotional Life and Moral Living' is an expanded version of my article 'Our Emotional Life: its contribution to right living', *The Furrow*, May 1998, pp 270 -281. The second half of this chapter is a revised version of my article 'Anger and After', *Intercom*, November 1994, pp 16-19; Chapter 5 appeared substantially as three articles in *Word*, Divine Word Missionaries, Donamon, in March, April & May 2000; Chapter 6, 'A Christian Understanding of Sexuality' is a revised and significantly expanded version of my article of the same title, *The Furrow*, June 1979, pp 361-371; Chapter 7, 'Understanding Marriage Today' is a revised and significantly expanded version of my article 'A Christian Understanding of Marriage', *Petrus* (Magazine of St Peter's Seminary, Wexford), 1979, pp 71-76; Chapter 8 is reprinted in a slightly revised and expanded form from *Doctrine and Life*, February 1998, pp 105-112; Chapter 9 is a significantly revised and expanded version of my article of the same title, *The Furrow*, August 1986, pp 506 - 516. (This latter article was also published as a booklet, *Theology of Liberation*, Veritas, Dublin 1987.) Chapter 10 is a revised and expanded version of my article 'Church Teaching on Religious Liberty: its development and influence', *Petrus*, 1990, pp 66-69 along with a slightly revised version of my article 'Voting in a Divorce Referendum', *Intercom*, September 1995, pp 6-8; Chapter 11 is a revised and significantly expanded version of my article of the same title, *The Furrow*, September 1995, pp 501-509 and includes also a revised version of my article 'Asceticism in Christian Living', *The Furrow*, April 1978, pp 79-84. My article 'Moral Character' in *The Furrow*, January 2000, pp 24-33 is a summary of Chapter 2 of this book; My article 'Understanding Sin Today', *The Furrow*, October 1999, pp 538-547 is a summary of Chapter 4 of this book.

Copyright © 2001, Bill Cosgrave

Contents

Introduction

This book has its origins in a series of articles that were written over a period of more than twenty years from 1979 to 2000 and published in Irish church magazines. Each article was written because at the time I had a special interest in the topic, due to the fact that it was my duty to teach it and/or it was being given widespread attention in theological and church circles. I wrote the articles because I felt I had something to say that was fresh, that would build on the Catholic moral tradition and bring to the attention of readers some of the new ideas that were emerging in those years as the fruit of the renewal in theology which was sparked off by the Second Vatican Council. In the main, then, these essays contain mainstream theology from the post-Vatican II period. They are basically summaries of what the top moral and other theologians have been saying on the topics chosen here in the 35 years since the Council. The selection of the subjects under discussion is mine as is the arrangement of the material in each chapter. Otherwise, you might say, the real thinking has been done by the church's best moralists of recent decades, among whom must be numbered such influential Irish theologians as Enda McDonagh, Vincent MacNamara, Donal Dorr and Patrick Hannon. From these noted theological thinkers I have learned a great deal and am most grateful for their many valuable insights.

I have collected these essays in book form and revised and expanded them, in general because of the positive reaction to the original publications but also because the ideas they contain remain valuable and enriching and may well have something to contribute to interested readers in this new century. The nature of the material in these 11 chapters points to the readership which will, hopefully, find most of interest here. The book will

7

appeal most and be of most value to those readers who are
reasonably familiar with church matters, have some interest in
theology and wish to improve their theological understanding,
at least to some degree, of the matters discussed in these pages.
There is little here for moral theologians to learn, though some
of them may find several of the chapters of value in connection
with their undergraduate lectures and courses. One might say
that this book contains 'theology for middlebrows' and so includes material that may prove useful to some preachers and
some teachers of second level RE. I have tried to write clearly,
logically and positively so that readers will be helped to understand better their own moral and spiritual experience and that of
the church community of our day. That, hopefully, will facilitate
better Christian living and a deeper commitment to the Christian
vision of human life.

William Cosgrave
Monageer, Ferns,
Co Wexford
Easter 2001

CHAPTER 1

Models of the Christian Moral Life

In the current renewal of moral theology one of the many significant and influential developments concerns what are frequently referred to as models of or approaches to Christian truth and life. The importance of models in theology has been increasingly recognised in recent years, especially since the publication in 1974 of Avery Dulles's classic work *Models of the Church*. This development has affected moral theology also and as a result one hears a great deal about different approaches to understanding the Christian moral life and pluralism in regard to images and metaphors used to illuminate that understanding.

In this opening chapter we will focus our attention on this issue of models of the Christian moral life, explaining and evaluating two of the more popular models that are to be found in the Christian moral tradition and in contemporary reflection. Our aim will be to facilitate and to improve our understanding of the moral life of Christians. In doing this we will be gathering the fruits of contemporary moral thinking in the church and summarising it, so as to provide a clearer understanding of how the church, past and present, has endeavoured to explain the good news about how human beings should live their lives. In other words, we are consulting the mainstream moral tradition of the Christian community in an effort to throw light on the church's understanding of the moral life Christians in our day are called to lead as disciples of Christ.

Models in contemporary theology
We may begin with a brief account of how theologians in our day understand and use models in theology. Dulles in his opening chapter gives us such an account. In theology (as in the physical sciences) models are understood as images (or metaphors or analogies or symbols) which are taken from ordinary life and relationships and used in reference to particular religious or theo-

9

logical realities or objects with the intention of illuminating the nature and meaning of those realities and objects. Models, then, help us to understand realities which we cannot describe literally and they do this by providing us with a pictorial or analogical representation of the realities in question. In religion and theology, where many of the things involved are deeply mysterious and hard to understand, models or images are particularly necessary and helpful. Such models or images have always been used and will always be used, whether we call them models and are aware of their importance and function or not. These models or images or analogies appeal to our imagination as well as to our intellect and, by so doing, can strengthen our attachment to the mystery or sacred person being talked about, in addition to promoting our understanding. Many examples of these images or analogies are to be found in theology and even in the Bible: God is called father, creator, shepherd, husband, etc.; Jesus is referred to as messiah, lord, saviour, son, shepherd, liberator, etc.; the church is called a body, a house, a flock, a bride, etc.

In theology a model can be used in an explanatory and in an exploratory manner, the former to clarify and illuminate the reality in question, the latter to reveal some further aspects or elements of it. In addition, it is usually the case, especially in theology, that one makes use of many models or images or metaphors in the effort to arrive at a fuller understanding of a particular truth or reality. In this way one provides a number of beams of light, as it were, to illuminate the truth or reality under discussion; one endeavours to present it from a variety of angles that are usually complementary and that, therefore, give one a fuller and more adequate view of it.

No one model or image or metaphor in theology is by itself adequate to present the full reality of any truth or mystery and we should not use it as if it were adequate. Each model or image has its strong points and advantages and it is these that make it illuminating and valuable when applied to some truth or reality of our Christian faith. Every model or image is limited and needs others to fill out and compensate for its limitations, inadequacies and weak points. We may, however, use a particular model or image as our central or main one but not as the only one that is needed or valid in relation to a specific truth or mystery of the faith. Some models or images are better than others as they express our religious or moral experience more clearly and adequately and involve less difficulties and possible distortions of that experience. However, we need to use all our images or models with care and discernment, lest we push them too far, use aspects of them that don't fit or take them literally and so distort the truth or reality, mislead people and maybe even fall into error.

Experience teaches us that models or images vary in their appeal and illuminating power from person to person, from culture to culture and from generation to generation. Thus, some that were widely used and helpful in the past are no longer found to be of great value today, while others that were once largely ignored, have regained popularity and are found to provide significant illumination in relation to one or other area of the Christian faith. A similar thing can happen in different societies and cultures at a particular time, when one society finds great illuminating and sometimes great motivating power in a particular metaphor or model, while people elsewhere in the world don't respond to it at all or with any great interest or enthusiasm.

We usually judge or assess models or images by their consequences for our understanding of the mysteries and truths of the faith, that is, by the amount of illumination they give us about a particular truth or reality that we are trying to understand better. In addition, we judge by the inspiration or motivation any model gives us and by its practical results among us as a community of believers.[1]

Models of the Christian moral life
Models have long been used in the church (and outside it) in connection with morality and moral issues, even if the word 'model' itself wasn't mentioned. Many different analogies or images or metaphors for aspects of or realities in the moral life can be found in the Bible and in the Christian moral tradition, e.g. morality as law, as love, as discipleship, as liberation. In fact such analogies or images or models are essential, if we are to come to any understanding of morality; we need them to illuminate

---

1. Avery Dulles, *Models of the Church* (Gill & Macmillan, Dublin, 1976), chapter 1. See Charles E Curran, *The Catholic Moral Tradition Today: A Synthesis* (Georgetown University Press, Washington DC, 1999), chapter 3. Also John F O'Grady, *Models of Jesus* (Image Books, New York, 1982), chapter 1.

what is meant by moral living and its various aspects and dimensions. It would seem too that the use of different models or images in our moral reflection can be not just a help and a source of illumination, but also an important contributing factor to the emergence of different approaches to and styles of doing morality. It may at times also be a factor in the development of not fully complementary understandings of the moral life and even conflicting ways of presenting moral realities. This will become clearer later in our reflections.

These points make it imperative, therefore, that we look closely, even if not at great length, at this fundamental but often neglected matter of models in the moral life and in moral reflection. Doing so will bring the matter more fully to our awareness, clarify the issues in question and show how our use of different models or analogies affects our doing of morality, often enough in not insignificant ways. In thus reflecting on models in morality we will be in line with an increasing number of Catholic and other moralists today. We will be in the mainstream of contemporary Catholic moral theology in our concern with this matter.

Here we will consider only two out of many models or ways of understanding morality. We will present the main elements of each, pointing out the positive and negative aspects they display and giving a brief evaluation of them as ways of expressing or articulating our moral experience. While each of these models is valid and valuable in its own way, it will be clear that they are not of equal value or helpfulness in relation to illuminating our moral experience. Hence, a definite preference will be expressed as it is in moral theology generally today. The two models we will deal with are the legal one and the relational one.

The legal model of the Christian moral life
What I am here calling the legal model has been the primary and the dominant way of conceptualising and understanding the moral life in Catholic moral theology and in Catholic teaching, preaching and spirituality for centuries, so dominant in fact that it was considered *the* way or even the only way to do so up to Vatican II. The Manuals of Moral Theology, in use from shortly after the Council of Trent (ended in 1563) until the Vatican Council (1962-5), contain an understanding of the moral life that is an obvious example of the legal model.

Basically the legal model understands morality and the

moral life in legal terms, i.e. in language and categories borrowed from the legal system in the state. In other words, it translates moral experience into legal terminology and concepts and considers that this provides us with an accurate and an adequate understanding of that experience.

In more practical terms the legal model sees the moral life as essentially a series of laws that originate from human nature, the state, the church or God and are presented to us Christians as binding norms for moral living. From these laws arise our moral obligations and duties. Our response to these laws and obligations ought to be obedience and conformity. Hence, in this understanding of the moral life of Christians, laws are very central and prominent and in practice obedience is the primary virtue. Thus, there was in pre-Vatican II times great stress on the ten commandments and on other laws of God and the church, especially sex laws, fasting laws and laws forbidding Catholics to attend non-Catholic services.

All this has the great advantage of being clear and definite; the Catholic has only to come to know the law to be clear on his/her obligations and duties in the moral life. So, the legal model scores heavily in terms of clarity, though in the light of recent insights it is seen to be, at times, a false clarity that doesn't do full justice to the complexity and, sometimes, the obscurity of some areas of our moral experience and, hence, of some moral realities, e.g. mortal sin. The legal model also has the advantage of stressing objectivity and making it very clear that particular actions are objectively wrong and, hence, prohibited by specific moral laws. We are obliged to conform to these moral laws or rules, whatever any individual moral agent may think or decide.[2]

Prominent also in the legal understanding of the Christian moral life, as in the legal system in the state, are the ideas of reward and punishment, in particular the latter. There is also talk about merit and how one can merit grace, and even salvation. Catholics were, thus, very conscious of the fact that there is punishment for sin either in this life on earth or, most certainly, in the next. In consequence, some saw bad luck, accidents and injuries as God's punishment of their sinful deeds, while everyone was well aware that purgatory and hell were punishments for sin, venial and mortal. In this context it is understandable that

---

2. Curran, p 65. Donal Harrington, *What is morality?* (Columba Press, Dublin, 1996), p 11.

many Catholics were anxious and fearful in their moral lives, lest they fall into sin and incur punishment for it. A legal morality, thus, tends to be a morality of fear, as many will remember from the days before Vatican II.

Common also in a legal morality is the tendency to become over-anxious about keeping the rules, even in their smallest details. If one adds to this the inclination to slide into legalism, where obeying the law becomes an end in itself, then one can begin to understand how and why many Catholics tended towards scrupulosity, thus suffering from what has in the past been called the Catholic disease. (Scrupulosity is now clearly understood to be an irrational fear of or anxiety about sinning or having sinned, especially in the sexual area of life. It is an emotional illness that distorts one's conscience judgment about one's own sins.) Today, as the legal model of the Catholic moral life fades out, so also, thankfully, do the scourges of legalism and scrupulosity.

Fundamental to the legal model of the Christian moral life is a particular image or understanding of God. Here the dominant image of God is that of lawmaker *par excellence* and, like any lawmaker, God wishes to ensure that God's laws are obeyed. Hence, God is viewed as also having a policeman's role. In addition, God is seen, naturally enough in this model, as a judge who sees to the enforcement of his laws by appropriate penalties. Here arises also the idea of God as punisher of breaches of the divine laws and, not infrequently, as a kind of super-accountant totting up all the good and bad deeds people do, so as to decide their eternal destiny. All this has the result that God's forgiveness is relegated to a secondary place, if not altogether forgotten. It is easy to understand that this whole presentation of God tends to increase the Christian's fear and anxiety and also to promote legalistic and even scrupulous attitudes and tendencies, which, as we all know, were a common feature of Catholic moral living up to about 1970.

It may be mentioned here that this legal model of the moral life in the Catholic Church was reinforced by the institutional model or understanding of the church itself, a model that was dominant for centuries before the Second Vatican Council. Since stress in this understanding of the church was on authority and its powers and the duty to obey, it is not hard to see that the legal model of morality was very much in tune with that ecclesiology.

They fed into and off each other. Not surprisingly, authoritarian attitudes and practices were common. Total and even blind obedience was widely demanded and just as widely given in Catholic life, being at its most complete and destructive perhaps in institutions of religious women.

Examples of legal morality
Two examples of the legal model of the moral life may be illuminating here. Marriage in legal terms was viewed as a contract, giving husband and wife rights and duties in relation to sexual relations and being itself indissoluble by any human power. Confession was conceived as a tribunal in which the judge (the priest) conducted a kind of trial of the accused (the penitent), questioned him/her, pronounced his verdict (the absolution) and gave an appropriate punishment (the penance). The penitent had to list all his/her crimes (serious sins) and be sorry for them. In this understanding confession was often experienced as an ordeal, provoking fear and anxiety. When it was over, the overwhelming feeling was one of relief.

Evaluation of the legal model
Despite its good points, especially its clarity, definiteness and stress on objectivity and the binding nature of moral laws, this legal model of the moral life of Christians has, as will already be clear, significant weaknesses and deficiencies. It gives law too much prominence, making it central in the moral life. Law should not be the primary reality in the Christian moral life, though it has a real and necessary place. This model also tends towards rigidity of outlook or spirit and is inclined to breed legalistic tendencies and attitudes and even to promote legalism. It tends also to promote conformism and passivity and, above all, it distorts the image of God notably. It usually brings with it fear and anxiety and does little to promote moral growth and maturity. Another distortion it frequently leads to is that of putting undue emphasis on places in the moral life where laws exist and overlooking other significant aspects of moral living, e.g. concern for our relationships and community living. The legal model tends also to be a very act-centred understanding of morality, where the emphasis is on specific moral acts that a moral agent has done or might do. In this context moral goodness tends to be understood as the sum total of one's good acts

and moral badness as the accumulated fruits of all the immoral actions one has done. As a result there is little emphasis on the moral subject/agent and his/her moral condition or character, and, in consequence, the virtues and vices as well as the relational and social dimensions of morality tend to be neglected.

In consequence of all these weaknesses and deficiencies, it is clear that this legal model should not be the main one in our understanding of Christian morality and is, in fact, better given a secondary place. This does not imply that there is no place for laws and rules in morality but it does mean that such laws and rules should not be seen as the primary elements of or realities in Christian morality.

The relational model of the Christian moral life
This is the most widely accepted and used model or understanding of the Christian moral life in moral theology and in preaching, teaching and the spiritual life in the Catholic Church in our day. It is regularly referred to also as the personalist model. It is not, of course, the only one but because of its wide acceptance and use it deserves our attention here.

Human life and hence also the moral life consists essentially of a complex set of relationships between persons, whether individuals, groups or communities. We live and act within these relationships. It follows, then, that the moral life is fundamentally about persons in relationship and in community. It is in this context of relationships and community living that moral obligations arise and that the moral call is heard. The other person or persons is/are a gift or blessing and from him/her/them comes the call/invitation or obligation to respond positively in the situation in which one is. This call or invitation is experienced as coming from the other person(s) but ultimately from God. To that invitation a response needs to be given, a response that is loving and appropriate to the circumstances. So, being moral is a matter of being faithful to the fact of our interrelatedness and to the demands of relationship.[3]

In the relational model of Christian morality that we are considering, there is a significant effort to stress the social and not just the personal aspects of the moral life. We live in groups and communities and these have an essential moral dimension; moral obligations arise within them and moral responses are

3. Harrington, p 16.

called for by individuals and by groups. However, Catholic moral theology is as yet only struggling to understand this social dimension of Christian morality. Much remains to be understood and done here. Still, progress has been made in our understanding of the group as moral subject, despite the undoubted complexities and difficulties.This is clear as the widespread discussion of and concern about issues like social justice and social sin indicate.[4]

Nowadays we are aware also of what is often referred to as institutional or systemic justice and injustice. This concerns the fact that groups and communities are called to practise justice both in relation to their own members and to people and groups outside. This is not always done, however. Hence, there are many examples of institutional injustice practised by states, institutions, companies, and even churches, in the various areas of life, e.g. economic, political, social, religious, etc.[5]

As a result of the rise of ecological or environmental awareness or consciousness in recent years, we are now also aware of the relationship of us humans to the cosmos, to the material world of nature in which we live and on which we depend so essentially. This gives rise to a moral call that is being heard and heeded by increasing numbers of people. It is a call to desist from the still widespread exploitation of that material world, and an invitation to appreciate and respect God's gift of creation, and relate to it in a way that enhances human life for all, while ensuring that the material world is itself preserved and protected in the long term as well as in the short and medium term.[6]

The relational model also gives a lot of attention to the moral subject, the person or group living and acting in relationship with others. It is not adequate just to take note of a person's or group's individual actions and assess these morally. The legal model, as we saw, confined itself largely to this only. We must also take into account what the person or group has become and

4. See Enda McDonagh, *Social Ethics and the Christian: Towards freedom in communion* (Manchester University Press, 1979), especially chapters 1 & 2; Also McDonagh's *The Gracing of Society* (Gill & Macmillan, Dublin, 1989), Part 1.
5. See chapter 4 below under 'social sin'.
6. As one good example of this ecological concern in a now vast literature, see Seán McDonagh, *To Care for the Earth: a call to a new theology* (Bear & Company, Sante Fe, New Mexico, USA, 1987).

is as a human person or group, i.e. morally speaking. In a word, it is essential to focus on the moral character of the agent(s), because that is the primary moral reality as far as any moral agent is concerned.[7] This involves attention to what is often referred to in contemporary moral theology as the subject's basic orientation or direction in life. This is one's deepest moral choice and stance, i.e. whether at the deepest level one is a loving or a selfish person, is God- and other-centred or self-centred.

The relational model of the Christian moral life also stresses the historical or temporal dimension of the person, group and community. This refers to the fact that we all have a past, present and future, that we live in time and move through time and in doing so change as persons, as groups and as communities, either by growing morally or sinking further into sin and diminishing morally. In addition, we belong to a particular society and culture and, consequently, we are socially and culturally conditioned. This has important implications for our moral lives as persons, groups and communities and for the morality of the actions we do or do not do.

Arising from this understanding of the basic elements of morality, theologians using the relational model give a great deal of attention to freedom and responsibility. Each of us is free and responsible, i.e. we are capable of responding to others morally and also we are accountable for the responses we make and do not make, for the actions we do and do not do. We are also responsible for what we have made of ourselves as persons and as communities over the years. In a real sense, then, we can say that the moral life of Christians, as of other people, is about being responsible in relationships and in community. This involves becoming ever more truly free as a person and learning to make ever better and more appropriate responses.[8]

In this context there arises naturally a stress on growth and maturity in the moral life. We are called to grow to the fulness of our potential as human persons and as groups and communities. Hence, we need to take a positive and dynamic attitude to

---

7. See Chapter 2 on Moral Character.
8. See H. Richard Niebuhr, *The Responsible Self: An Essay in Christian Moral Philosophy* (Harper & Row Publishers, New York, Evanston and London),1963; Albert R. Jonsen, *Responsibility in Modern Religious Ethics* (Corpus Books, Washington/Cleveland, USA), 1968.

ourselves and our moral development, not being content with being passive and static, but doing all we can to become the best person we can be. Here again we are touching on the question of our moral character and its formation and growth (See Chapter 2). This points up the basic moral call or duty of each person and group: become what God calls you to become as a person or group, whether Christian or not. How to do this is complex and difficult but it is captured essentially in the statement of Jesus that the greatest commandment of the Christian way is to love God and one's neighbour and that the goal of Christian community living is to build God's kingdom or rule of justice and peace, freedom and truth.

In the model of the moral life that we are reflecting on, we find an image of God which emphasises that God is personal, loving and forgiving rather than punishing and to be feared. God is triune or trinity and, hence, is in relationship and in community; in fact God *is* community in perfection. As such God loves us and invites us humans to respond in love to God's love and so to become more human and more divinised. Jesus the Christ is God's revelation and God's love incarnate, while at the same time he is humanity's perfect response as he loves God the Father perfectly. We humans are, then, called to live our lives in imitation of Christ. That's what the Christian moral life essentially is.

The emphasis on the person and her/his relationships in the model of the Christian moral life that we are considering would seem to be linked with the contemporary concern in morality and in theology with human experience, moral and religious. Great weight is given today to experience, personal and communal, in the task of coming to a better understanding of morality and of our Christian faith. The appeal to experience as a source of moral and religious insight has a powerful attraction for contemporary searchers after truth, and what rings true to experience is much more likely to be acceptable to the modern person, Christian and non-Christian. In consequence of this, some speak today of an 'experience culture' that is replacing the 'obedience culture' of the pre-Vatican II era. This 'obedience culture' was a powerful force in the church of those times and provided a context in which the legal model of morality could and did flourish. It meant that the appeal to authority and its teaching on faith and morality was for all practical purposes absolutely decisive for the Catholic. Today this is no longer the case. What people in our day find convincing, especially in relation to moral issues, is what they have learned from and find congruent with their moral experience in their day to day living and that of the communities of which they are members.[9]

It would seem fairly clear that the relational model of the Christian moral life provides an understanding of the Christian way of living that is closer to the experience of many Christians today than the legal model. Hence, its greater appeal for contemporary Christians.

The relational model is, of course, quite compatible with the Catholic moral tradition of natural law. This means that, in this view of the moral life of Christians, it is the nature of the person-in-relationship-and-in-community that ultimately provides the basis for our morality and grounds our moral values and judgments. And it is by using our reasoning faculties to reflect on our nature as human persons and our experience of being human that we discover moral truth. However, the relational model of morality gives rise to a more personalist and a more relational understanding of human nature and human morality and seeks to avoid the tendency in the legal model, and especially in the approach of the Manuals of Moral Theology, to construct not just a legal view of natural law, but also a physicalist one. As a result of this one finds that when it comes down to specific moral judgments on particular human actions, there arises some questioning of earlier church formulations. Hence, the widespread adoption of the relational model has proved to be a contributory factor in relation to some of the controversy in the Catholic Church in recent decades on specific moral matters.

We may add here that the model of the church that was most prominent in Vatican II, and that is widely accepted and used in contemporary ecclesiology, is a model that supports and reinforces the relational model of the moral life. We may call it the community model of the church. It fosters active participation by all, the taking of initiatives and the building of equal relationships, as well as the formation of committed and active groups and communities within the wider community of the church universal. One area where these models are particularly close is

9. See Michael Paul Gallagher SJ, *Help my Unbelief* (Veritas, Dublin, 1983), chapter 9, especially pp 68-9; Dermot A Lane, *The Experience of God* (Veritas, Dublin, 1981), chapter 1.

in relation to authority and how it is understood and exercised. They both see authority, and especially teaching authority, as a service to the whole church, the service of leadership that enables and coordinates the talents and energies of the members at the various levels of the church and that facilitates and guides the search for truth throughout the whole community.[10]

At this point it may be mentioned that the issue of dissent from the official teaching of the church's magisterium, especially on moral matters, is greatly illuminated when considered in terms of the relational or personalist model of morality and the community model of the church. To speak in terms of dissent from church teaching is to buy into the legal model of morality and the institutional model of the church and its teaching authority. As such, the assent-dissent approach is very defective and is far from doing justice to either the church's role as moral teacher or the conscientious position of the theologian or individual Catholic who is in disagreement with some specific teaching.[11]

In this area it is imperative to continue to work with the relational model of the moral life and the community model of the church and its teaching authority. In such an approach the whole church is seen as both learning and teaching in relation to the truth of Christ, while, of course, the essential role of the church's central teaching office is recognised and accepted. In moral matters it is not a question of imposing and obeying moral principles and rules. That is a legal way of looking at the issue. Rather is it a question of all participating in the common search for the truth, with the magisterium exercising its leadership by proposing moral teaching for the acceptance of all the church's members, while they assist in the discovery of truth by their best efforts to understand and to make the magisterium's understanding their own. In this context, there would be no temptation to think of rival moral authorities in competition and the hierarchy of truths would be respected by all. The occasional disagreement of an individual theologian or church member with a teaching of the magisterium would not be unexpected or regarded as plain disobedience to be punished and stamped out. Rather the focus would be on how best to understand and artic-

10. Dulles, chapter 3.
11. Linda Hogan, *Confronting the Truth: Conscience in the Catholic Tradition* (Darton, Longman & Todd, London, 2001), 174-9.

ulate the good and the loving thing to do in each situation and how to harmonise the insights of each perspective. The main effort would, then, be to create a dialogue to achieve agreement and to find ways of living fruitfully in the midst of difference.[12]

Examples of relational morality
In the relational model, marriage is understood primarily as a relationship or community of love in which two equal and different partners seek the good of each other and each other's fullest growth as persons. Their love will be creative of better persons and procreative of new persons, children. Confession is now transformed into the sacrament of reconciliation, in which the individual or group seeks to restore his/her/its relationship with the church and with God by repentance for his/her/their serious (and other) sins. In response to this, the church grants forgiveness, a forgiveness that comes ultimately from God. So, the reconciliation with the church is the symbol or sacrament of one's reconciliation with God. Achieving this reconciliation brings joy to the repentant sinner or community.

Evaluation of the relational model
This model of the Christian moral life is much closer to our experience of human life today and resonates better with contemporary Christians. It puts the person and his/her relationships at the centre and is strong on freedom and responsibility. It is also more biblical and is illuminating when applied to specific realities in the Christian life, as we have just seen. It can, however, be taken in an individualistic sense and that needs to be guarded against. In comparison to the legal model, it may seem vague and imprecise but this must be seen, not as a fault or weakness, but rather as a gain in realism and as something that reflects better what the moral realities actually are.

Further Reading
Curran, Charles E., *The Catholic Moral Tradition Today: A Synthesis* (Georgetown University Press, Washington DC, USA, 1999), chapter 3;
Dulles Avery, *Models of the Church* (Gill & Macmillan, Dublin, 1976), chapter 1.

12. Hogan, 177-9; William Cosgrave, 'Models of the Christian Moral Life', *The Furrow*, September 1983, 566.

CHAPTER 2

Moral Character: Becoming a Good Person

In this chapter we wish to consider a topic that has been largely neglected in Catholic moral theology, spirituality and pastoral practice, not just in pre-Vatican II times but up to very recently. We will begin with a brief consideration of the reasons for this neglect and that will involve us in a summary discussion of the legal understanding or model of the Christian moral life, as already outlined in chapter 1. We will turn, then, to our main concern. This is moral character, as seen in the context of what is now the dominant understanding or model of our moral lives as Christians, namely, the relational or personalist understanding. We will explain what moral character is, what are its various aspects and dimensions and the implications of giving it such a central position in our moral thinking and living. This will enable us to see more clearly why there is so much interest in moral character (and the virtues) in contemporary Catholic theological, spiritual and pastoral reflection.

The legal understanding and moral character
The legal understanding of the Christian moral life is generally seen as being very act-centred. Its main focus and interest is the individual moral actions a person performs. The impression then comes to be given that the whole moral life consists mainly of doing as many right acts and avoiding as many wrong ones as is possible. This focus on actions brings with it a significant neglect of concern for the person, the moral subject and moral agent, and what is happening to her/him as these actions are being performed. There is here little reference to the moral subject's growth or failure to grow in goodness and what sort of person he/she is becoming as his/her life history unfolds. In consequence, there is in such a theology little about moral character. Involved here also is a neglect of the virtues and vices, all of which are dimensions of one's moral character and of great significance in the Christian moral life.

It is true that one can refer to the understanding of the Christian moral life in the legal model as an ethic of virtue. But even a brief look at the Manuals of Moral Theology from the pre-Vatican II era in which the legal model was dominant will show that, despite this fact, the presentation of the moral life there was basically act-centred and not person- or character-centred. The reason for this is that in those textbooks the virtues were not seen as constituting the dynamics of the Christian moral life or as the various dimensions, areas or ideals of that life but rather they were reduced largely to sources of obligation for the Christian. Practising the virtues meant doing and being called to do more good actions, and avoiding the vices meant not doing a whole lot of other specific actions. So the potential of what was referred to as an ethic of virtue was not realised and the legal model remained and remains a predominantly act-centred ethic that pays scant attention to moral character or to the virtues properly understood.[1]

Here we find another reason why there has been a very widespread move away from the legal model in contemporary moral theology, spirituality and pastoral practice and a consequent search for a better understanding of the Christian moral life. The relational model provides such an alternative and has found widespread favour throughout the church in post-Vatican II times. To that we now turn.

Moral character in the relational understanding of the moral life
In this understanding or model of the Christian moral life the main emphasis and focus is on the person-in-relationship-and-in-community. Specific actions are not, of course, neglected but the first and primary concern is the moral subject and her/his relationships. In this context it is essential to develop and work with an adequate understanding of the human person, since such an understanding or anthropology is needed to provide us with the basis for our moral reflections and conclusions, and also to furnish us with the fundamental criterion or norm by

---

1. See John A. Gallagher, *Time Past, Time Future: An Historical Study of Catholic Moral Theology* (Paulist Press, New York, 1990), pp 56-62; William C Spohn SJ, 'The Return of the Virtues', *Theological Studies*, March 1992, p 60.

which one is to judge the person, the community and their actions from the moral viewpoint.[2]

Clearly such an anthropology will also be essential for our development of an understanding of moral character. In this chapter we will assume this account of the human person and focus on the person as a moral being and how he/she builds character or becomes a morally good or bad person, and how this is affected by what the person does or does not do over the course of her/his lifetime.

What is moral character?
We know from experience that certain people are generally consistent in the way they react to situations. We can rely on them to make a certain type of response in most circumstances. They are predictable and seem to have certain stable characteristics. This predictability and reliability seem to come from these people's commitment to particular values and from their maintaining certain attitudes and intentions. People often refer to this predictability and stability as the person's character. That is the word we will use here. Others call it integrity.[3]

This character, which manifests itself through one's actions and is clearly a moral reality, refers to who one is as a human being. One's character is one's moral identity as a person, one's moral self. My moral character is who I have made myself and become as a result of my life experiences and in particular as a result of my moral choices and actions over my lifetime. Each person's moral character consists of a very specific and personal configuration or arrangement of virtues and vices, affections, intentions, dispositions, beliefs, values and priorities. One's character gives one a particular direction or orientation in and to life, so that one acts in a consistent way, either doing good or evil. The character one has built represents the characteristic way one has of determining what it is appropriate for one to do in any particular situation. Everyone's character is unique, but no one type of character is normative for all.[4]

2. See Richard M Gula SS, *Reason Informed by Faith: Foundations of Catholic Morality* (Paulist Press, New York, 1989), chapter 5.
3. James M Gustafson, *Christian Ethics and the Community* (Pilgrim Press, Philadelphia, USA, 1971), pp 166-172.
4. Stanley Hauerwas, *Character and the Christian Life: A Study in Theological Ethics*, (Trinity University Press, San Antonio, USA, 1975) p 127.

The issue of character is, then, the basic question for each person in her/his moral life. This is confirmed by experience where we discover that, along with the call to do good deeds, we also experience the call, from the depths of our being as persons and ultimately from God, to become good persons. Hence, our moral lives must be concerned above all about the kind of persons we are, are becoming and ought to become. It will be important for us, then, to reflect well on this question of our moral character, so as to understand it and its central importance better, and do all possible to build that character more fully.

Building moral character – our basic moral obligation
As human beings we all have important duties or obligations to do good in various ways and forms. At the same time, as was noted just now, we can discern in our deeper selves a call or invitation to become a good person, to build our moral self or character, so that we become the best human being we can become. Hence, while it is important to be kind, just and generous, it is more important for each individual to become a good person, to build one's moral character to its highest level. This moral duty is reinforced for us Christians, who experience a call from God through Jesus, not just to do good but to become good and be the best disciples of Christ we can be. Thus we become fully mature with the fulness of Christ (Eph 4:13).

Building one's moral character can only be achieved, of course, through the particular choices and actions one performs. These choices arise from one's goodness of character, and confirm and strengthen that goodness. Despite this importance that attaches to our particular choices, however, focusing on one's call to character building remains primary and essential. This focus will ensure that we avoid an act-centred moral outlook, get our priorities right and keep in mind the process nature of the journey towards maturity as a human being and a Christian.

Moral character and moral choices
The two core points here may be stated simply as follows.
   a) Our moral choices shape and form our moral character.
   b) Our moral character gives rise to and conditions our moral choices.

In other words, there is a reciprocal or two-way influence and conditioning between one's character and one's choices and actions.

On the one hand, our choices over our lifetime make us who and what we have become and are as persons. In choosing to adopt one or another course of action, we make ourselves into certain sorts of persons. But the other side of this coin has equal validity and importance. Character gives rise to moral choices. Who and what we are now powerfully influences and conditions what we choose to do or refrain from doing in any and all situations. Examples of both principles are abundant. If a person over many years performs acts of kindness and generosity in most of the situations she/he is in, then that person will become a kind and generous person; her/his moral character or self will acquire the virtues of kindness and generosity. Similarly with vices like miserliness and laziness. As for examples of the power and influence of our character on our choices, most of us have the experience that people who are just and fair usually behave in just and fair ways, while people who are intemperate and imprudent frequently perform acts that should be described as intemperate and imprudent. In other words, we usually act, as they say, in character.

We should note here that in qualifying the statement in the previous two sentences by the word 'usually', we are adverting to the fact of common experience that very few people always act justly and fairly or always act intemperately or imprudently. Even the best people can and do act out of character occasionally, and even the worst can and do perform good deeds from time to time. Stated differently, this amounts to saying that from experience it seems to be the case that few if any people are totally good and few if any are totally bad or evil, even in particular areas of their lives, not to talk of their life as a whole. There is evidently some good in the worst of us and some bad in the best of us. In a word, one's moral character is always only predominantly good or bad, not totally so.

This would seem to imply that there can be degrees of goodness or badness in one's character. One person can be, say, 90% good in his/her moral character, while another person is only 70% or less good; and similarly on the negative side. It may even be that one's character is such that we simply meet each situation as it comes, not trying to determine the direction of our lives, but letting the direction vary from one decision to another.[5]

---

5. See Hauerwas, p 122.

The impact of our moral choices on our character
It should be clear from what has been said above that our choices and actions, because they are free and are performed by a free self-determining agent or subject, have a twofold effect. Firstly and most obviously, any particular choice I make, or action I do, affects or has an impact on a specific situation in which I am, e.g. I come to the assistance of an injured person much as the Good Samaritan did, or I steal another's money and leave that person materially deprived. But at a deeper and more personal level, my choice and action also have an impact on myself as a person, as a moral subject. They form my character in a real way; they make me more or less a good person, thus determining to some degree what I will be and do in the future. Thus my act of generosity relieves another's material needs but it also builds my moral character and makes me in some degree a more generous and so a more virtuous and good person. In the same way, sinful or immoral choices and actions do damage to some person or persons but they also damage me myself as a moral agent and subject, because they make me more selfish and less good. They deform my moral character, lessen my goodness as a person and thus make me a lesser human being and Christian. In the legal model of sin these effects of one's sinful actions are referred to as the punishments for sin. Here we see them as the natural effects of our sins on ourselves as moral subjects and agents, or, in other words, as the damage done to one's moral character by one's sins.

Different sinful choices will do damage in different degrees, some minor, some significant. In this context it is possible to think of a particularly deep and wholehearted choice or action that will change one's character profoundly. From being a good and loving person, basically if not totally, one can be transformed by such a profound choice and become a basically selfish and unloving person. One's moral character is, as it were, deconstructed and rebuilt in the reverse direction. Similarly one could perform a basically good act that would make one a basically good person, where before one had been basically sinful. Such profound choices will clearly be rare, because they will be difficult to make, but they are possible. Today they are referred to by theologians and in official church teaching as fundamental options or basic choices. While there is some disagreement about what precisely is involved in such choices, everyone accepts that they are possible and that they profoundly alter our moral character.

The core point in all this, then, is that, while our choices and actions are important because of their effects on other people and situations, they have added importance because of the way they condition and form ourselves as moral agents and subjects. They build up or damage our moral character and so are the means by which we become better or worse persons. Thus what we do is all important for what we have become and are as persons and for what we will make of ourselves in the future. Our doing impacts on our being and makes us what we are.

Character and choices: goodness and rightness

A further point needs to be made in this context. In distinguishing but also relating a person and his/her actions, character and choices, we have been making use of an important distinction that deserves brief explicit treatment. When we talk of the person and his/her moral character, we use the terms good and bad or good and evil. We speak of a person's moral goodness or badness or of good and bad moral character. This use of this terminology is accurate and in itself presents no difficulty. Where possible confusion and even mistakes may arise is when we use also the terms right and wrong. Strictly speaking, these terms refer to and are to be used only in relation to choices or actions, not persons or their moral character. So, choices and actions are spoken of as right or wrong; persons and their characters as good or bad. Goodness and badness pertain to persons and their characters only, whereas rightness and wrongness are attributed only to choices or actions that persons make or do.

This distinction in our moral language points up the reasons why moral character and its formation and growth are of such central significance in Christian (or any) morality and life, and why they must be given the priority in our moral concern. We may mention three of these reasons.[6]

a) We speak of persons and their moral character as moral in the full sense, whereas choices and actions can be called moral only in an analogous sense. In other words, morality refers and

---

6. Russell B Connors, Jun. & Patrick T McCormick, *Character, Choices and Community: The Three Faces of Christian Ethics* (Paulist Press, New York, 1998), pp 22-24; See Bernard House, *Proportionalism: The American Debate and its European Roots* (Georgetown University Press, USA, 1987), chapter 3; Josef Fuchs SJ, *Christian Ethics in a Secular Age* (Gill & Macmillan, Dublin, 1984), chapter 4.

is applicable to persons and character in the first place and to choices and actions only in a secondary sense.

b) Only persons can be moral agents and what they choose and do as agents flows from, and is shaped by, their moral character. Only persons can thus be the source of actions. Hence, forming persons morally or building character has the priority for this reason also.

c) Only persons can construct moral or just communities and for this moral character is essential. In fact, the moral quality of those communities will depend to a large extent on the moral characters of their members, and reform and development of moral character will be an important means of constructing a truly just society.

A group or community character?

It is possible to speak of a group or a community of people having a moral character, though here we are much less clear on what is involved and there are important limitations on what character can mean in such a context. Since character results from our moral choices and actions, we can say that a group or community has a character to the extent that that group or community is based on, and is held together by, its common choices and activities. Its character arises from the choices it has made, choices that first constituted it and now maintain it as a group or community of free people. Thus we can speak of a particular marriage as a community that has a specific character arising from the couple's choice to marry each other and their subsequent choices that maintain and strengthen (or weaken) their union. In a similar way, one may refer to the moral character of a family or neighbourhood or even a political community or society. In the latter case, such a political community may well lack many of the features of a true community. Still, it is possible, e.g. to speak of the 'Irish character', this being constituted by the Irish people's choice of and commitment to democracy, its shared recognition of the equality of all its members and the consequent requirements of justice and fairness along with other values and virtues.[7]

In this context we can speak of the Christian community, the

---

7. Germain Grisez & Russell Shaw, *Fulfillment in Christ: A Summary of Christian Moral Principles* (University of Notre Dame, Notre Dame & London, 1991), pp 24-5.

church, as a community that has a quite definite moral character. This character arises from and is maintained by the church's
commitment to and action in support of the gospel and kingdom
values and virtues which Jesus originally preached, exemplified
in his life and gave to his followers to pass on to others. As such
a community, the church powerfully influences and shapes the
characters of its members. But these members can also influence
the church and its character in a variety of ways. Undoubtedly
also the church's moral character can be and is influenced by the
society in which it exists and functions at any particular time,
while the influence can and does often go in the reverse direction as the church's character and activities make their mark on
society itself.

Formation of moral character
It will be clear from what has already been said that each person's moral character becomes what it is, and what it will be at
the end of life, only by a long and complex process of formation.
This will involve growth and development over many years and
in many ways but also perhaps regression and failure, immorality and sin.

When we talk here about character formation, we are really
talking about the formation of the person as a moral being.
Today, with the added attention being given to the ethic of
virtue, some would prefer to speak simply of formation in
virtue, while others again say that what we are discussing is the
formation of conscience in the human person, since at its deepest level conscience refers to the person as a moral subject and
agent who lives by certain values, ideals and principles and
makes moral judgments and decisions out of that moral foundation. It is clearly the case, then, that what forms the person forms
his/her character, his/her virtue, his/her conscience. All three
refer to the same human reality looked at from somewhat differ-
ing angles.[8]

Whatever approach one takes, the main aim in forming our
moral character is that we may become good or virtuous persons, morally or humanly mature people. This will enable us to
actualise our potential for being and doing good or, simply, for
being loving persons and acting in loving ways. For the

8. See Linda Hogan, *Confronting the Truth: Conscience in the Catholic
Tradition* (Darton, Longman & Todd, London, 2001), pp 128-135.

Christian this can be stated in terms of loving God and our neighbour in imitation of Christ and in the power of the Holy Spirit. Such formation of character requires that we form good relationships with others and with God and do what we can to build a just society in which the kingdom values of truth and freedom, justice and peace will flourish. This will be an essential element in God's kingdom or rule on earth.

In the light of all this, any discussion of the formation of moral character will of necessity be complex and many-sided, since the process of character formation is itself complex, many-sided and always ongoing. Here, however, only some main points will be touched on.

Factors within the person that condition moral character
In order that we form our moral character so as to become good, virtuous or morally mature people, we must attend especially to three internal factors and develop them as fully as possible.[9]

a) Knowledge: Here we refer, not so much to abstract ideas and intellectual theories, as to our knowledge of moral values. But this is not just conceptual or academic knowledge such as a professor of ethics or moral theology might have. Rather we need what is often referred to nowadays as evaluative knowledge or a real appreciation at the level of our deeper selves of what moral values and dis-values are and involve. This refers above all to an appreciation of persons and what contributes to their welfare and what goes contrary to that welfare.

But most important of all here is knowledge of oneself, self-awareness. This means knowing and being aware of one's values, attitudes, dispositions, intentions, feelings, needs, weaknesses, blind spots, limitations and level of moral development or stage of moral maturity. All this will be essential so that one may realistically make moral choices and decisions that will be right in one's personal circumstances and will thus contribute to one's moral growth and the formation of one's character in goodness and virtue. In short, as Gula says (p 28), becoming aware of one's self is the cornerstone of moral, spiritual and psychological growth.

b) Freedom: To form one's character in goodness one has to have true freedom, so that one is able to take responsibility both

9. Richard M Gula, SS, *Moral Discernment* (Paulist Press, New York, 1997),pp 27-40.

for one's moral choices and actions and for what one has made of oneself as a person and what one is making of oneself. There are clearly limits to our freedom, but there are degrees of freedom too. The greater that freedom from internal and external obstacles, the more we are in charge of our own house, as it were, and so the more we can make of ourselves as moral beings and the more we can put ourselves into the choices we make. Hence, formation in character and virtue requires us to work for greater freedom and so a greater ability to take responsibility for ourselves and our choices. While factors like genetic endowment, family background, social class, education or lack of it, shape and perhaps limit our freedom, we still retain true freedom and with it the ability and the responsibility to form our character in a truly human and Christian way by making choices for good in the various situations we find ourselves in.

Theologians today speak not just of our freedom to choose particular actions, but also of our freedom to choose who and what we will become as persons, whether good or bad. This freedom is referred to as basic freedom and it is expressed in and through our specific choices of X or Y. It is a freedom that we exercise when we make a basic choice or fundamental option for good or evil and, as noted earlier, any exercise of this basic freedom will profoundly shape and indeed transform our moral character for good or for ill.

c) Emotions: Our emotions have a very powerful and often overlooked role to play in the development of moral character and in influencing how one's character impacts on one's moral judgments and choices. In the past this role and influence were conceived in largely negative terms and, as a result, reason and emotion or affectivity were separated and even presented as opposed to each other. Today we understand our affectivity much better and so we can appreciate its very significant contribution to character building and moral choice more fully and more positively.

A person's morality or moral sense has its roots in his/her feelings and it is from them that that morality gets its nourishment and power to shape character and choice. In other words, the springs of morality are in the heart, and the origins of our moral experience are in our affections or feelings. Now, our basic moral experience is that of value, in particular the value of persons. Here we find the foundation of our morality, a foundation that contains an emotional element, namely, our appreciation of and concern and care for the human person. Values or goods are appreciated emotionally or affectively as well as intellectually; in fact our primary response to value is an affective one. This response is not, however, a blind emotional reaction. Rather it has an element of judgment or evaluation in it, giving us an immediate preliminary moral assessment of the situation we are in, or the action with which we are faced, e.g. anger in the face of injustice, sadness or anguish in relation to a severely handicapped baby, uneasiness at some new technique of human reproduction or some proposed manner of acting. Whether these affective responses are confirmed by subsequent moral reflection and logical analysis or not, the point here is that emotion pervades all our moral knowledge and contributes notably to our moral choices and the building of our character. Thus feelings can guide our perceptions and moral judgments and they are what gives energy and strength to our commitments to good (or evil) and to becoming a good person. In fact, for a person who has formed a good moral character, one's feelings in relation to a particular value or values can make appropriate moral choices second nature, as it were, to that person. This is explained by the fact that often our affections or feelings give rise to a deeper insight into the values we love and appreciate and facilitate us in judging and choosing wisely and well in their regard. Thus is moral character influenced and formed in significant ways by our emotions or affections.[10]

All this helps explain why the emotionally immature person will very likely have a diminished level of moral maturity or of character formation, and so may well act immorally more frequently and thus have less success in building moral character than if he/she were more mature emotionally. This can be seen clearly in relation to bad anger or mood control and lack of empathy. These give rise to conflict, damaged relationships and a low level of care for others. On the positive side, a similar close link can be seen between our levels of emotional and moral maturity. Here too one's ability to control one's moods and feelings such as 'bad humour', moodiness, anger, jealousy and hate, will

10. See Gula, *Moral Discernment*, pp 34-39 and 87-91; also Daniel Maguire, *Moral Choice* (Winston Press, Minneapolis, USA, 1979), pp 71-77, 263-7, 281-308; also John Macquarrie, *Studies in Christian Existentialism*, (SCM, London, 1966), chapter 3, 'Feelings and Understanding'.

enable one to act in a more moral manner and so to build one's moral character better. But perhaps more important will be one's level of empathy. Empathy means feeling with and for another or others; it means being sensitive to others. It is a short step from that to caring for them. So the greater one's empathy or care for others the more will one's character be formed in moral goodness and the more will one be enabled to love others by making better moral choices that promote their welfare as persons.[11]

Social influences on moral character formation

The fact that we form our own character in and through our patterns of moral choices does not exclude the fact that all of us as persons-in-relationships-and-in-community are powerfully influenced and shaped by the people around us, in our family, neighbourhood, society and world and, for us Christians, also by the church, the community of Christians.

Social groups and communities

In a real sense it is true that people make groups but, on the other hand, it is also the case that groups make people. This latter holds true from the family up to society itself and, in important ways today, the world community too. This deep moulding of us as persons takes place because as members of many groups and communities we internalise and make our own the patterns of thinking, communicating and behaving of these groups and usually also their beliefs, values and virtues, at least to some considerable extent. In the communities of our family, friends, ethnic group, neighbourhood, school and the wider society, we learn what it is we are to value about persons. We identify instinctively with the ways of thinking and acting that we see supported by these communities. The ways we experience people treating each other in these communities are for us moral lessons, and each community has built-in moral messages about what is expected of a good member. Morality is, then, in significant ways, socially conditioned or a social product. Especially significant in forming our moral outlook and character are people who influence us by their wisdom, moral commitment and moral maturity. These function as role models and so they contribute powerfully to our formation of character. Other influ-

---

11. See Chapter 3 below, 43-50, 52-53.

ences in our groups and communities that are important here
are authority figures and experts, and also values, principles
and laws that are held in and by our groups.[12]

The Christian community, the church
There can be no doubt that for Christians, and especially for us
Catholics, the Christian community, the church, through its
vision of human life with its beliefs, stories, traditions, images
and rituals, moral ideals, values, principles and virtues, is a
powerful shaper of our moral character, though obviously the
extent of this will vary from person to person. Particularly important here will be the Bible, Jesus' example and teaching and
the life of the church itself, especially its internal relationships,
structures, teaching and preaching, tradition, liturgy, laws, pastoral ministry and, of course, the great witness of its many saints
and other outstanding personages. All this will shape our vision
of life very significantly and, hence, also our perspectives, dispositions, affections and intentions. And as a result, our choices
will be informed and conditioned in very notable ways by the
church to which we belong.[13]

Of course, the extent to which the church or any community
will condition our moral character will depend on how we respond to what we experience as members of the Christian community or those other communities. It is this response that
makes us who we are and forms our moral character. Since this
response will be uniquely personal, so will our character be.[14]

Ways of describing good moral character
There are many ways in which to describe what the ideal of a
good moral character is. These are not new and indeed most of
them have been mentioned in passing earlier. But in the context
of our present discussion it will be helpful to set out briefly four
expressions of, or ways of describing, this ideal. These are quite
common, not just in moral theology, but also in spirituality,
pastoral practice and daily Christian discourse. They are four
different ways of answering the question, what would a good

12. Gula, *Moral Discernment*, pp 64-74.
13. Gula, *Reason Informed by Faith*, pp 140-145, 186-188, 200-203; Gula,
Moral Discernment, pp 58-64.
14. Connors & McCormick, pp 20-21; Gula, *Reason Informed by Faith*, pp
200-207.

moral character look like? or what does 'good' mean in this context?

a) Being fully human

One way of expressing the fact that a person has acquired a good moral character is to say that she/he has made significant progress towards being fully human. No one arrives at the fulness of being human in this earthly existence; only Jesus achieved that. But many come close and we are all called to try. So to be good in the fullest sense is to be fully human, i.e. to have to a large extent achieved fulfilment as a person and to have realised substantially one's potential as a human being. It is clear from this way of expressing the matter that growing in moral goodness or forming one's character morally is something that humanises us, i.e. makes us more human, better human beings. Doing good and becoming good enhances our humanity, makes us more what God calls us to be. It is encouraging as well as challenging to realise that moral living is not, then, some kind of task or burden imposed on us by some external agent like the church or society or God. Rather it is what our very nature as human persons-in-relationship-and-in-community calls for and pushes us to do. It will be obvious here too that building a good moral character or becoming fully human is a lifelong project that is always in the making and is never complete in this life.

b) Being a loving person

A good person is one who loves self, others and God. One is good to the extent that one is loving and to that extent too one has built a good moral character. What does loving mean? It means caring for oneself, others and God in an unselfish and mature manner. It involves entering into caring relationships with others in ways that are appropriate to the situation of those in the relationship. It requires us to reach out to others with compassion and empathy. In other words, we can say that to be loving involves and requires one to have all the virtues in some real degree, because love expresses itself in and through those virtues, e.g. kindness, patience, generosity, justice, chastity, temperance. So the loving person is the one who is virtuous or has developed a good moral character.

c) Being a virtuous person

This is yet another way of saying that one has a good moral character. To be virtuous is to have acquired those moral habits, attitudes, affections and beliefs that we call the virtues and to

practise them consistently in our daily lives. Practising the
virtues leads to genuine human and Christian fulfilment for individuals and for groups too. Doing so makes us good persons
and builds good moral character.

We may add here that in moral theology today the virtues
are getting a lot more attention and study than they got before
Vatican II. This is due to the fact that they did not fit into the
legal model of the Christian moral life very well, largely because
that approach to the moral life was very act-centred and saw the
virtues as basically sources of further obligations for individual
persons.[15]

But the virtues do fit into the relational understanding of the
moral life, and in consequence moral character is restored to its
true central and basic place in the Christian life. In fact we hear a
good deal nowadays about the Christian ethic being an ethic of
virtue. In that context the focus moves to the question, what
should I become as a person? and only subsequently to the issue
of what should I do? So when we talk of a virtuous person, we
are describing that person's moral character and asserting that
he/she has acquired such a character over the course of his/her
life up to the present.

   d) Being a morally mature person

This way of expressing the fact that one has a good moral
character is closely related to a) above, where we spoke of the
good person being fully human. It indicates that one has grown
morally or in one's humanity to a level appropriate to one's
stage in life's journey. It also points to the importance of emotional, personal and relational growth and maturity as foundations required for the building of moral maturity. Without
these it will not be possible to become a truly mature person and
so one will have difficulty acquiring a good moral character. In
short then we can say that being morally mature is another way
of saying that one has a good moral character.

Practical implications for our daily living
We may mention very briefly some significant implications of
our emphasis on moral character and its formation as central in
the Christian life.

   i. It is important to move away from an act-centred view of
one's Christian moral life and focus, first and primarily, on one-

---

15. See above p 24.

self as a person and what one has made and is making of oneself morally speaking. Emphasising moral character is one way that enables us to do that.

ii. It is important to emphasise that growth and decline in Christian virtue or character is a process that goes on over time and requires continuing effort and attention. Improvement will tend to be gradual, often hardly noticeable and never automatic or guaranteed. Awareness, commitment and struggle are called for, if progress is to be made in building moral character.

iii. The same holds in relation to conversion from sinfulness and sins, and particularly from habits of sin, sinful attitudes, tendencies and dispositions and faulty values and priorities. Awareness here is the beginning of success and that needs to be accompanied by the will to be converted and the sustained effort to accomplish that conversion in all its dimensions.

iv. It may be possible to 'get away' with a sin in the sense that other people may not find out about it. But such 'getting away' with it is not possible in the sense of avoiding the damage the sin itself does to the sinner. This damage is automatic, as it were, and so, when one sins, one is rendered less loving, more inclined to sin in future and one's moral character is in some degree weakened.

v. Similarly, when one does a good or virtuous act, one automatically develops one's moral character to some extent and makes oneself a better person.

vi. The better one becomes as a person and the more one builds one's moral character in goodness, so the more one is inclined to do further good acts and the less one will tend to engage in sinful activity. So, if one's heart is in the right place and one has been doing one's best to be a good Christian for years, one should not be anxious or fearful about sinning. One can be at peace, knowing that one's virtue is strong, one's character is good and God holds us in the palm of God's hand.

vii. There can be no room for complacency, however, since one can always act out of character, even if that is unlikely for one of really good moral character.

viii. One will need to respond positively but critically to the messages and influences of the various groups and communities to which one belongs, including presentday Western society and culture. In this the guidance of the church's teaching will be essential and will provide us with both direction and directions.

ix. To assess oneself or one's character morally or, in more

traditional terminology, to examine one's conscience, it may
help to look at particular virtues (and vices) and also at the quality of one's part in one's various relationships, extending from
the family circle through one's relatives and neighbours to one's
work colleagues and one's friends. How one relates to one's
local community and one's parish community also needs to be
considered.

x. Finally, for one's peace of mind and serenity of soul it is
important to realise clearly that one cannot attain perfection of
character here on earth. Perfection is for heaven only. We will, in
other words, always be imperfect here below. One's task in life,
then, is to continue to develop one's moral character and to
grow in virtue. Then, in God's good time, we can hope to arrive
at the perfection of virtue and character that we all desire and
that God has promised can be ours as a result of our living like
sons and daughters of God in Jesus the Son of God.

Further Reading
Connors, Russell B., & McCormick, Patrick T., *Character, Choices and
Community: The Three Faces of Christian Ethics*, (Paulist Press, New York,
1998), chapter 2;
Cosgrave, William, 'Moral Character', *The Furrow*, January 2000, 24 - 33.
This article is essentially a summary of the present chapter.
Grisez, Germain & Shaw, Russell, *Fulfillment in Christ: A summary of
Christian Moral Principles* (University of Notre Dame, Notre Dame &
London, 1991), pp 23-25, 84-85;
Gula, Richard M., *Moral Discernment* (Paulist Press, New York, 1997),
pp 22-24, 27-40, chapters 3-5;
Gula, Richard M., *Reason Informed by Faith: Foundations of Catholic
Morality* (Paulist Press, New York, 1989), pp 138-146, 186-188, 199-206;
Gustafson, James M., *Christian Ethics and the Community* (Pilgrim Press,
Philadelphia, USA, 1971), pp166-172;
Hauerwas, Stanley, *A Community of Character: Towards a Constructive
Christian Social Ethic* (University of Notre Dame Press, Notre Dame,
1981), chapters 6 and 7;
Hauerwas, Stanley, *Character and the Christian Life: A Study in Theological
Ethics* (Trinity University Press, San Antonio, USA, 1975), chapters 1-3.

CHAPTER 3

Our Emotional Life and Moral Living

People from the Co Wexford won't need to be reminded that in September 1996 the Wexford team won the All-Ireland senior hurling championship. That was an occasion of great excitement and rejoicing for us in Wexford; we were thrilled in a way not experienced among us for many years. For many of us this magnificant victory at the national level was a very emotional experence. It involved, of course, the winning of a hurling match but, in addition, our very identity as Wexford people was somehow re-affirmed and our feeling that it is good to be from Wexford was dramatically reinforced.

Now most people who know about hurling would probably agree that that response to our team's All-Ireland triumph was very understandable, appropriate and rational for us Wexford people, given the very special occasion that it was. While we were very excited and emotionally moved, few of us lost the run of ourselves. On the contrary, one could say that, because of our state of high feeling, our response to our county's success was not just intelligent but more intelligent than if we had taken a detached, logical, from-the-neck-up attitude. Few from Wexford would regard the latter kind of reaction as appropriate and many would likely brand it as odd, insufficient and indeed quite unintelligent.

The point being made here is not primarily about hurling, as the reader may well have discerned. Rather is it about our emotions. We are really saying that our emotions don't always, or indeed often, lead us into trouble and result in irrational, disruptive and even immoral behaviour. On the contrary, they have an intelligence of their own which, when properly understood and deployed, leads to attitudes, choices and actions that are not less but more intelligent and human than the purely rational or academic. In a word, we are affirming that our emotions or passions, when maturely integrated and exercised, have real wisdom; they guide our thinking, our valuing and our decision-making, and, in consequence, make an essential and basic contribution to truly intelligent and truly moral living. What follows in the first part of this chapter is largely an attempt to explain how this is so and what it involves.

The negative tradition: emotion as suspect and requiring rigid control
In the ordinary run of life most of us, and especially us males, don't give much thought to our feelings or emotions. We simply experience them, at times without a great deal of explicit awareness of their presence and power in our lives. Very likely, then, we don't understand our emotions very well and in all probability don't give much time or attention either to understanding them, managing them better or integrating them more fully into our personality by efforts to achieve emotional maturity. In consequence many of us are to some degree at the mercy of our emotions. We may well be somewhat emotionally undeveloped, perhaps even emotionally illiterate and hence we may find ourselves carried away by some sudden surge of feeling that seems to have a mind of its own, e.g. anger, fear, sexual passion, jealousy, revenge, loneliness.

This kind of experience of our emotions has led many, and especially many Christians, to understand our emotional life as an irrational, almost uncontrollable dimension of our personality and life. Perhaps celibate males have been particularly prone to take this viewpoint. In this perspective our emotions came to be viewed as very liable to escape the control of reason and run wild in ways that can be very destructive, not just of our relationships and communities but even of ourselves as persons and moral beings. One has only to think of what can happen when one flies into a rage or experiences strong feelings of jealousy or revenge. Thus, our emotions (or passions, as they were usually called in the church) have come to be seen as morally suspect, with the proper approach to them being the ascetical or penitential one: rigid control aided by stern mortification of the senses and appetites and unremitting self-denial, especially in relation to all sexual feelings and fantasies.[1]

---

1. See William Spohn SJ, 'Passion and Principles', *Theological Studies*, March 1991,69; Pat Collins CM, *Intimacy and the Hungers of the Heart* (Dublin: Columba Press, 1991),43; G. Simon Harak SJ, *Virtuous Passions: The Foundations of Christian Character* (New York: Paulist Press, 1993), 7-12.

This attitude to our emotions goes back many centuries in history generally and in Christian history too. It has found many advocates among Christian pastors and moralists and has often been accompanied by negative and even hostile attitudes to the human body, especially the female body and, in consequence, to women as well. Not surprisingly this dualistic viewpoint has not infrequently made its way into spirituality and given rise to unfortunate anti-body thinking and to practices that were more geared to suppress one's emotional life rather than to enhance and integrate it. Thankfully in our day these negative attitudes and practices are clearly recognised for what they are, and are being laid aside as dualistic, damaging and ultimately unChristian and anti-human. In place of them major efforts are being made to develop a positive understanding of our emotional life, to discover how best to integrate our emotions into our personality and humanity generally, and to do all possible to appreciate and enhance the essential contribution of emotion to intelligent living and to the moral life.[2]

The remainder of our reflections in the first part of this chapter will be devoted to an effort to summarise and explain these developments.

Emotions and Intelligence

Our emotions are, as the word itself implies, a source of movement within us; they are an impulse to act. Thus anger pushes us towards vigorous activity in defence or attack; fear serves to warn us of danger and gets us ready for fight or flight. Our emotional reactions are swifter than our rational responses to situations or persons, and so our emotions provide us with a sort of instant understanding of a situation and an almost automatic reaction. The rational mind, however, takes longer to understand, judge and act. In a sense, one could say, we seem to have two minds or two streams feeding into our intelligence, the emotional and the rational. These usually operate in close harmony and in balance, providing us with information and decisions that guide us through life. Our emotions feed into and inform the operations of the rational mind and the rational mind refines and

2. Spohn, 69; Collins, 43-4; Daniel Goleman, *Emotional Intelligence: Why it can matter more than IQ* (London: Bloomsbury, 1996), pp XI-XII. This book is a main source of much of the remainder of the first part of this chapter.

sometimes vetoes the input of the emotions. It seems clear, then, that our feelings are essential to thought and thought is essential to feeling. It remains true, nevertheless, that we can be carried away by a powerful emotion, so that reason is overwhelmed and rational considerations are cast aside. But this is normally a rare event and the interaction and balance between the rational and the emotional usually works so as to facilitate more intelligent and wiser thinking and decision-making. This means that how we do in life and the success we have are due not just to rational factors or the IQ we have been gifted with. Rather they result from the integration and harmony of what some call our rational and our emotional intelligence. These two complement and support each other and only their regular cooperation will enable us to have a full and happy life. Clearly, then, one of our main tasks in life is to integrate and harmonise reason and emotion, head and heart, so that we live a fully intelligent and human life. When we do this, reason and emotion will each have its due and essential place in our lives, with neither dominating or in subordination to the other but with an intelligent balance being struck between them.[3]

Emotions contribute to intelligent living
Experts tell us today that our IQ or academic intelligence contributes only about 20% to the factors that determine success in life. In other words, 'brains' accounts for only about a fifth of what we may call a happy and successful life. 80% of that success and happiness is due to other factors. This fact alone would seem to indicate that we have dramatically overestimated the importance of IQ in and for our lives; we have placed too much emphasis on the rational or intellectual dimension of our personality and too little on the other factors, most of which are in the emotional area and which many refer to nowadays as emotional intelligence or simply affective maturity. We may note too that academic intelligence has little to do with our emotional life or level of happiness, as is clear from many instances of very intelligent people making a complete mess of their lives. Of course many people of high IQ are very successful in life but many are not, and the reason for this lies in the 80% of factors just referred to, and central to these is the issue of how we handle our emotions.

3. Spohn, 69; Goleman, 27-9.

This focus on handling our emotions and its relation to success and happiness is a new emphasis and hence it is not as yet fully understood or fully explored. But numerous studies show its importance and afford more than enough evidence to warrant our concentration on it here.

Experience shows that some people are more emotionally mature or adept than others and many studies highlight the fact that this maturity or adeptness is crucial to understanding why one person thrives in life, while another, of equal or even greater academic intelligence, fails or under-achieves. It seems clear, then, that emotional development and skill are basic in determining how well we can use whatever skills we have, including our 'brains'. There is now plenty of evidence that people who have acquired significant emotional maturity are at an advantage in all areas of life and are more likely to be content and effective, whatever they choose to do in life. On the other hand, those who cannot exercise real control over their emotional life find that they are hamstrung as far as using their intellectual gifts in the service of clear thinking and effective career work are concerned. Success and happiness tend to elude them.[4]

Areas where emotions enhance intelligent living
It is clear from what has been said so far that scholars today are understanding intelligence in a much wider sense than previously. It will be important, then, to outline what this wider understanding involves or embraces, and in particular to clarify what is meant by emotional intelligence. In other words, what areas or elements of life are we talking about when we say that our emotions enhance and foster intelligent, successful and happy living?

Goleman in his recent book, *Emotional Intelligence*,[5] discusses

4. Goleman, 33-43; Spohn, 59; Raymond Studzinski OSB, 'Feelings', in Michael Downey, Editor, *The New Dictionary of Catholic Spirituality* (Dublin: Gill & Macmallan, 1993), 392-3; See Claude Steiner PhD, *Achieving Emotional Literacy: A Personal Programme to Increase your Emotional Intelligence* (Bloomsbury, London, 1999), chapter 1; and Frances Wilks, *Intelligent Emotion: How to Succeed Through Transforming Your Feelings* (Arrow Books, London, 1998), chapters 1 & 2.
5. Chapters 4 through 8. For a brief summary of Golemen's ideas here see Maureen Gaffney, *The Way We Live Now* (Dublin: Gill & Macmillan, 1996), 62-3. This whole chapter, 'How Feelings Count', 61-67 in Gaffney's book, is a review article of Golemen's book. See also Steiner, 24-5.

five main areas or domains where we can see intelligence in our emotions and where intelligence can be brought to our emotions. We may summarise these insights briefly in the following manner.

i) Knowing one's emotions as they occur

This is the central element in emotional competence or maturity. Being aware of one's emotions or feelings as they happen is essential, if one is to have good psychological insight and understand oneself well. Self-awareness is basic for the task of managing one's emotions constructively and that management is, as already indicated, vital to success and happiness in life, not just in personal relationships but also in relation to decision-making about anything from who to marry to what job to take. It is clear here that being attuned to one's feelings is very important for the exercise of one's reasoning powers in making decisions. It is now evident that our feelings play a very significant role in all our decisions in our personal life and that there is no such thing as a purely rational or intellectual choice. Experiments have shown that one who has lost touch with his/her emotions is quite unable to make any decision or choice and can't use his/her reasoning powers at all adequately. Such a person, who completely lacks emotional self-awareness, appears as quite emotionally flat, unresponsive to feelings, boring and in fact incapable of personal relationships. On the other hand, the person who is strong in awareness of his/her emotional life tends to be independent, sure of his/her boundaries, is in good psychological health and has a positive outlook on life. He/she is better able to manage his/her emotions and to make good and appropriate personal choices and decisions. Women tend to be more in touch with their feelings than men but, for both, awareness of their emotions as they occur is basic to happiness and success in life.[6]

ii) Managing one's emotions appropriately

The degree or level of one's awareness of one's emotions is fundamental in the task of managing or integrating one's emotional life in an appropriate and balanced way. The better one's self-awareness the better chance one has of achieving emotional balance or maturity. If, however, one is largely out of touch with one's emotions, one will very likely be at the mercy of one's moods. In this matter of emotional management, the ideal is

6. See Wilks, chapter 3.

neither repression nor giving free rein to one's feelings. Rather is that ideal to be found in the middle way between these two extremes and its name is, to use the traditional words, temperance or moderation. All will agree that allowing one's emotions to run riot in one's life is a recipe for disaster and unhappiness, while repressing them results in a dull, cold, featureless existence which lacks any worthwhile relationships and anything one could realistically call happiness. Integrating one's emotions or passions into one's personality and life is, then, the task to be undertaken and carried through, if one is to live an intelligent and truly human and Christian life. And it may be noted at once that studies have discovered that there is little connection between one's IQ level and one's level of emotional wellbeing or maturity.

Central to appropriate balance in one's emotional life is the ability to keep one's distressing or negative feelings in check, so as to avoid being carried away by them and being in their grip over long periods. The main feelings we are talking about here are anger, anxiety and sadness or depression. If these are anyway strong, they can be very hard to manage. There are no magic answers in this area but some methods have been shown to be helpful. With effort and time one can learn to control these common emotions in an intelligent manner. People who are good at this emotional skill of managing their feelings tend to bounce back quickly from whatever setbacks they encounter and to have a life rich in personal relationships, success and happiness. Those who are poor in this area are constantly in the throes of some deep negative emotion and can experience great distress and unhappiness.[7]

iii) Controlling impulse and motivating oneself

Studies have found that two vitally important emotional skills that facilitate the full use of one's talents and abilities are, firstly, controlling one's impulses so as to delay gratification and persist in one's efforts to achieve a goal one has set oneself, and secondly, motivating oneself so as to be successful despite setbacks and the tendency to give up the struggle. Those who have acquired these skills will be more successful in life, because they will use their natural abilities better. This applies in academic matters, in sport, in business and even in prayer. If one wants instant gratification or is poor at controlling one's moods and

---

7. Goleman, 59-75; Wilks, chapter 6; Steiner, chapters 3, 4, 5 & 6.

impulses, one will be less successful academically, in sport, socially, etc. In addition the presence of hope, optimism and positive thinking has been found to help greatly in one's efforts to do well in all areas of life. One's beliefs and feelings about one's abilities have a profound effect on those abilities and how one uses or fails to use them. If one thinks positively, is hopeful and optimistic, one will very likely do better than the person who thinks in a negative way and is not hopeful or optimistic about his/her abilities and possibilities.

In short, then, channelling one's emotions towards a productive end is an emotional skill of great significance and proven positive results. Those who have acquired it are living examples of the power of emotion to guide effective effort and they demonstrate again the profound importance of emotional maturity and competence in living an intelligent and so a successful and happy life.

iv) Being sensitive to others' feelings

Here we are on slightly more familiar ground and are already aware of the importance for living, and especially for relationships, of being sensitive to how others are feeling. This emotional ability or skill is today referred to as empathy, and we need little convincing that the more empathic one is the better one will succeed in relationships and the more emotionally intelligent one will be. The person who scores high on the empathy scale will be one who is well adjusted emotionally and, in consequence, is one who will be more sensitive to others' feelings, will be more outgoing and in tune with others, and so will be more popular and well liked. This means that such a person will be better at making personal relationships and friendships and hence will be better also in relationships with the other sex. In general, women are better than men at this kind of empathy and there are some people who lack this empathy almost totally. These latter are the people we call psychopaths, and because they can't empathise with or be sensitive to the feelings of others, they can inflict pain and do damage to those others without any revulsion or twinge of conscience. Their emotional deficiency is the root of their brutal and immoral behaviour. Some murderers, rapists and child molesters fall into this category.

It is clear also that it is possible to acquire this emotional skill of empathy and to develop one's ability to be sensitive to the feelings of others. It is also easy to see, from all that has been said

here about empathy, that there will very likely be a close link between one's level of empathy and one's level of caring for others.
To feel with another is really to begin to care for that other and
so we can say that to empathise with another is the root of caring
for that person. This leads to the reflection that the degree of
one's empathy will shape significantly the morality one lives by,
and in particular the moral values and principles one acts out of
and the moral judgments one makes. In a sense, then, the roots
of morality are to be found in empathy and those of immorality
in lack of empathy. Here we find a clear link between one's emotional life and one's moral life: the more emotionally skilled or
mature one is in this area, the more moral one is likely to be, and
vice versa. One's level of emotional growth will have a direct effect on one's level of moral maturity. This will be particularly
true in regard to caring for others, justice and fairness and providing for the most needy in society.

v) Making and managing relationships

The fifth and final area where our emotions can enhance and
foster intelligent living concerns relationships with other people. It is easy to see that empathy is a basic skill in this area of
life. Being able to discern and manage emotions in others is the
core of the art of handling human relationships. But a deficiency
in this emotional skill will probably result in even the intellectually bright floundering in their relationships and being socially
incompetent. Being good at empathy will, however, enable one
to shine in social skills: put others at ease, influence and per-
suade them, inspire them to action, set the tone in interpersonal
meetings and make friends, etc. Other elements of what may be
called social intelligence are being skilled at organising and
leading groups and having a talent for resolving conflicts that
can arise in such groups.

We may conclude this section, in which we have discussed
the five areas where emotional intelligence is at work, by saying
that the role and importance of our emotions in these areas provides a firm basis for broadening our understanding of intelligence
beyond the purely rational or academic. Thus truly intelligent
and human living is only to be found in the person who has
achieved a suitable level of emotional maturity or competence
and has integrated that with his/her rational or academic intelligence. Such a person alone can make a real success of life and be
a happy and contented person, who has realised her/his potential

substantially if not totally and so has arrived at living a full and truly human and Christian life.

Implications of these perspectives
Comments have already been made that point to some of the consequences or implications of the above thinking about how our emotions contribute to intelligent human living. We may tease out these implications in regard to the intelligence in our emotions by adding some further remarks under three headings.

a) Leadership
It will come as no surprise that the level of one's emotional competence or integration will be of great significance in relation to how successful those in leadership positions will or can be. Since one's emotional maturity is vital for making and managing human relationships of all sorts, one who is deficient in this area will have a very uphill job indeed in the task of being a good leader, whether that is in business, in government, in sport, in the Christian ministry or any other area of life.

We have often heard it said that leadership demands one's head not one's heart. Studies in recent years have shown, however, that this view is outmoded and indeed counter-productive. In this area too intelligence needs to be understood in its wider sense and, hence, a leader needs to attend to and be competent in the five areas of emotional intelligence already outlined, if he/she is to be successful as a leader. This is easily illustrated. If a leader is given to angry outbursts or is quite insensitive to the feelings of those around him/her, then clearly, those under his/her leadership will be upset, probably fearful and distracted and will function much less well than they otherwise would. If a leader is unpredictable and given to mood swings, then too those around him/her suffer and so will his/her effectiveness as a leader. Even if such a leader sees leadership as domination and getting his/her own way, it is unlikely that that way will always be very balanced or that the decisions he/she makes will be the best for the enterprise in question even most of the time. In addition, this leader's staff and co-workers will suffer great stress and will probably function very ineffectively. In other areas of leadership too, how one deals as leader with the people around will be crucial. The giving and receiving of criticism is one such area. If criticism is delivered in a harsh or angry or sarcastic manner, and as almost a personal attack on the one to whom it is directed, then that will have serious effects on motivation, energy, confidence and cooperation, and great damage will have been done not just to the one criticised but to the relationship with the leader and so to the part the one criticised will in future play in the enterprise or group. Bias or discrimination by the leader on any grounds will also tend to have profoundly negative effects. From recent studies it seems that the crucial difference between run-of-the-mill leaders and the stars in leadership is that the latter put a lot of energy into building up informal networks involving good relationships with key people in their organisation. This involves good communication, the gradual building of trust between the leader and the key people and so the availability of those people to help out when problems arise.[8]

b) Health

It is now clear from various studies that strong distressing emotions, and especially anger, anxiety and depression, can have serious negative effects on one's medical condition or state of health. Like smoking or high cholesterol, these emotions can pose a major threat to health. Anger is an emotion that, above all others, can do serious damage to one's heart. Since being angry increases one's heart rate and blood pressure, a lot of damage can be done to one's heart when such increases are repeated over and over again by a person who is habitually angry. Anger is particularly lethal in those who already have heart disease, and if anger becomes chronic, then it is at its most dangerous. Luckily one can reduce one's levels of anger and so lessen the damage to one's heart. Stress or anxiety is another emotion that is toxic for one's health. It can weaken one's immune system, i.e. lower one's resistance to infection, and so increase one's chances of getting a variety of diseases, e.g. colds, flu, asthma, ulcers, diabetes, etc. The stress or strain that goes with high-powered jobs and high-pressure performance in the workplace is included here, so that one's job can take its toll on one's health. Depression, it is becoming clear, can also inflict damage on one's health, because it tends to make one's sickness worse and one's recovery more difficult.

The other side of this medical coin is that positive emotions can improve one's state of health at least to some degree, e.g. an optimistic outlook, hope for recovery, having friends to share

8. Goleman, 148-163.

one's deep feelings with and to support one in an illness, can all have a positive influence on one's health.

In short, then, attending to emotional needs is medically very beneficial and medical care that neglects how people feel is no longer adequate.[9]

c) Morality

There is a negative and positive side to the ways in which one's level of emotional well-being can affect one's morality.

If one is emotionally immature or unintelligent, then the level of one's moral maturity will be affected in a negative way. For example, one who is prone to angry outbursts or fits of jealousy will very likely not have a great deal of self-control in these areas and so may well get into conflict, and damage his/her relationships with others by selfish and aggressive behaviour. One who is deficient in empathy will tend to be insensitive to the needs and difficulties of others and so will probably be limited and even at fault in regard to care, compassion and altruism. A person who has poor impulse control will tend to act to satisfy his/her own needs or wants, ignoring the impact this may have on others. Thus he/she may act selfishly. It can be seen, then, that emotional immaturity is closely linked to, and may well be the cause of, moral immaturity.

On the positive side, a similar close link between the emotional and the moral can be seen. As has been noted, one's level of empathy has a strong connection with one's level of caring, compassion and altruism, so that the more empathic one is, the more one displays these morally positive attitudes towards others. Similarly, if one has learned to manage one's anger well, one will be a person who practises the virtue of meekness to a high degree. And if one has acquired the ability to make and manage personal relationships maturely or intelligently, then one will love others maturely and competently. It will be obvious too that being able to motivate oneself will be vitally important in regard to fulfilling one's duties, especially those one finds it hard to warm to, and in persisting in one's efforts despite failure and difficulties. Delaying gratification and disciplining oneself also have major moral implications in relation to our moral choices, behaviour, character-building and moral development.

In short then, it can be safely stated that being emotionally intelligent has great significance for one's moral life and one's

---

9. Goleman, 164-185.

level of moral intelligence or maturity. So much so in fact that it can be clearly seen that we have a real duty to do all possible to reach emotional maturity, in order that we may then live a morally mature or intelligent life, whether we are Christians or not.[10]

MANAGING ANGER INTELLIGENTLY

What has been discussed so far has concerned our emotional life in general. It may be of value at this point to focus in more detail on one particular emotion or feeling and reflect on it and how to manage it when we experience it. This will enable us to see how to be emotionally intelligent in connection with an emotion that is very much part of our daily lives and in the process to take a look at the moral dimension of anger.[11]

From our ordinary experience of living, all of us know what anger is. We have all experienced it at first hand, having been angry on occasions ourselves and having been on the receiving end of others' anger now and again. The question is, then, how we should understand it and handle it, so as to be emotionally intelligent in this area of our lives.

Faulty attitudes

In the past, and even today, faulty attitudes in relation to anger can be discerned, not least among Christians. We have tended to moralise and spiritualise in regard to this emotion. Some feel that it is morally wrong to be angry, especially with authority figures like one's bishop, parish priest, religious superior, the pope, etc, or with those we love or ought to love, like spouse, parent, friend. Even still the occasional penitent will confess that 'I was angry, Father', as if that were sinful in itself. We spiritualise our anger when we say such things as '(s)he's so holy or sick or likeable, I can't be angry with him/her'. Or it is not right to be angry with God, the church or the dead. We rationalise our anger when we say such things as, 'it won't do any good to express my anger', or 'my anger may be irrational', or 'expressing it may destroy our relationship'. The result of these attitudes is that we repress our anger, because we feel bad about being angry. Such repression is nowadays seen to be psychologically

10. Goleman, 104-110, 285-6; Spohn, 69-87; Harak, chapters 4 through 6.
11. The following pages are a slightly revised version of my article, 'Anger and After', *Intercom*, Dublin, November 1994, 16-19.

unhealthy and damaging to ourselves, and often enough is of little help in regard to our relationships. In consequence of this we need to find a better approach to anger and managing it, one that has more constructive and positive results for ourselves, for others and for our relationships.

Understanding anger
Anger is an emotion or feeling and as such is simply a psychological or psychic fact that is neither good nor bad in itself. Being angry is, then, morally neutral; it is neither right nor wrong in itself. After all, Jesus was angry on some occasions. Also, anger is a positive reality placed in our very being for a good purpose. It is a form of energy which we can use in a constructive or destructive manner and, if used in the latter way, there may be question of wrongdoing or misuse of the energy which this feeling provides for us.

Anger can arise in a great variety of situations in daily life. It is perhaps one of the feelings we most commonly experience in ourselves and in others. Many things can provoke anger in us but, in general, we can say that anger is the human person's emotional or deeply personal response to his/her perception that some need he/she has is not being met or is being blocked, frustrated or threatened. Examples are plentiful. I may get angry if my need for food or shelter is being denied, or if someone makes me feel rejected, or incompetent or foolish, or if I am unfairly treated or accused in the wrong. Similarly, if I am blocked in carrying out some project or my expectations are not met in a particular case. So when my anger rises, it is a signal to me that some need I have is not being met or I am being threatened in some way.

Experience makes it clear that there are many degrees of anger, ranging from mild irritation to violent rage. This anger may be suddenly provoked by a particular event or incident or may build up over a period and erupt, as it were, when some last straw triggers it. It frequently happens that our pattern of anger and our way of handling our anger are deeply influenced by our childhood experiences, especially those with our parents. If your father was an explosive type or if your mother always repressed her anger or handled it well, then you will instinctively tend to imitate what you saw your parents doing. And you may still be doing just that, for better or for worse.

Another influential factor in relation to anger in one's life is the level of self-esteem or inner personal security which one has attained. If that self-esteem is good, the chances are that one will be good at managing one's anger in a balanced way. If it is not good, then one will more easily feel under threat and as a result may get angry more frequently and handle it less constructively.

Kinds of anger

It will be helpful to divide anger into the following types or kinds.

Expressed and repressed: Expressed anger arises when a person gives outward expression to the anger he/she is now feeling, so that the anger is communicated to the other person(s) or at least to someone. Such expression of anger may be appropriate or inappropriate, constructive or destructive and as such is subject to moral assessment. It will be right or wrong morally.

Repressed anger is anger that is not expressed but is kept within the person. When this is done consciously the process is referred to as suppression and it may be appropriate or inappropriate, depending on the circumstances. When it is done subconsciously, it is called repression. It is generally held that this repression of anger is not a psychologically healthy thing to do, because it involves burying the energy of the anger within one's psyche. If this is continued over a period, it is likely to give rise to a variety of physical symptoms, since the energy attached to one's anger seeks an outlet and, being denied its usual expression, will find some expression. Hence, repressed anger may be at the root of ailments like headaches or pains that don't seem to have an identifiable cause; it can cause tension within a person, ulcers, asthma, depression, etc. Trying to become aware of the fact that one represses anger will, therefore, be very important for one's emotional health.

Direct and indirect: Direct anger is anger that is expressed directly, usually to the person(s) who has provided the circumstances in which one gets angry. Such direct anger will be appropriate or inappropriate, since it may be excessive or destructive or the opposite of these. Direct anger usually arises from and within some specific situation. But it is possible that a person may have become an angry person whose anger is, as it were, free-floating and somewhat indiscriminate. Then it can erupt against nearly anyone who gives even a tiny reason for triggering it off. Often enough such anger will be targeted on the weak and vulnerable and those in no position to defend themselves or respond in kind.

Indirect anger is more subtle and devious than direct anger and is an interesting emotional tool frequently employed by many of us, often quite unconsciously. This kind of anger is disguised anger; it is outwardly not anger at all but it is in intention and effects. It is used by many people, because they are afraid to engage in direct anger but it can be just as hurtful and damaging to the one at whom it is directed. Examples are plentiful. Sarcasm, cynicism, resentment or humorous remarks with a sting in the tail are common instances. Forgetting things like an appointment, keeping a promise, an anniversary, etc, are other example of indirect anger. Here one doesn't really want to remember; in fact one subconsciously wants to forget, in order to get back at someone whom we feel has hurt or offended us. Thus another name for indirect anger is passive aggression, since one is being aggressive but in a disguised or passive way. Classic examples of this form of aggression are the apparently absent-minded person who frequently 'forgets' and the person who regularly turns up late for appointments, in both cases to the inconvenience and annoyance of some other person or persons. On the surface the passive aggressive person may be very pleasant and even apologetic for 'forgetting' or being late. But subconsciously this is a planned expression of their anger. The test of whether an activity is indirect anger is whether it causes inconvenience and annoyance to some other(s).

Moral and immoral expressions of anger
While anger itself is morally neutral, expressions of anger, or actions motivated even in part by anger, will have a moral character. They will be right or wrong, whether in a major or minor way, because they involve the free activity of a free person. We may refer to an action expressing anger that is morally appropriate as morally right or rational anger. An angry action that is inappropriate or destructive can be said to be immoral or irrational. Others again use the terms righteous and unrighteous anger in this context.

Rational or righteous anger is that expressed by Jesus when he ejected the dealers from the temple. A person's anger can be righteous when he/she is responding to injustice or some other kind of evil. This anger is here a spur to action for justice or good and as such is a help to us to live morally and to make an appropriate moral response in a specific case. Having this capacity for righteous anger is a sign that we care about people and values; it is a sign that we love. If, however, we have little or no capacity for this kind of anger, that indicates that we have little or no capacity for justice or love, that we really don't care much about people or values. Clearly, then, being righteously angry is the ideal to aim at in this area of anger management; it is the moral response to anger-provoking situations.

On the other hand irrational or immoral anger is anger and action that are inappropriate and destructive in any particular situation. A lot of our angry responses fall into this category, though often enough there may not be anything serious in what we do. At times one's anger may be justified but the way one goes about responding to a particular situation may be aggressive or damaging and so do more harm than good. The moral call for all of us is to eliminate all irrational anger from our lives.

Rational or righteous anger has traditionally been spoken of in terms of the virtue of meekness. This virtue is usually classed as one of the basic virtues of the moral life, just as irrational anger is placed among the seven deadly sins or vices. One possesses meekness, not when one is, as we often say, meek and mild and inoffensive. Rather when one expresses one's anger consistently in a constructive and rational way, then one can be said to have the virtue of meekness. A modern word for this virtue is assertiveness. It involves controlling one's anger and yet acting in a positive and constructive way to undo an evil or work for justice.

We may sum up these moral reflections on anger by quoting the very apt and demanding words of Aristotle. He said: 'Anyone can become angry – that is easy. But to be angry with the right person, to the right degree, at the right time, for the right purpose, and in the right way – this is not easy.'[12]

And, we may add, it is the morally ideal way to manage one's anger. Such anger is truly righteous.

Anger and sin
Anger, as already noted, has long been spoken of as a capital or

---

12. Aristotle, *The Nicomachean Ethics*, as quoted in Goleman, *Emotional Intelligence*, ix.

deadly sin, i.e. one of the main roots of our sins. There is an important truth here which it will be helpful to spell out a little. It is quite normal and not at all sinful to be angry in certain circumstances. This is righteous anger. But we can sin because of the way we handle our anger. While repressing anger is usually psychologically damaging and unhealthy, it is better not to speak of this as sinful, since it is usually not free activity. The usual way in which sin can enter our lives in the area of anger is when we express our anger destructively, i.e. in an aggressive and/or excessive way. Such angry actions hurt other people and can do great harm to our relationships and/or communities. They may even damage oneself. Hence, if our anger erupts explosively or we angrily browbeat or berate others or simply let our anger loose in an uncontrolled self-serving way, then there will likely be moral wrong and some degree of sinfulness. This happens not infrequently at all levels of the Christian community and outside it too.

We need, then, to work on the management of our anger, so as to move from a destructive use (hurting others and damaging our relationships with them) and a repressive use (hurting ourselves) to a constructive or assertive use of it, in which we acknowledge our angry state and channel the energy generated by our anger in reasonable and positive ways. This will have good results for ourselves, for our relationships and our community.

Anger and forgiveness
All of us know from experience that it is sometimes very difficult to forgive another for his/her offence against us, especially in a serious matter. It will be helpful to realise, here, the reason why such forgiveness is so difficult. It is because we have been hurt emotionally by the offence and our anger has very likely been stirred up. As a result, forgiveness is usually not just a matter of mind and will but will have an emotional element also. Unless we deal constructively with our hurt feelings, our forgiving will remain largely at the intellectual level and so will not be really effective. We need, then, to come to grips with our anger and hurt in order that our forgiveness be fully personal and so complete. We must let go of our anger in order truly to forgive the other, and this applies even in the case where we go to confession and confess our lack of forgiveness. A similar process may be needed in relation to forgiving ourselves for our faults

and failures. We need to let go of our anger against ourselves, so that we can fully forgive ourselves and be at peace. This applies also in regard to forgiving God, whom we sometimes blame for the tragedies and losses that befall us.

Managing our anger constructively
The two extremes to be avoided here are repression of our anger and explosiveness or the destructive expression of that anger. The golden mean between these two, and the virtuous or emotionally intelligent way to manage one's anger, is to do so assertively or in the spirit of true meekness. This involves directing the energy created by one's anger into constructive channels, so that good is done and the welfare of all involved is promoted. This rational or assertive management of anger requires a series of steps to achieve.

i) One must become aware that one is angry. Some people aren't so aware and deny they are angry. This renders good management of anger very difficult.

ii) We must learn to name our anger accurately and not cover it up or play it down with euphemisms. This is part of being fully aware that we are angry.

iii) It is important to own one's anger, i.e. to accept the fact that this is my anger and is not caused by others. Blaming others for making me angry can be an element in denying I am angry. Others, by their actions, may well trigger my anger or provoke it, but it is factors in my personal make-up which cause me to be angry in precisely the way I am angry. Someone else might react differently to such provocation.

iv) Become clear on why you are angry; what exactly has triggered it, e.g. a threatening event, an authority figure, a chance remark, etc? At times we may misunderstand and so get angry unnecessarily or for the wrong reason or excessively.

v) Now one has to try to control one's anger rationally or in an emotionally intelligent way. This is often the most difficult step in the process of good anger management, but it is also the key step. One may have to learn to do it over a period of time, so that gradually one moves from being aggressive or repressive to being assertive. Growth in self-confidence will be a big help here, since the more confident one becomes, the more assertive one can be.

Being assertive rather than repressive or aggressive will have very good consequences for oneself and one's relationships. It will involve one in staying calm in face of provocation or another's anger and expressing your viewpoint patiently yet firmly. If you have learned to be assertive, it will mean that you handle other people's anger well and are not intimidated by it, no more than you are carried away by your own anger. This will help to avoid hurt to the other and your relationship with him/her, and go a long way towards avoiding an escalation of angry remarks. So, for example, if you say, 'I get angry when you come late for our appointment or haven't prepared the document you promised to prepare for our meeting', this statement focuses on the issue at hand and gives the parties involved a chance to address the problem calmly and positively. When this is done, then the chances are the people involved will face and perhaps resolve their bone of contention without damage to their relationship or any unnecessary stress or tension. At times this assertive expression of anger will not be possible, because the other person is absent or is very aggressive. Then one may need to go to a sympathetic third party to let off steam, as it were, or may be forced to deal with one's own anger by oneself. In the latter case it may help to go for a walk, dig the garden, play some game, work at one's hobby or even beat a pillow.

Further Reading
Cosgrave, William, 'Our Emotional Life – its contribution to right living', *The Furrow*, May 1998, 270-281. The first part of the present chapter is a slightly revised version of this article.
Goleman, Daniel, *Emotional Intelligence – Why it can matter more than IQ* (Bloomsbury, London, 1996);
Sofield, Loughlan,ST, Juliano, Carroll, SHCJ, & Hammett, Rosine, CSC, *Design for Wholeness – Dealing with Anger, Learning to Forgive, Building Self-Esteem* (Ave Maria Press, Notre Dame, Indiana, USA, 1990), chapters 1 & 2;
Steiner, Claude, *Achieving Emotional Literacy* (Bloomsbury, London 1999);
Whitehead, James D., & Whitehead, Evelyn Eaton, *Shadows of the Heart: A Spirituality of the Painful Emotions* (Crossroad, New York, 1996), Parts One & Two & chapter 10;
Wilks, Frances, *Intelligent Emotion: How to Succeed through Transforming your Feelings* (Arrow Books, London, 1998).

CHAPTER 4

Understanding Sin Today

Few will disagree with the statement that there is less talk about sin among Catholics nowadays than there was before Vatican II (1962-5) and what talk there is is in important ways quite different from what was the common coinage of the church for centuries before the council in this area of the Christian moral life. Some see here a crisis involving the loss of the very sense of sin itself. Others are not so negative and alarmed and feel that overall there has been development and improvement in our understanding of sin and where and how it is to be found in our lives as Christians. If we take this latter view as the more accurate assessment of the situation today, we may usefully focus our attention on a central element of our sense of sin which we will here seek to expound and explain. This central element is the nature of sin itself.

There can be little doubt that our understanding of sin has changed in recent times. An illuminating and helpful way of discussing this change is to look at sin in terms of models or images or approaches. This method of understanding sin clarifies the concept of sin we are using, enables us to see the ideas that flow from our starting point, or basic concept of sin, and brings these ideas together in a coherent whole that greatly facilitates understanding.

We intend in this chapter to examine two models of sin: the pre-Vatican II legal model and the contemporary relational model. There is truth in both these ways of looking at the reality of sin but, since all models are limited and imperfect and some are better than others, we will come to see that the legal model is beset by grave weaknesses and faults, while the relational one has many advantages, not least that it facilitates a better understanding of the contemporary experience of sin. It is also the dominant model of sin in the church today and is much to be preferred.

PART ONE: THE LEGAL MODEL OF SIN

The legal model of sin is one element or expression of the legal model of morality generally. In this model morality is understood in terms of law. In other words, moral experience is conceptualised and articulated in legal categories borrowed from the system of law in the state. Human beings have been using such legal categories in relation to morality from very early times and it is an understanding of morality that has significant values and advantages, e.g. morality is clearly objective and imposes obligations.[1]

What is sin?
In regard to sin, this approach or viewpoint understands sin as primarily the breaking of a law, whether human or divine, e.g. one of the ten commandments. Sin is here seen as a moral crime, an offence against God through breaking some law. And since laws are to be obeyed, sin is an act of disobedience. It may even be branded as wilful rebellion against God's will as expressed in natural, divine positive and human laws. It follows then, that the sinner is disobedient, a law breaker, a criminal, even a rebel. And he/she will be worse if these offences are repeated and develop into habits of sin.

From our vantage point today we can see clearly that the understanding or concept of sin that dominated Catholic moral theology and spirituality for centuries up to Vatican II and beyond was what we are here calling the legal model of sin. We are now very much aware that this model is just one among many ways of understanding the reality of sin, though in pre-Vatican II times it was seen as *the* way in which to do so. We will proceed now to expand on this legal model, pointing out its strengths as well as its weaknesses. This will enable us to understand why this manner of viewing sin is widely judged today to be misleading and inadequate in significant ways, despite being basically valid as an approach to the topic.

---

1. For a brief account of the legal model of the Christian moral life generally see chapter 1 above, pp 12-16; also William Cosgrave, 'Models of the Christian moral life', *The Furrow*, September 1983, pp 562-3; Donal Harrington, *What is Morality?* (The Columba Press, Dublin, 1996), pp 11-12, 62.

Tendencies in and implications of the legal model
Act-centred view of sin

When we understand morality in legal terms, there is a tendency to think of sin as, primarily, a specific identifiable action or event done at a particular time and place. This is the sort of reality that law usually concerns itself with and the sort of thing a breach of the law normally is. And of course sin is often such an action. But in a legal morality there tends to be an over-emphasis on such acts and a relative neglect of other aspects of sin. In the legal model there has been much less talk about sin in terms of attitudes, dispositions, tendencies, values, goals and priorities. Nor has there been much emphasis on the person or the person's character or heart as sinful. Here we see a major weakness in the legal view of sin and one that was very much in evidence in pre-Vatican II times, both in theory and in pastoral practice. In a word, the legal model of sin was in a narrow and one-sided way very act-centred.

Since in the legal model sin is a matter of breaking a law, there developed the tendency to look for sin in the areas where there were clear laws to break and also to give an exaggerated importance to sins in those areas, with a consequent neglect of sin in areas where laws weren't so clear or so plentiful. So we find in the legal morality of the pre-Vatican II era a great stress on the ten commandments, on laws and rules in the sexual area and on church laws like fasting and abstinence. We also find such statements as: it is a mortal sin to miss Mass on Sunday, to eat meat on a Friday. In this context one didn't hear a great deal about sin in our relationships, communities or in society itself. In short, then, the legal model of sin tends to focus on sin in relation to laws, to exaggerate the sinfulness of breaking those laws and to overlook sin where laws are not so prominent.

Another obvious weakness of the legal model of sin was its individualistic nature. The sinner was nearly always an individual person, just as, most frequently, laws are broken by individuals. So sin was found nearly exclusively in the actions of individuals and there was very little emphasis on or interest in sin in its communal or social manifestations, not to speak of its institutional, international and global dimensions and structures.

The matter as the primary element in sin

In the legal understanding of sin there is an in-built tendency to put great stress on the matter of a sin, on the thing done, the external act. Most theologians and ordinary Catholics before Vatican II tended to view the matter, the thing proscribed or prescribed by the law, as the most important element of a sin. The presumption was that, if you did the external deed which was forbidden, then you had committed some sort of sin, since you had done the primary thing required for a sin. Lessening of freedom and knowledge was, of course, taken account of, but the main thing in a sin was the matter or object and the freedom and knowledge seem often to have been taken for granted. In this context there emerged such misleading and ultimately false statements as, it is a mortal sin to miss Mass on a Sunday or Holyday, to break the fast, to engage in masturbation, to use contraception, etc. This is typical of a morality that makes the matter the chief element in deciding the moral quality of an action.

This point may be expressed differently by saying that a legal model of sin has a tendency to collapse the distinction between immorality and sinfulness. To say X is immoral is to express a judgment on the objective morality of X, a particular external action or object of an action which is thus said to be wrong apart from the attitude, knowledge and freedom of any person who performs it. But to say that an action is sinful is to make a statement about both the action and the person who does it, not just about the action alone.[2] It includes a judgment that the person knowingly and willingly performed the action. Now this may be true in a specific case where the action has already taken place. One cannot, however, make such a statement about a whole class of actions. But that is precisely what one does if one makes a statement like, it is a (mortal) sin to miss Mass on Sunday, to tell an untruth, engage in masturbation, etc. One cannot know in these cases what the agent's outlook, knowledge and freedom will or might be and in what circumstances he/she will or might be. Hence, one cannot speak of sinfulness in such a general way.

When making such general statements, then, one must confine oneself to speaking of immorality and leave the issue of sinfulness or lack of it to each particular agent who does the act, to his/her confessor and to God.

---

2. Harrington, 66.

Mortal and venial sin

This excessive emphasis on the matter of a sin led to a proliferation of sins and of mortal sins in particular, so that it was generally assumed that there were many mortal sins and that they were relatively easy to commit. Hence, the pre-Vatican II conviction among the faithful generally, priests, bishops and theologians included, that mortal sin was lurking around almost every corner, even for the best of Catholics, and that most people were in real danger of committing one or other of them, especially in the sexual area of life. In fact it seems that most Catholics believed that they, not infrequently, did actually commit mortal sin.

In pre-Vatican II moral thinking there was heavy emphasis on the distinction between mortal and venial sin. The reason for this was that mortal sin had several very important practical consequences, namely, one could not go to communion, one was obliged to go to confession and, above all, one was liable to hell fire. Hence, it was vital to know whether one's sin was mortal. A lot of effort was put into finding out if it was.

This emphasis on mortal sin gave rise to a tendency to think of venial sins as in practice minor things that didn't matter that much and need not be worried about. There was here a fairly obvious danger of a minimalism which was content to avoid mortal sin and not bother too much about venial sin. 'How far can I go without committing mortal sin?' could be said to be a likely attitude in such a way of thinking. It was a temptation that was not always resisted by Catholics in the pre-conciliar era.

Legalism, scrupulosity and act-counting

Another danger of a legal morality and a legal view of sin was that of legalism, i.e. making obeying the law in the letter an end in itself. Not infrequently this attitude was found in the moral lives of Catholics. Allied to this was the tendency to give excessive attention to the minutiae of the law and to become overly fearful about breaking laws and thereby committing sin. So in the times when a legal morality and a legal model of sin were dominant in the Catholic Church, many were beset by fear and anxiety about falling into sin, especially mortal sin, and not a few were found to suffer from what some called the Catholic disease, scrupulosity. This irrational fear of sinning has largely faded out in recent years as the legal model of morality and of sin has itself declined in the church.

In an act-centred understanding of sin, such as the legal model proved to be, there was a tendency for people to assess their virtue and their sinfulness by counting up the number of acts of virtue and sin they had performed. This tendency was probably furthered by the official regulation that one tell in confession all one's mortal sin-acts and the number of times one had committed each of them. God was even imagined as a kind of super-accountant, totting up the good and bad deeds of all and giving a verdict on that basis in relation to their eternal destiny. Here all the stress was on one's acts of sin, with little attention being paid to the sin or sinfulness in the person's heart.

Punishment, image of God and view of repentance
It was taken as axiomatic in the legal model that sin is and should be punished. When a civil or an ecclesiastical law is broken, some form of penalty or punishment is frequently imposed. So in the legal view of morality sin deserves punishment, because it is wilful disobedience to the divinely established order of things in the moral world. Hence, some people came to believe that illness or misfortune was a punishment from God for their sins. More frequently, it was accepted that sin would be punished by God in the next life, that is, in purgatory or hell, and it was further assumed that purgatory and hell were rightly thought of as places of punishment for sin.

In this scheme of things the great Christian realities of forgiveness and reconciliation got, in practice, less than the central roles they have in the message of Jesus and the New Testament authors. They did not fit well with the legal view of sin and punishment and neither did talk of mercy and compassion for the sinner. Of course, these things were never denied and were in fact universally preached. However, since sin was a crime that upset the moral order established by God, punishment was needed to restore the balance disturbed by the sin and it was on this punishment that the emphasis lay in the legal model of sin. Punishment here was usually presented as imposed by some external agent after the sin had been committed. Thus we heard talk of God 'throwing' a mortal sinner into hell. In consequence of this stress on punishment for sin, there was widespread fear and anxiety among Catholics in regard to their moral lives and especially their mortal sins.

Perhaps the most noteworthy, and from our viewpoint

today, the most unfortunate aspect of the legal model of sin is that it tends to give rise to and to reinforce a very distorted and faulty image of God. It sees God as primarily a lawmaker, a policeman, a judge and a punisher of sin. Such a God is to be feared and it will be of central concern for the Christian to keep on the right side of such a God, since God is watching one's every move and will punish transgressions severely. In this context it is no wonder that in pre-Vatican II times many Catholics lived their moral lives in the church in fear and anxiety, and often succumbed to legalistic attitudes and even scrupulosity in observing the many laws of this demanding and strict God. In line with this current of thought, many confessors were harsh and judgmental in their ministry, thus imitating the God whom they had created in their own image.

Because it sees sin, even mortal sin, as rather easily committed, the legal view of sin is inclined to assume that the sinner can just as easily repent and give up his/her evil ways. All that is needed really is an act of the will, a decision to repent. Full freedom to do this tends to be taken for granted and little attention is given to social or psychological or emotional factors that can, as we now know, make such a view of repentance/conversion seem naïve and unrealistic. In a word, then, the idea of repentance/conversion as, at least sometimes, a long and difficult process, especially in relation to habits of sin, and perhaps requiring emotional and psychological growth and even social change, is little understood in the legal model of sin and, hence, is rarely taken into consideration. In consequence many resolutions to improve, or purposes of amendment as they were called, were ineffective.

Confession in the legal model
Finally, the legal model of sin was very probably both a cause and a consequence of the legal understanding of confession that was dominant in the church for centuries before Vatican II. In other words, the legal understandings of sin and confession tended to reinforce each other.

In this legal view of the sacrament of penance, confession was understood in terms of the courtroom analogy that was so central to the Council of Trent (1551 AD): the sacrament is a kind of tribunal or court in which the priest acts as a judge who, like most judges in the state legal system, behaves in a formal and severe manner, while the penitent is the accused (and accuser) who has to give a full account of his/her serious crimes (sins), including their number and their different kinds, be questioned, when the confessor deems it necessary or useful, have the verdict pronounced (get absolution or have it refused) and receive an appropriate sentence or punishment (the penance). Confession, thus understood, was frequently experienced by penitents as an ordeal and relief was the dominant feeling afterwards.

Evaluation of the legal model of sin
The strengths of this approach to sin may be listed briefly. It is strong on clarity and definiteness, as is usually the case in matters of law. It emphasises the objectivity of morality and of sin. It highlights the most visible aspect of sin, namely, sin as a specific deed that breaks a law, and it also takes a strong stand in regard to uprooting sin from one's Christian life by repentance and a purpose of amendment. This model was also widely approved of, or at least accepted and used in authoritative statements over the centuries. Up to the Second Vatican Council it was almost universally accepted in the Catholic Church as providing the best and indeed the only authoritatively approved way of understanding the reality we call sin.

The weaknesses and faults of this legal model of sin are, however, much more significant than its values and provide the reasons for the shift away from it in the church in recent times. Most of these weaknesses have been mentioned already or will be alluded to later, at least by implication, as we discuss the relational model of sin. It will suffice here then to list the main points on which the legal model of sin is criticised today.

i. It tends to neglect or at least under-emphasise attitudes, dispositions, tendencies, intentions, values and priorities as realities in which sinfulness can be found. In addition, it gives little attention to the way sin affects the sinner and forms character. There is not much talk about sinfulness in the person or about a sinful character from which individual sins spring. In short, the legal understanding of sin is superficial.

ii. This understanding of sin causes too much stress and value to be placed on moral laws and rules and as a result one is inclined to overlook sin in areas of life where laws are not so prominent, e.g. relationships, communities, or where arrangements are approved and supported by law, e.g. structures, institutions.

iii. This view of sin is very individualistic, as is the legal view of morality generally and, hence, it pays little attention to the social dimension of sin, e.g., sin in and by communities and societies, structures and institutions.

iv.It tends to collapse the distinction between immorality and sinfulness and so leads people to see sin where it may not exist.

v. This model of sin devalues both mortal and venial sin by effectively lessening the commitment to evil required for mortal sin and by giving the impression that venial sins are trivial and of little significance.

vi. The superficial understanding of freedom and knowledge in this model of sin has caused many to misconceive how sin happens and also the degree of its seriousness. In addition, the legal model has an inadequate concept of repentance and conversion.

vii. Its openness to minimalistic attitudes is unhelpful and dangerous in the Christian moral life.

viii. It tends also to foster attitudes of passivity, immaturity and legalism and, hence, tends to stifle moral growth, a sense of responsibility and creativity.

ix. By its concept of punishment for sin and the emphasis it places on this idea, this model radically distorts the moral life and the very idea of sin itself. This breeds fear, anxiety and even scrupulosity.

x. The image of God in this model, though it can be found in the Bible, is a travesty of the Christian concept of God as a loving and forgiving Father. Such an image of God has done untold damage to the spiritual lives of innumerable Catholics over the centuries.

PART TWO: THE RELATIONAL MODEL OF SIN

The relational model of sin is one element in the relational model of the Christian moral life generally, a model that is dominant in Catholic moral theology today.[3]

In this section we will outline the basic elements of this relational model of sin, beginning with a brief description of sin

3. For a brief account of the relational model of the Christian moral life in general, see chapter 1 above, pp 16-22; also Cosgrave, 'Models of the Christian Moral Life', *The Furrow*, September 1983, pp 564-7; Richard M Gula, *Reason Informed by Faith: Foundations of Catholic Morality* (Paulist Press, New York, 1989), pp 63-4; Harrington, pp 16-17.

itself and moving on to discuss the main presuppositions and
implications of that starting point as they emerge in this understanding.

What is sin?
As the name indicates, the relational model of sin sees the moral
life of the Christian, and hence also sin, as being concerned with
and taking place in relationships between people. Christian
morality is a relational reality and so too is sin. The Christian
community and its members are called to live their lives in these
relationships with other people and in community and to do this
in a loving manner. This they do by relating responsibly and appropriately to the individuals, groups and communities they
come into relationship with. In this context sin is understood as
any selfish attitude, disposition, tendency, habit or activity that
damages or destroys a relationship a person or persons
has/have with another person, group or community. It is unloving activity; it is a failure or refusal to love another or others. It
involves saying no to a person(s) in a relationship. In a word, sin
is selfishness in relationship. This means that to commit sin is to
be irresponsible in our relationships, to fail to respond positively
and appropriately to others, to fail to love.

For the Christian this failure or selfishness in human relationships involves failure and selfishness in our relationship
with God, since to fail to love other human persons is to fail to
love God. It follows that sin is, at one and the same time, both a
refusal to love another human person or persons and a refusal to
love God. Refusing to love others is refusing to love God. To offend against another human person or persons is to offend
against God. It may be mentioned here that it is also possible to
sin against oneself in one's relationship with oneself, i.e. to fail to
love oneself appropriately, e.g. by damaging one's health
through over-work, by substance abuse, by over- or under-
nourishing oneself physically, by isolating oneself excessively
from relationships.

Personal and social dimensions of sin
In Catholic theological thinking on the moral life today, there is
a noticeable shift from talk about human nature to talk about the
human person. Thus Christian morality is seen today as, above
all, personal, involving persons in relationship and in community.
In this context there is a concern to take account of the fact that

human activity must be judged morally by reference to the human person integrally and adequately considered. This means that the human person adequately considered is the criterion by which we discover whether an act is morally right or wrong. Hence, we need a good Christian anthropology, or understanding of the human person, if we are to think fruitfully about morality and live well as moral beings.

In this context, it will be clear that sin, like morality generally, concerns persons or groups of persons, not in isolation but in relationship with other individuals and in community. It is persons who sin, whether individually or in groups, but it is also persons who are affected by sin and who suffer damage in one way or another. Sin hurts people in their persons and in their relationships. It also hurts or damages the sinner, because it makes him/her more selfish and less loving and so less human.

Special attention needs to be given to the communal or group dimension of sin, since this has been neglected in the past and even today is poorly understood and inadequately presented in Catholic moral theology. We have done, and still do, most of our thinking and theologising about morality and about sin in terms of individual persons. While this is basic, it is not by itself adequate. Some improvement has taken place in this matter in recent times and we find, in consequence, valuable reflections on immorality and sin from the group, communal, social, national, international, structural, institutional and systemic points of view. We are still, however, far from having an adequate theology of social immorality and social sin. In particular we need a fuller account of the group as moral agent and as sinful, and of structures, institutions and systems in their relation to causal and even moral responsibility. See below under social sin, pp 85-88.

Sinfulness and sins

Our focus on persons in all their dimensions enables us to look for and find sin in areas other than specific actions or individual concrete deeds. As a result there is in the relational model a tendency to speak of sinfulness as well as sins, or of sin as distinct from, though not opposed to, sins. This arises from the fact that sin is more than a specific act done at a particular time and place. We can be sinful in our attitudes, tendencies, dispositions, habits, intentions, values, goals and priorities, and this sinfulness can and will express itself in concrete choices and actions. Here we find the sources or roots of our individual acts of sin and these sources or roots are in important ways more significant than the fruit they bear. In other words, the sinfulness in a person or within a group is the primary reality; the sins that flow from that sinfulness are, of course, important but they are not the source or root of the evil. In this context it makes sense to speak of sin as a condition or state of the person or group or even of a whole community, nation, institution or system. Some, like St Paul, consider sin as a power within us pushing us to commit particular sinful acts. So sin is primarily in the heart of the sinner or deep within the group or community. This is sin at its deepest and most significant and it is in relation to this sinfulness within that conversion and reconciliation are most needed but usually most difficult.

One can easily understand that sinfulness in the sense intended here, as well as the individual sinful acts that flow from it, may well have very serious consequences for and effects on one's relationships or those in a group or community. Such sinfulness or selfishness will weaken and perhaps destroy some of our relationships, since the person or group concerned is selfish in some real degree and so is less capable of loving others and of responding to them positively and appropriately. There are, of course, degrees or levels of sinfulness and these vary from person to person and from group/community to group/community as well as from time to time. These degrees or levels can range from minor to basic or profound. Experience would seem to indicate that every person and group/community has some degree of sinfulness and commits some sins.

Sin as primarily a choice for evil
One of the criticisms of the legal model of sin is that it gives too much importance to the matter, the external deed, and underplays the significance of the other factors in the choice to commit a sin. The relational model seeks to redress this distortion and so changes the emphasis in relation to the factors that are central in the commission of sin. This results in sin being described as primarily a free choice for evil, where the main element of the sin is the commitment of the sinner to the evil on which he/she has set his/her heart. Care is taken to avoid identifying the sin with the external deed and, in consequence, sin is seen as being, first of all, in the choice the agent makes of some particular evil or im-

moral reality. What really makes an action sinful (as distinct from just being immoral) is the degree to which the sinner puts his/her heart into it and makes the evil in it his/her own. Hence, sin is seen as being, firstly, in the heart, in one's commitment to evil, and this expresses itself in and through one's choice of a particular immoral deed or evil.

This does not mean that the external deed, the matter of the sin, is unimportant. It is very important, because one's choice expresses itself in the doing of that external deed. When one chooses morally, one has to choose something. One's choice has to have an object, a reality one decides to commit oneself to in some real degree, in this case, some evil. We can say in fact that the object of one's choice evokes that choice and in a sense determines it. So, the matter is a pointer to the sin and to the degree of sinfulness in the choice. But it is no more than that, since in some cases one can make a deep choice about a small thing or a superficial choice in relation to a major evil. So then, the sin remains primarily in the choice as expressed in what one does. Hence, the object chosen, the external deed, is in itself correctly spoken of as immoral rather than sinful. One can, then, observe or see the immoral deed, the external act, but the sin considered as one's choice of evil is rooted deep in the sinner's heart.

We cannot, therefore, know with certainty if another has committed a sin, and even less can we know the degree to which he/she has committed her/himself to the evil involved in the choice made. Only the sinner can know that, and even he/she cannot always be certain. Clearly, then, we should refrain from saying such things as, Michael has committed a serious sin; Joan has fallen into mortal sin. We should, rather, confine ourselves to saying something like, Michael has done something immoral; Joan's action is gravely wrong. Leave the judgment about sinfulness to the person him/herself, to the confessor and to God.

In the light of this line of thought, it seems clear that it will often be far from easy to distinguish between serious (or mortal) and non-serious sin, certainly in regard to other people and even in one's own case. This is true but it is not of primary importance, since the main thing is to repent of one's sin and not agonise over which category of sin it is to be put in.

Sin as a process
It would seem to emerge fairly clearly from what has been said

above that sinfulness or sin, as distinct from specific sin-acts, is not usually something that happens in an instant or on the spot, as it were. There is fairly obviously an element of process about our becoming sinful persons or groups. It takes time and effort; it is something that happens gradually and usually imperceptibly. It seems true also that some of our individual sinful actions do not take place in an instant but involve a process that can go on over quite some time. We may consider these points briefly here.

In relation to the person (or group) becoming sinful, it seems clear that one does not normally become a sinful person in one fell swoop, in an instant. Generally, one grows into sinfulness over a period of months and even years, until finally one is in fact a sinful person in some degree. (The same sort of process takes place, it would seem, in relation to becoming a virtuous or holy person.) Such growth is a process and it would seem to consist of many individual choices for evil, serious and not so serious. One's sinfulness, like one's virtue, builds up gradually and usually seems to occur without any very noteworthy, much less spectacular, actions on the surface of one's life. Many people don't even notice this development in sinfulness or vice in themselves. It seems to creep up on them without them being explicitly aware of it. And yet one must be aware of it at some level, since it involves one's free commitment of oneself to evil. It will be obvious from experience also that one's sinfulness or sin can vary in depth and strength, and can become stronger or weaker, depending on the moral choices the person (or group) makes from time to time.

In regard to individual sinful actions, not all of them seem to take place in an instant or solely at the time and place when the external deed is done. Some do, especially the smaller or more superficial ones, e.g. a minor theft, a small lie. But it can and does happen that a particular sin or moral choice for evil may take quite some time to get under way and come to completion. Since a human action is not to be identified with a particular visible object or thing done, we must reckon with the fact that a person (or group) may make a choice for evil that takes time to work itself out in external behaviour. In other words, an individual sinful action may involve a process, spread over a notable interval, that is made up of many lesser choices for evil (venial sins), as the major or deeper choice unfolds. We have only to think of a vocation to the priesthood or to marriage and all that is required for and involved in such a profound choice to see this. This would seem to be true also, at least sometimes, in relation to significant choices for evil like adultery, murder, serious theft. Such immoral and sinful actions are not to be identified with the external event of physical sex or physical killing or actually putting the money in one's pocket. It will likely be the case here that these sins will have begun long before the external deeds or physical acts themselves actually occur. Such sins will probably include selfish desires and attitudes, deteriorating relationships and perhaps increasing conflict, with much thinking and planning beforehand, etc. Doing the external deed would, then, be the culmination of a long and profound internal process, the visible expression of a single but complex human choice for evil, a major sin. In a word, these sins involve a process and take time and effort to bring to completion.

Awareness and conditioning in relation to sin
The above discussion of the person as sinful and of individual sinful actions brings with it, in contemporary moral theology, an important reflection on the levels of awareness that we have in our human choices, whether for good or for evil. Today two such levels are usually distinguished. In our specific choices for evil, i.e. our acts of sin that fall into a particular category like lying or theft, we are explicitly aware of what we are choosing and doing. This is referred to as explicit or reflexive awareness or consciousness and means that we are thinking about our choice and have concepts about it in our head, e.g. when one decides to steal a sum of money and does so. Implicit or non-reflexive awareness, on the other hand, is the awareness or consciousness which we have of ourselves as subjects, as we make a basic choice for evil (i.e. commit a mortal sin) or for good. This awareness is obscure and elusive, since the choice is too personal to be viewed as one views an object or even a specific deed one does. Hence, it is difficult to be sure one has committed a mortal sin or is in the state of mortal sinfulness (or of grace). This fact would seem to be borne out in our experience.

In the relational model of sin, it is also presupposed that freedom and knowledge in the sinner are always conditioned, situated, limited and frequently imperfect. This is simply how the human condition is. Part of this conditioning and limiting is due to social influences and attitudes, and part of it comes from psychological and emotional factors within the agent(s). It will clearly be very important to take account of this in assessing the sinfulness of oneself or one's action in any particular case. In short, we must reckon with the fact that responsibility for sin is real but seldom total.

Distinguishing kinds of sin

In this relational model of sin one soon comes to realise that it may be rather difficult to make a clear distinction, in practice at least, between the different kinds of sin and in particular between mortal and venial sin. In many cases there seems to be no very obvious dividing line between them, even if in theory we can and should distinguish them, as we will attempt to do shortly. When we emphasise that sin is primarily in the subject, in the sinner and in her/his choice for and commitment to evil and selfishness, and only in the second place in the matter or external deed, then it becomes clear that we cannot always in practice distinguish mortal and venial sin as neatly as in the legal model of sin. The boundary line between the human free choices involved in serious and minor sin can be somewhat blurred and far from always clearly discernible in our daily experience. This seems to be how things are in reality and we must live with this relative lack of clarity. It may be said to be compensated for by the greater sense of realism that attends this relational understanding of these kinds of sin as compared to that in the legal model. This understanding rings truer to our experience, it seems to many, and that points to its basic correctness.

It will be important to add here that in the majority of cases there is no pressing need for a person or group to spend a lot of time trying to decide if a particular sin is mortal or venial; much less should they worry about it. The reason for this is that, when a person or group has sinned, the primary thing is to repent of and be converted from that sin. It is less important and very often not really a priority to be able to label one's sin as mortal or venial. One will normally have a general impression about its seriousness or lack of it and that usually suffices.

Mortal sin

In the relational model of sin, our understanding of mortal sin runs along the following lines. Avoiding identifying the sin with the external deed, as tended to happen in practice at least in the legal model, and remembering that what really makes an action sinful, as distinct from simply immoral, is the degree to which the sinner puts her/his heart into it and makes the evil her/his own, we may describe mortal sin as follows. Mortal sin is one's deep personal commitment to evil, a profound choice of selfishness. To make such a commitment or choice one has to have a real appreciation of the values and evils involved in one's choice; one has to gather one's resources as a person, as it were, and then one has to commit oneself to evil in a big way, in and with one's heart or deepest self. Mortal sin in this sense is referred to today by theologians as a fundamental option for evil, a basic choice not to love, to be selfish. Such a deeply personal choice is difficult to make; it cannot happen by accident or on the spur of the moment. It will usually take time and involve a process that includes lesser or more superficial choices (venial or minor sins), until finally one completes or finalises one's basic choice and commits mortal sin. Thus one comes to be in the state of mortal sinfulness, which means that one is now a basically selfish, unloving person, who has broken her/his relationship with God and her/his relationships with other people and so has lost the state of grace. Mortal sin thus understood is, of course, a specific human action but, since it is a choice made deep within the agent, even the person who does it will find it hard to identify it as a mortal sin. We may add that such a mortal sin will shape the person who does it profoundly. By it he/she takes up a particular stance or direction morally or as a person: one is now directed towards evil and selfishness and away from other people and from God. And this stance or direction is fundamental, as the choice for evil was. In short, the fundamental option for evil that is mortal sin gives rise to a fundamental stance or direction in the agent that is also set on evil or selfishness.

Viewed in this manner, it would seem correct to say that mortal sin can come about in two ways. One may commit a mortal sin as one makes a wholehearted choice of a specific gravely evil object or matter, e.g. murder, adultery, major theft. Such a choice, because it is so basic and profoundly personal, will very likely have an element of process in it; it will take time and develop gradually within the agent, as he/she moves towards completing his/her commitment to the major evil involved. On the other hand, there is the possibility, as experience would seem to indicate, that one can make a fundamental option or

basic choice for evil in a more hidden, subtle manner and without necessarily doing any specific external deed that is spectacu-
larly evil. Such a basic choice will also come to completion gradually as one moves deeper and deeper into selfishness over
quite a long time. The end result in both these cases is that one
loses the state of grace and enters the state of mortal sinfulness.[4]

In this conception it will be true to say that mortal sin will be
a rare thing in the life of a Christian, especially if one is trying to
live a good life. It will be rare, because it involves a profound
and difficult choice and we do not make many such choices. In
addition, it will be a choice that only one with significant moral
maturity can make. Only those with such a level of moral maturity will have the personal capacity to make a deep personal
commitment such as is required for mortal sin. In other words,
mortal sin is an adult reality; it is not something of which children are capable. So only those who are adults in the moral sense
can commit mortal sin. Furthermore, it is important to say that,
though it is hard to be sure one is in mortal sin oneself and virtually impossible to know if others are, this is not a matter for
worry. It is generally not of prime importance to have certainty
about this. Since conversion or repentance is the main thing, one
should focus on that and do all possible to achieve it.

We have said above that it is hard to commit a mortal sin and
get into the state of mortal sinfulness. This is a reassuring and
comforting point, particularly since the legal model of sin gave
the impression that it was rather easy to fall into mortal sin. We
may add in this context, then, that it is highly unlikely that a person who has lived a good life for decades will fall into mortal sin
at the last minute and so be lost for all eternity. On the other
hand, it has to be said that a sudden death-bed conversion after
a seriously sinful life is equally unlikely.

Mortal Sin: the three essential requirements
In the legal view of sin it was usual to state that three conditions
were essential for a mortal sin. These were full knowledge, full
consent and serious matter. While this is, of course, correct, it
seems clear to theologians today that these requirements
weren't always understood with full accuracy in that model of

---

4. See Harrington, p 71; Kevin T Kelly, *New Directions in Moral Theology:
The Challenge of Being human* (Geoffrey Chapman, London, 1992), p 133;
Richard M Gula, *Reason Informed by Faith: Foundations of Catholic
Morality* (Paulist Press, New York, 1989), p 111.

sin. The tendency was to hold that all three were present in some particular actions when in fact they may not have been. So, today in the relational or personalist understanding of sin, care is taken to ensure fuller accuracy in this matter. Full knowledge is now held to be present only when one has a realistic evaluation or appreciation of the values and evils involved in the action one is thinking of doing. A mere head or academic knowledge is not really full knowledge. Full consent is not just a facile, superficial 'yes' to what one is about to do. It requires the exercise of one's basic freedom, involving one's heartfelt commitment to the evil in the proposed action. This alone is capable of changing one from being a basically loving person to being a basically selfish one, a change which mortal sin alone is capable of bringing about and which is the distinctive effect of mortal sin.

In this context, serious matter is seen as the kind of object or external deed or thing one might do which is likely to evoke a choice that is made with full knowledge and full consent, i.e. a basic choice or fundamental option. There are not many of those objects or external deeds around. There are certainly fewer of them than we were led to believe when thinking of mortal sin in terms of the legal model.

So the three conditions or requirements for mortal sin can be met or fulfilled, but not so frequently as we once thought. Mortal sin is harder to commit than seemed the case in the legal view of sin, because its three conditions are more difficult to fulfil in the one action than was often assumed in the past.

Three kinds of sin: mortal, serious and venial?
In recent years some Catholic theologians have suggested that, instead of distinguishing just two types of sin, mortal and venial, it is a more adequate and accurate description of our experience to use three categories of sin, mortal, serious and venial. The reasons for taking this position may be stated as follows.

In the relational understanding of sin as outlined above, mortal sin is presented as such a deeply personal choice for evil that it will be very difficult to commit and hence very rare in the ordinary Christian's life. On the other hand, venial sin involves only a superficial choice for evil and concerns relatively minor faults. There seems, then, to be a major difference between these two types of sin, a big gap between the two kinds of free personal choice involved. Experience tells us that some of our sinful choices are not so deeply personal as mortal sin and yet they don't seem to be as minor as venial sin. In other words, between these two types of sinful choice there would seem to be another third type which is less fundamental than mortal sin but more significant than venial sin. This choice for evil is referred to by these theologians as serious sin.

We may mention some examples of sins or choices for evil that would seem to fit into the category called serious: a significant theft done with real commitment to the evil in it, deliberately telling an important untruth, noteworthy and intended aggression against another, important neglect of one's duties at work without any excusing reason, a significant habit of being domineering or aggressive.

Serious sin is, then, an important free choice for evil and self-ishness that is not fundamental enough to make one basically sinful, i.e. to lose the state of grace, but yet is too significant to be designated as only minor.

What is to be said of this line of thinking? It would seem to be realistic and reasonably true to our experience of sin in our lives. Thus it may be said to provide us with a helpful analysis of that experience that in important ways seems to be an advance on the twofold division of sin. In the last few years, however, one finds Catholic moralists being less inclined to favour this three-fold categorisation of sin and reverting to the traditional position. This seems to be happening because they do not think that, pastorally or practically speaking, this new set of categories is very illuminating or helpful. It may even confuse people, give too much attention to putting a label on our sins and distract us from our primary task of repentance and conversion.

One can accept this latter position and continue to use the traditional two categories of sin, provided one adjusts one's understanding of venial sin. It will be clear from what was said earlier that the legal model of sin tended to trivialise venial sin as it put nearly all the emphasis on mortal sin and its practical consequences. Thus, in practice in the legal understanding a venial sin meant a minor or insignificant sin or fault, and since it was only venial, one didn't have to worry too much about it. In daily living this often led people in practice to ignore their venial sins and carry on as if they weren't really sins at all. But in the re-lational model of sin this minimalistic attitude is unacceptable, firstly, because venial sins are really sinful and selfish and dam-age our relationships and ourselves; and, secondly, because these sins are often far from trivial. They can be quite significant and damaging. The only truly Christian attitude to them, as to all sins, is that they are morally bad, must be uprooted and require our best efforts to do so as quickly as possible.

The roots of personal sins
It is the experience of many people that some of our sins, and in particular some habits of sin, are very difficult to uproot. Despite our best efforts they seem to persist and resist all attempts to banish them. Examples are plentiful: vulgar language, aggressiveness and badly controlled anger, jealousy, attention-seeking, bullying and bossiness, 'bad' thoughts (sexual fantasies) and masturbation. The question is why? And how does one break these sinful habits and make one's purpose of amendment or commitment to improve a reality, something that actually happens, rather than just another failure?

Modern psychology provides us with some very helpful insights here. These point to the fact that our sins and especially our habits of sin are often, if not always, rooted in or closely related to our emotional lives. All of us have some emotional wounds or hurts which we received in the course of our upbringing, some serious and some minor. These wounds can have a very significant influence on our personality and our manner of relating to ourselves and to others. They can, therefore, have an impact on our free choices, whether these are virtuous or sinful. The reason for this is that our emotional hurts or scars affect the way we feel about ourselves, about other people and about our relationships with them and with God too. This is true even, and perhaps especially, when we are quite unaware of these emotional factors and their impact on us.

In relation to our sins and habits of sin, this emotional influence will be clearer if we look at a few examples. Aggressiveness, with the conflicts and destructive actions that frequently result from it, often has its roots in a lack of self-confidence. Because one feels insecure and under threat, one is inclined to go on the attack as a means of self-defence and so one becomes aggressive in one's attitudes and actions verbally or even physically. Jealousy has its roots in a poor self-image or low self-esteem, a condition that causes one to fear losing a relationship or a position of prominence, and in consequence may lead to actions motivated by jealousy. The habit of masturbation can be a symptom of some personality difficulty or some emotional state like stress, tensions, loneliness, anxiety, sexual frustration.

It will be clear from what has here been said that our persist-
ent sins, or habits of sin, are likely to continue to plague us if we
do not remove the emotional roots from which they very likely
spring. We must heal these emotional wounds by some process
of therapy, if we are to overcome our sinful habits. This will require increased self-awareness, sharing with at least one other
person about our emotional scars, a great deal of positive thinking about oneself and others, reading and learning about the
emotional dimension of our personality and life, so as to understand them better, and perseverance in all this over quite some
time. As and when we grow in emotional maturity, as outlined
here, we will also grow in moral maturity and the sinful habits
we are discussing will gradually fade out of our lives. Without
this emotional growth, however, our sinful habits will persist
and no amount of other supposed remedies, like prayer,
penance, purpose of amendment or will power, will make any
worthwhile difference.[5]

We may add here that in relation to religious or spiritual
matters a similar point can be made. Many spiritual difficulties
are rooted in psychological or emotional ones and the former
will not be resolved unless and until the latter are. E.g. strong
feelings of anger and/or rejection towards one's father and/or
mother that have been buried since childhood may well make
relating to God as Father difficult or even impossible. More positively, the more we are in touch with ourselves and the more
mature we are emotionally and personally, the better placed we
are to engage in the search for God in the depths of our selves
and the more likely we will be to establish a deep and truly personal relationship with God in prayer and in our Christian lives
generally .[6]

Punishment for sin?
If one asks how does one understand punishment for sin – an
idea that is taken for granted in the legal model of sin – when
one is thinking in terms of the relational model, the answer is
that one finds it necessary to re-interpret this concept. The best
approach seems to be to 'translate', as it were, the language of

5. On this area see my article 'The Roots of Sin', *Intercom,* May 1994, pp
12-14.
6. See Tony Baggott, 'Getting the Spiritual Life Together', *The Furrow,*
November 1991, pp 628-35.

punishment into more personal and relational categories, thus getting at the deeper meaning behind the legal terminology. What the language of punishment was trying to express, in its legal and rather inadequate terms, was that sin has bad effects on the sinner and on one's relationships with others. Sin damages the sinner by making him/her more selfish, more inclined to sin again and less able to be and to do good. In a word, it makes the person less loving and less able to love. It thus isolates and alienates the sinner from other people, from God and even from him/herself. Thus, by sin relationships are weakened or even broken and other people and God are put at a greater distance from the sinner by the sinner's own choice.

It is sometimes said that sin is its own punishment. This is true in the sense that sin brings its own negative effects with it. But it seems better to re-interpret even this usage of the language of punishment, since it too can mislead us about sin and about morality generally. In particular, talk of punishment can give the impression that this so-called punishment is imposed by some external agent after one's sin rather than being an intrinsic element in, or consequence of, the sin itself.

It follows from what has been said here that we should see purgatory and hell, not as punishments for sin, but rather as the natural and inevitable consequences in the afterlife of sinning either venially or mortally. If we commit venial sin and stay in it till death, then we need the process of purification or maturing that we call purgatory to prepare us for the perfection of heaven. This process is painful and, hence, the image of fire is often used in relation to it. If we commit mortal sin and remain in it till death, then we enter the state we call hell, i.e. the condition of being totally selfish and cut off from others and God. This is a state of total isolation and alienation, even from oneself; it is self-chosen and eternal. This state is even more painful than purgatory, being utterly contrary to the deepest nature of the human person, and so the image of fire and flames is supremely apt in its regard. It is clear in this conception of the matter that God does not 'throw' one into hell; one chooses it for oneself by sinning mortally and not repenting.

Sin and the image of God
In the relational understanding of sin, the image of God as lawmaker, policeman, judge and punisher is transformed as the

central New Testament conception of the God of Jesus Christ is taken on board and used in elaborating our understanding of God in relation to us as sinners. God is here seen as a loving Father who calls God's people to live as Jesus lived and who enables us to do so by the gift of the Holy Spirit. When we fail to imitate Jesus and commit sin, God shows us that God is totally forgiving, a God of forgiveness. The Father works through the Holy Spirit and the church to bring us to repentance, to conversion of heart and thus to reconcile us with ourselves, with others, with the community, with the church and with God. This is memorably illustrated by the parable of the forgiving father welcoming back the prodigal son after the latter's life of sin (Lk 15). In this understanding of God in relation to us as sinners, then, we see God as a forgiving and reconciling God, not a punishing one. We are called to be like that God, forgiving and reconciling but not punishing.

Repentance/conversion in the relational model
The legal model of sin gave the impression that repentance/conversion was relatively easy, in the same way that committing sin, even mortal sin, was relatively easy. But we have seen that that approach was misleading and inaccurate in important ways, both in relation to sin and to repentance also. Since the relational model is clear that committing sin, especially serious sin, is often a process that may take time and effort, it understands that repentance/conversion may well also involve a process and is usually not instantaneous or a quick and easy achievement. Experience bears this out. We have seen examples of this in our discussion of habits of sin and it holds also in regard to serious or mortal sin. It may well take time, effort and not a little struggle to turn one's heart from such sins, leave them behind and return to the path of virtue. So simply saying an 'act of contrition' or making 'a purpose of amendment' can't be taken as in themselves equivalent to the full reality of repentance or conversion. They may signal the desire to achieve this repentance; they may point to the presence of a real sorrow or regret for having sinned and a commitment to making an effort to avoid the sin in the future. But that doesn't in itself mean repentance has taken place or one has actually been converted from the particular sin. More is needed. One has actually to give up the sin, turn one's heart from that form of selfishness, remove

the damage to oneself and one's relationships that the sin has done and return to virtuous living. Then one can say one is actually converted from one's sin; one has truly repented.

A helpful parallel here may be giving up heavy smoking or excessive drinking. Regretting having been involved in doing these things, desiring to give them up and determining to do that are important, but they are not equivalent to actually giving them up. More is needed. One must actually do so with the change of attitude and perhaps lifestyle that must go with that. Then the reality of having given up these practices will be in place.

The sacrament of reconciliation

This new name for the sacrament signals a renewed understanding. Now it is seen as concerned with restoring broken relationships between the serious sinner and the church and God. The repentant sinner or penitent comes to the church, represented by the priest, and says he/she is sorry and converted from a particular serious sin or sins. The church responds by expressing its and God's forgiveness. The result is the reconciliation of the serious sinner with both the church and God. Like the father in the parable of the prodigal son, the priest receives the penitent compassionately and gladly reconciles him/her. The penitent, knowing this, comes without fear or anxiety and rejoices to be reconciled. Hence, the sacrament should be a warm and friendly meeting and be joyful in its result, reconciliation. It is valid to use the word tribunal about the sacrament here, as Trent did, but the emphasis would be on that tribunal as one of mercy rather than one of strict justice.

Social sin

This is another relatively new concept, though it is now widely and officially used in the Catholic Church at all levels, even if not without some hesitations. It represents a renewed and welcome emphasis on the social dimension of morality and, in particular, of immorality in its communal, national, international, global and even environmental aspects. In contemporary theology one finds a variety of terms used for what we are here calling social sin. Some prefer to call it social immorality for the reasons discussed above in relation to immorality and sin. Some refer to it as the sin of the world; others speak of solidarity in sin, while phrases like structural sin or sinful social structures are also commonly used.[7]

Social sin cannot really be discussed without talking about personal sin, so closely are they linked. So, instead of giving a definition of social sin, theologians often approach the matter by focusing on how personal and social sin are related. We may mention four viewpoints on this issue.[8]

1) Some say that social sin refers simply to the social effects of personal sins. There are such effects, as has long been recognised. However, most theologians do not see this as an adequate account of the reality being referred to as social sin.

2) Some view social sin as the embodiment of personal sin. Here personal sin is sin in the full and proper sense and social sin is sin only by analogy. Personal sin is the ultimate root of social sin, since it often happens that personal sin gives rise to situations, structures, institutions and systems that are immoral and sinful. Thus personal sin becomes embodied in these social realities and its evil effects can continue, become consolidated and prove very difficult to remove. This understanding of social sin is the one the Pope and some Catholic theologians favour at the present time. They speak regularly of structures of sin. Basically, this understanding sees social sin as a form of the previous position, i.e. 1) above, so that social sin is at root a social effect of personal sin. In such a view groups, structures and institutions cannot, strictly speaking, commit sin; only persons can.[9]

Some questions are, however, raised about this position. It is suggested that it is not fully adequate, because it feeds into and supports the individualism that is so strong in western culture nowadays and, in addition, it may well give credence to the view that, in the end, change or conversion of heart is enough to get rid of social sin in all its forms.[10]

3) A third position goes a step further and sees personal and social sin as co-essential, i.e. these two kinds or dimensions of sin are always present and are equally important. Sin is always

7. Mark O'Keefe OSB, *What are they saying about Social Sin?* (Paulist Press, New York, 1990), pp 26-35.
8. O'Keefe, pp 17-24.
9. O'Keefe, pp 19, 31-2, 69-75.
10. Thomas F Schindler, *Ethics: The Social Dimension* (Michael Glazier, Delaware, USA,1989), pp 135-140.

both personal and social in the sense that sin is experienced as involving personal freedom and responsibility but also as being external, social and powerful in relation to individuals. This position seems significantly different from the first two we have examined but the differences should not be exaggerated.

4) A few theologians, none of whom are Catholics, see social sin as the primary reality and personal sin is viewed as a manifestation of this social sin. In other words, personal sin refers to the ways in which individuals actively participate in sin as a social reality. In this understanding social sin is not a mere consequence of personal sin. Rather sin is understood in a wider sense than has been usual in the Catholic tradition and refers to all opposition to God's reign and the historical and social forms that opposition takes. The sins of individuals are, then, expressions or concrete realisations of that wider and deeper reality called sin as such.

In Catholic thinking about social sin today positions 2) and 3) above are the most common approaches and seem to hold out most promise of providing the foundations for an adequate theology of social sin. As already mentioned, one specific need that most recognise here is for the elaboration of a theology of the group as moral subject and moral agent and the relation of structures, institutions and systems to causal and in particular moral responsibility.[11]

Structural or institutional sin
It may be helpful to say a few words about social sin in this form. Structures in society, or even between societies or regions, can be unjust and sinful in that they may have their origin in unjust actions and decisions by individuals and/or groups. In addition, they may give rise to consequences that are themselves unjust and sinful. These structures may, then, be said to embody injustice and social sin and to be themselves unjust and sinful. Examples are the following: the apartheid system in South Africa, the Communist regime in the USSR, the national security regimes in South America, the First World economic system that lives off the Third World and exploits it, both ecologically and humanly, the structures of patriarchy that discriminate against

11. See Judith A Merkle's article 'Sin' in *The New Dictionary of Catholic Social Thought* (Gill & Macmillan, Dublin, 1994), Ed., Judith A. Dwyer, p 888. See also Enda McDonagh, *Social Ethics and the Christian: Towards Freedom in Communion* (Manchester University Press, 1979), pp 15, 19.

and oppress women. Structural or institutional sin is in important ways the most serious form of social sin, but it is also the most difficult form to tackle and the most resistant to efforts to promote social justice for all. It can become a reality in any community or institution or system, the church included.

Evaluation of the relational model of sin
The relational model of sin is the most widely accepted one in contemporary moral theology, at least in the western church. One hopes that the values and positive aspects of this model will have become clear during the course of our exposition of it in the preceding pages, especially as one contrasts it with the legal model and the weaknesses in that. It may be of value, however, to present here a very brief evaluation of this relational model, focusing on its strengths but adverting also to its weaknesses.

Strengths
We may list these as follows:
1. It is firmly grounded in scripture and is compatible with the central strand of the main Christian moral tradition.
2. It places the person at the centre and is concerned to see him/her in the context of his/her relationships and social setting. Thus it is both personalist and communitarian or social.
3. It seems to be closer to and more in tune with the contemporary moral experience of Christians in the church.
4. It stresses freedom and responsibility and so fosters growth and creativity in the moral subject.
5. It puts the emphasis in regard to sin on the personal choice of the sinner and sees the matter/object chosen as important but not primary.
6. It gives adequate attention to the historical aspect of both the sinner and the process by which a sin, especially a major sin, happens, and so is more realistic and balanced than the legal model of sin.
7. Its concept of mortal sin seems to resonate well with the contemporary Christian's experience and so seems realistic and helpful.
8. The discussion of the roots of our sinful habits is illuminating, consoling and challenging all at once and represents a valuable and necessary growth in our understanding of sin.
9. The focus on social sin fills a big gap in the usual presentation of sin and is an important advance in regard to arriving at an adequate theology of sin.

Weaknesses

The relational model of sin is not without its weaknesses and undeveloped aspects. We may mention the following:

1. The relational model of sin is at times less clear and more difficult to understand fully than the legal model. This could appear to some as a disadvantage, but one has also to remember that this model gains in realism and accuracy what it loses in clarity. And anyway, we can now see that the clarity of the legal model is in some areas a false one that does not do full justice to our moral experience of sin.

2. There may be a temptation to understand the relational model in individualistic terms in a distorted conception of its personalist dimension and to the neglect of its focus on social sin.

3. Much remains to be done in relation to our understanding of social sin.

4. As in regard to the theology of morality in general, this contemporary understanding of sin needs a great deal of development in the matter of the religious or theological dimension of sin, as we seek to work out a richer theology of sin, and not be content with just a morality of it.

Further Reading

Cosgrave, William, 'Understanding Sin Today', *The Furrow*, October 1999, pp 538-547. This article is a summary of the present chapter.

Gaffney, James, *Sin Reconsidered* (Paulist Press, New York, 1983), especially chapters 1, 8 & 10;

Gula, Richard M, *Reason Informed by Faith: Foundations of Catholic Morality* (Paulist Press, New York, 1989), chapters 7 & 8;

Gula, Richard M, *To Walk Together Again: The Sacrament of Reconciliation* (Paulist Press, New York, 1984), chapter 4;

John Paul II, Apostolic Exhortation, *Reconciliation and Penance* (1984), nn. 13-18;

May, William E, 'Sin' in *The New Dictionary of Theology*, edited by J Komonchak, M Collins & D Lane (Gill & Macmillan, Dublin, 1987), pp 954-96/;

O'Connell, Timothy E, *Principles for a Catholic Morality*, Revised Edition (Harper & Row, San Francisco, 1990), chapters 7 & 8;

O'Keefe, Mark, OSB, *What are they saying about social sin?* (Paulist Press, New York, 1990).

CHAPTER 5

The Sacrament of Reconciliation Today

In this chapter we turn to the ceremony or ritual which Catholics have for many centuries of Christian history associated very closely with sin and its remission, namely, Confession or the Sacrament of Penance or, to use its more recent name, the Sacrament of Reconciliation. To begin we will make a very brief sketch of the history of the sacrament and then move on to consider the sacrament today from the theological point of view. Our last section will treat of pastoral practice in relation to the sacrament as we discuss the values and benefits of the various rites of the sacrament, the demanding tasks of repenting, forgiving and reconciling and, finally, the place of the sacrament in the spiritual life today.

CONFESSION: HOW IT DEVELOPED OVER TWENTY CENTURIES

In relation to the history of confession, which we will summarise very briefly here, an important point to get firmly into our minds is that what we know as confession is the product of almost 2000 years of growth and development in which very extensive evolution took place, so extensive, one contemporary theologian has said, that if it had not already taken place, most would say it could not happen, because it has affected the very substance of the sacrament.

Ancient Penance (The New Testament to 500 AD)
As a significant part of his ministry, Jesus frequently and with great compassion forgave sin and reconciled sinners to God. In addition, he commissioned his followers, the community of the church, to do the same, saying they were to forgive and retain sins (Jn 20:23) and bind and loose in relation to sin and other matters (Mt 16:18-9, 18:18).

Now it is important to note that, for the early church as for the Jewish community at that time, sin and especially serious and public sin was not simply a private matter concerning only the person who had sinned and God. Rather such sins were viewed as affecting the church community and damaging or wounding it as the community of salvation and reconciliation. Because of this, the church from very early on felt it necessary to take measures in relation to serious sinners, for their reconciliation with the church and the protection of the church's holiness. Without such reconciliation these sinners could not be saved or at least be assured of salvation.

Procedures for the reconciliation of serious sinners
In the New Testament church the baptism of adults was the primary procedure or ritual in and through which the church carried out its commission from Jesus to forgive sin (Jn 20:23). In relation to sin after (adult) baptism, Jesus left no liturgy or ritual by which to reconcile serious sinners with the church. The early church did, however, confront the issue of serious sin after baptism, at least in some places, and, in imitation of the Jewish practice, took two steps in the process of reconciling serious sinners with itself. The first was binding, i.e. segregating these sinners within the church, forbidding them to exercise their active role as members of the faithful and prohibiting them from sharing eucharistic communion. The second step was loosing, i.e. reconciling repentant sinners with the church, a reconciliation that was symbolised by the sinner going immediately afterwards to the eucharist, the sacrament of reconciliation. The ceremonies of binding and loosing were public ones, taking place during the eucharist, where they were performed by the bishop. Thus they were also liturgical and part of the public worship of the church. The church community, by its prayers, supported the repenting sinners as they did their penances.

How this binding and loosing was carried out is not fully clear, and also there was no universal agreement on which serious public sins had to be submitted to this ecclesial (church related) penance, though in time all accepted that murder, adultery and apostasy should be among them.

Further developments
In the third century, the rites and procedures for reconciling serious sinners became more developed as the Order of Penitents emerged. Since this ecclesial penance was seen as a second

chance for reconciliation (adult baptism was the first), it came to be the practice that, like baptism, this penance was available only once in one's lifetime. The acts of penance required of the repenting sinners in the Order of Penitents were often severe and lengthy, e.g. fasting, almsgiving, prayer, wearing sackcloth and ashes, etc. These activities were seen as expressions of the conversion or repentance in which the sinner was engaged, and when the penance was complete, it was assumed that the conversion was also. At that point the church judged that the repentant sinner was ready for official reconciliation.

Canonical Penance
In the fourth and fifth centuries, a more developed form of ecclesial penance called canonical penance was adopted. At this time penances became more severe and longer, with the result that many people postponed official church penance to the end of life. For those on their death-beds this penance tended to be reduced to a brief ritual. Of course only very few people needed or were allowed to undertake canonical penance anyway, and so for the vast majority of Christians it was irrelevant and no help. By about 500 AD it was for all practical purposes a dead letter, though it lingered on as the only official form of penance for about four more centuries, largely in the area around the Mediterranean.

The emphasis in canonical penance was on doing one's penance as the sign and proof that one's conversion was under way. Confessing one's sins was largely a preliminary that was not much emphasised. Canonical penance was also public and liturgical and involved the whole local community.

Church Penance in the Middle Ages
While the form of the sacrament of penance which we have been discussing was dying out in one area of the church, the seeds of a new growth in ecclesial penance were being sown in far away Ireland and Wales. Influenced by the Eastern Church, the Irish and Welsh monks, about 550 AD, began the practice of a monk going to his abbot or other holy monk for spiritual advice and often moral guidance. This spiritual guide would give a penance for the sins confessed and later, at the end of the penance, the sinner would go back to the eucharist. Soon this practice spread outside the monasteries and then people who were not monks

would come to the spiritual guides in the monastery. By 600 AD this form of 'confession' had made its way to Europe through the Irish missionaries. In time penitential books containing lists of sins and appropriate penances were compiled to help the 'confessors'.

Special features

The special features of this Celtic or monastic penance were that it took place in the context of spiritual direction, all sins could be brought to one's spiritual guide, and one could go to him as often as one wished. There was no rite of reconciliation (or absolution, as we'd say). In addition, this procedure was completely private and non-liturgical and in its earlier stages the spiritual guide was usually not a priest but rather an unordained monk or maybe even an 'ordinary' Christian. The emphasis was on one's sin-actions and as time went on a legal view of sin and penance began to predominate. The focus was on the relationship between the sinner and God, while the relationship with the church receded into the background. This form of ecclesial penance was unofficial for many centuries and in places met serious opposition from bishops and synods. Only about 800 AD was it accepted as an official form of church penance and then only in some places.

The continuing evolution of ecclesial penance

Around 800 AD a ritual of reconciliation or absolution was added and gradually the giving of this absolution was reserved to priests. The form of the absolution changed too, so that it came to be given in the form of a declaration of forgiveness ('I absolve you ...) rather than in the form of a prayer for forgiveness ('May God forgive you ...') as had previously been the case. So by about 1150 AD the absolution was seen as an exercise of the power of the keys and was heavily emphasised as essential to the sacrament.

Around 900 AD another innovation enabled penitents, for practical reasons, to do their penance after, not before the absolution was given, as had been the case up till then. With this the emphasis soon moved from doing one's penance to confessing one's sins in detail and getting absolution. The penance faded out largely and soon became only a token. In effect the sacrament was now simply the confession of sins and the absolution, a brief ritual that could take place in a very short time. This made going to the sacrament easier and quicker, of course, and so it was welcomed. But it contained hidden theological problems.

A problem created

The odd situation was now created where one could be absolved from one's sins before one was actually converted from them! In the past, doing one's long and often severe penance was the sign and proof that one was actually converted or repentant, and only when the penance was completed was one in a position to be reconciled with the church and with God. Now, however, all one needed to do to be reconciled was to confess one's mortal sin(s) and make an act of contrition. This meant that performing the brief ritual of confessing one's sins and getting absolution became, effectively, a substitute for the reality of conversion. So the idea was in practice lost that conversion or repentance is often a process that can be long and difficult. This is clear if one thinks of being absolved from a habit of sin or some grave sin. In the sacrament one is forgiven for the habit but one may be far from converted from it in any full sense, and it may very likely recur again fairly soon, as experience abundantly confirms. In relation to grave sin, full conversion is also often a process of considerable length and difficulty and may not be complete when the ritual of confession ends.

Given this situation, the danger was real that the sacrament could be seen as a kind of magic ritual, wiping out sin almost automatically, whether one was fully converted or not. This danger frequently became a reality in medieval times and later and was made more likely by the teaching that the sacrament is effective *ex opere operato*, i.e. by the very performance of the rite for those who don't put an obstacle in the way. Even today this problem is with us, since the fact that repentance or conversion is often a process is not adequately taken account of in the present rites of the sacrament.

In 1215 a church law was made that all who had reached the age of discretion (probably 14 years) are obliged to go to confession annually and to confess all mortal sins. This bit of legislation marked the official acceptance of Celtic penance in its developed form as the church's sacrament of penance for all its members.

Modern Penance (1551 to 1962)

The Council of Trent (1551) confirmed the developments we have noted and added some other points. It re-affirmed that Christ instituted the sacrament of penance (Jn 20:23) and that going to confession is necessary for salvation for those who have committed mortal sin. Penitents are to confess all their mortal sins not already confessed, along with the number of times each sin was committed and any circumstances that would change the nature of the sin. In other words, the mortal sinner is obliged to make a full or integral confession. Venial sins may be confessed. Trent spoke in legal terms and so saw confession as a kind of tribunal in which the priest is the judge (but also a healer) and the penitent is the accused (and the accuser). The core point here is that, like a judge in a court of law giving a verdict and passing a sentence, the priest's absolution is effective and actually forgives the sins confessed.

Trent to Vatican II

What Trent decreed prevailed for the following four hundred years down to Vatican II (1962-5). So relatively little had changed since Trent. The sacrament continued to be understood in a narrow legal and at times legalistic manner. An individualistic understanding and practice was dominant. There was a tendency to go to confession more often after Trent but that usually amounted to little more than annual confession in accordance with the law. Only in the twentieth century did people begin to go to the sacrament more frequently than this, namely, once a month or even weekly. This was due largely to Pope Pius X (1905) recommending frequent communion. Since people felt that they had to go to confession before going to communion, confession became more frequent as communion did. In this context, people with only venial sins also went to the sacrament regularly and indeed frequently as, in their view, this was a surer way of overcoming their sins and growing in virtue.

In the fifteenth century the confession box was introduced in some places but it was only in 1614 that, with its screen, it became an obligation for all. The main reason for this development was to prevent solicitation of women penitents and by women penitents in the sacrament. A secondary reason was to preserve the anonymity of penitents.

After Trent, other means of repenting became very secondary, though of value too, as the sacrament came in the eyes of many to be seen as the only sure place to achieve repentance and get forgiveness.

One may add, in conclusion, that for most penitents in the post-Tridentine and pre-Vatican II era going to confession was usually experienced as an ordeal and the dominant feeling afterwards was one of relief. Not infrequently, though, great peace of soul was experienced after the sacrament.

THE SACRAMENT OF RECONCILIATION TODAY

In this second section of our chapter on confession we will look briefly at the sacrament as it is today: firstly, the big decline in its use, and then how it is understood in and by the church community at the present time.

The decline in the use of the sacrament
It is plain to all that there is a major fall-off in the numbers of Catholics going to confession in recent years. Very few lay people, bishops, priests or religious, approach the sacrament as often as they used to do 20 or 30 years ago. So the decline is an accepted fact nowadays. It will help if we document that decline with a few statistics.

One US survey showed that between 1964 and 1974 monthly confession declined in the United States from 32% to 17%. Another poll discovered that 27% never go to confession, 25% go once a year and only 6% go monthly or more often. In relation to US priests, the same survey found that 8% go weekly, 27% monthly, 47% every few months and 18% once a year.

In Ireland surveys indicate similar trends and the more recent the survey the bigger the decline. Thus between 1974 and 1984 there was a drop of 20% in the rate of monthly confession, down from 46.5% to 26%. A 1989 poll saw this downward trend continuing: 18% go to the sacrament monthly and 11% never go. More recently a 1995 investigation lists 14% for monthly confession, while a 1998 survey reported that 40% of Catholics rarely or never go to confession, 1% go every 2 or 3 weeks, 24% every 1 to 3 months and 34% less often. Not surprisingly, young people go to confession much less frequently than the over-50s.

This decline in the use of the sacrament of penance is highlighted by the contrast with the increased frequency with which Catholics now go to communion. There was a 15% increase in going to communion in Ireland between 1974 and 1989, though that has now dropped to 11%, because, one assumes, of the drop in Mass attendance in the last few years.

Context of the decline: a look at history
In relation to confession, the following old and wise saying is particularly apt: those who don't know history are very likely to be prisoners of recent tradition. As was indicated in our first section, the vast majority of Christians never went to Ancient or Canonical Penance, because they were forbidden to do so, not having committed one of the few very serious public sins for which that form of the sacrament was reserved. The small number who did go would have shrunk to almost nothing during the many centuries after Ancient Penance became obsolete (500-800 AD), since there was in the church then no other official form of ecclesial penance. Celtic penance, which emerged about 550 AD, was unofficial for centuries and, by medieval and presentday theological standards, was not a sacrament and, in addition, was to be found only in some parts of the British Isles, and some areas of what are now called France, Switzerland, Italy and Spain. So up to about 850 AD the sacrament of penance was seldom if ever used by church members throughout the church. Even after the law of 1215 AD about annual confession was passed, confession-going remained in or around that minimum of once a year. It was only in the twentieth century that people began to go to confession really frequently, doing so in the 1950s and 1960s as often as monthly and even weekly.

It is clear, then, that the central church tradition about going to confession has been a nineteen-century-long practice of infrequent confession and even no confession. The twentieth century is the exception, an exception that is to be explained largely as a result of Pope Pius X's recommendation of frequent communion for all who had reached the age of reason.

In this context the present decline in confession-going appears far less alarming and can be seen as essentially a return to the situation in the church before 1905.

Why this major decline today?
We still need to ask this question, since church members disagree about the answer and the answer is, anyway, an interesting one. Those who are alarmed over present trends tend to attribute the

decline to our loss of the sense of sin (though what that means exactly is not fully clear), and/or to our lack of understanding and poor celebration of the sacrament of penance. Mention is also made of the secularisation and individualism of Western society today, as well as the general drift from the church in our day.

Those who see the drop in the numbers celebrating the sacrament of penance as basically nothing to worry about give quite different reasons for the present situation, the main ones of which are the following:

i) The virtual disappearance of the idea, long taken for granted, that one must go to confession before one goes to communion.

ii) The emergence of a more balanced understanding of sexual immorality and sexual sins.

iii) The decline of the legal understanding of confession and especially of the image of God as policeman, judge and punisher of sin.

iv) The realisation that mortal sin is hard to commit and so is rare.

v) The failure of many to experience frequent confession as a significant help to conversion and growth in holiness.

vi) The desire for quality in one's confession and the rejection of going to the sacrament as largely the regular enactment of a routine ritual.

In the light of this it seems best to conclude that the current big decline in confession-going has negative and positive elements, with the positive being perhaps more weighty than the negative. Whatever about that, if we ask about the future, we may with safety predict that, as in the past, the frequency of going to confession will in due course settle at a level that will be appropriate for the Catholics of our time. Remember, however, that the quality of our celebration of the sacrament of penance is of much greater importance than the frequency with which we approach it.

Understanding the sacrament of reconciliation today
The change of title of the sacrament points to a change of understanding and that's important. Up to recent decades the sacrament was understood in a legal way, as we have noted. Today this approach has been replaced by what is referred to as a relationship understanding and it is this which is indicated by the changed

title. The sacrament is now seen as being primarily concerned with healing the broken relationship between the serious sinner and the church and God. Serious (mortal) sin breaks this relationship and the sacrament of reconciliation is the church's official ritual or liturgy by which this relationship is restored and the parties reconciled. The penitent repents, the church expresses its forgiveness through the priest's absolution and, as a result, reconciliation is achieved between them. We can describe confession, then, as the sacrament of the serious sinner's reconciliation with the church and so with God.

A forgotten truth recovered

Note here the recovery of the forgotten truth that the sacrament involves as a central element reconciliation with the church. Sin wounds the church as a community of grace and salvation, and the sacrament reconciles the serious sinner with that community and so with God. The whole church community is active in this work of reconciliation: it calls us to conversion, introduces the sinner to penance, offers prayers for him/her/them, and provides spiritual direction and counselling when needed. The church is thus seen as the reconciled and reconciling community. It is implied here that, strictly speaking, reconciliation is needed only when the relationship of the sinner with the church has actually been broken and not just damaged. This occurs through serious sin only and hence, if a penitent has only venial, non-serious sin, then all that is needed in or outside the sacrament is fuller conversion or repentance but not reconciliation. (This is parallelled in ordinary relationships in our daily lives.) It is clear here, then, that the sacrament was and is designed to deal with serious sin. Venial sin is its secondary and optional object.

The sacrament as communal by nature

The 1973 Rite of Penance also makes clear that the sacrament of reconciliation is not a private ritual for an individual sinner, but rather a communal liturgical action of the church itself, which is performed or, better, celebrated, for the benefit of an individual sinful member or members of the church community. So the sacrament is a form of public worship; it is liturgy and so is communal by its very nature. It follows that the more communal the ritual or form of the sacrament, the more is the nature of the sacrament as communal respected and expressed. It would seem from this that the third form or rite of the sacrament in the 1973 official document, a form popularly called general absolution, is the best or ideal form of the sacrament, because it is the most communal. This makes it all the more difficult to understand why this rite is severely restricted in its use by Vatican regulations, and in Ireland effectively sidelined.

Conversion as process in the sacrament
As was mentioned in passing in dealing with the history of the sacrament, the three new rites of the sacrament of reconciliation do not handle very well the fact that conversion/repentance from serious sin is frequently not a quick and easily completed action, but a process that takes effort and time. These rites are brief rituals and their main structural elements are confessing one's sins and getting absolution. So one may be absolved before one is fully converted from one's serious sin or habit of sin. This may lead one to assume that one's conversion is complete as soon as one gets absolution. But, as experience would seem to confirm, it may well not be so. The penitent needs to take this into account and, if need be, work to bring conversion to completion. It would seem from this that a change in the structure of the rites of the sacrament would be beneficial, so as to cater for the process nature of repentance/conversion, as Ancient Penance catered for it in terms of its long penances which, when completed, were the sign and proof that one was fully converted from one's sin.

It needs to be kept in mind all the time that the penitent's main task in confession is conversion from sin. This is his/her chief contribution to the reconciliation the sacrament provides. On the other hand, the priest, representing the church and Christ, must show a Christ-like attitude of understanding and compassion as he welcomes the penitent and gladly extends to her/him the church's and Christ's forgiveness. Thus is reconciliation achieved and celebrated in joy and gratitude, a reconciliation that is modelled very effectively and movingly in the story of the prodigal son and his father in Luke 15.

Examination of conscience
In light of the contemporary theology of sin, one would be well advised to do more before confession than examine oneself on the ten commandments alone. They have value as a list of possible

immoral actions one might question oneself about, but they do not cover everything and are more helpful in a legal than in a relational approach to sin and confession. So, as noted earlier, one should look for sinfulness in oneself as a person, attending to one's attitudes, dispositions, tendencies, habits, values and priorities as well as one's actions. It will be helpful and necessary also to look at one's relationships and their moral quality. Perhaps it is in these, above all, that the sinfulness in oneself will show itself and have its primary impact. One could begin with the relationships in one's home and move out in circles, as it were, from there. One's practice of justice in its various aspects will also require attention, as will one's religious practice, personal and communal. In dealing with these relationships one will thereby also be dealing with one's relationship with God.

One should remember, however, that this examination of life or conscience ought not be seen, or turn into, a kind of moral and religious witch-hunt against oneself. Rather, it is preliminary and an aid to one's primary effort which is to repent and be converted. At the same time, knowledge of what one is called to repent of is essential, if one is to move out of sinfulness and sins and into greater virtue and better Christian living.

THE SACRAMENT OF RECONCILIATION IN THE CHRISTIAN LIFE TODAY

In this final section we wish to focus largely on some practical aspects of our use of the sacrament in our Christian lives. Clearly, the patterns of use of this sacrament of reconciliation have been undergoing extensive change among Catholics at all levels of the church in the last thirty years, as was adverted to above. This seems to involve also the deeper issue of a reassessment of the place of the sacrament in the Christian life and spirituality of a great many Catholics in our day. This change and reassessment are still ongoing and it is not at all clear what the future will hold. Our discussion of some practically significant points may, however, help to throw some light on the place to give to the sacrament in our spiritual lives in the future.

The values of each of the three official rites of the sacrament

If we assume, without any real reflection, that these three rites or forms of celebration are basically three different but essentially similar ways of doing the one thing, namely, reconciling serious sinners with the church and God, then we may use them in an indiscriminate manner that in effect says that one rite is as good as another, whatever sort of confession one wishes to make. This is, however, to fail to realise that these rites seem to be devised for different spiritual needs and situations. A word on each rite will clarify this.

Rite 3 (General Absolution): Here the congregation makes a general statement of sinfulness and repentance and the priest-presider gives absolution to all as a group without anyone having to go individually to him or another confessor. This quite new form of the sacrament is obviously fully communal but less fully personal. It would seem, then, that it is most appropriate for a group of people who wish to celebrate reconciliation sacramentally but who do not need detailed confession of their sins or individual spiritual counselling. One could say that it seems very suitable for a routine confession, and it looks ideal for childrens' confessions. One would not envisage an individual participating in the celebration of this rite with any frequency, even if it were allowed. It could become rather superficial and rather routine, a bit like the penitential rite at the beginning of Mass often tends to be. The great value of Rite 3 is that it reminds us that we all share a real solidarity in sin, while at the same time it enables us to ritualise and celebrate our solidarity in repentance / conversion and to support each other in that task. Rite 3 realises communal reconciliation as the sinful community repents and the priest extends to all the forgiveness of the holy church and the all-merciful God.

Rite 1 (Going to the priest-confessor personally and privately): This is the most personal and the least communal of the three rites. As such, it seems designed for use by a penitent who wishes to make an in-depth confession, perhaps with a need also for spiritual, moral and even psychological counsel. This rite gives one an opportunity to examine one's sinfulness, one's sins and their roots with the help of an experienced, understanding and official representative of the church. This should be very useful in promoting repentance and realising genuine reconciliation with the church and with God. Again it is hard to imagine an individual needing this form of the sacrament very often. It would seem to be the sort of encounter that would only be needed occasionally and which would be all the better in quality for being rather rare. To facilitate it, a face-to-face meeting with the priest rather than an anonymous coming together in a dark box would seem essential.

Rite 2 (Combining the communal and the personal): This rite is a kind of compromise or half-way house between the previous two rites. In ways it succeeds, in ways it does not. It is communal as the congregation gathers and expresses its sinfulness and repentance as a single community. It is personal in that each individual confesses her/his sins and is absolved personally by a priest-confessor. However, these two dimensions of the sacrament are only partially realised or expressed. This rite too seems designed for a more routine confession, where complexity is at a minimum and guidance is not a prime need.

Working for reconciliation in daily life

Confession as the liturgical or ritual celebration of reconciliation between the serious sinner and the church and God presupposes and assumes a great deal of repenting, forgiving and reconciling in our ordinary relationships and living. The sacrament is not at all a substitute for these daily realities, but builds on them and requires them as an essential foundation. So the place of the sacrament of reconciliation in our spiritual lives necessarily relates closely to this everyday repentance, forgiveness and reconciliation. Some reflection on this 'ordinary' experience will be valuable here.

Repentance/conversion in daily life

We all agree that apologising, saying sorry or repenting is part of what love means and often requires. But experience makes it quite plain that repentance or making an apology is usually a very difficult thing to do, especially in the case of a serious fault or sin against another or others. If we ask, why is this?, the answer must be that after such a fault and because of it, we usually feel guilty and perhaps ashamed. This dents our self-esteem and tends to give rise to feelings of regret, disappointment with oneself and maybe embarrassment. One feels small and humble and the prospect of having to go to the other(s) and say, 'I'm sorry' adds to these feelings. Clearly then, negative feelings are engaged in any repenting we do and that is what makes it so difficult. And of course, if one's self-esteem is already low and one's feelings about oneself rather negative, we can understand that it will be even more difficult to apologise and express one's sorrow. Hence, the difficulty intrinsic to repenting may be increased by these negative feelings, at times to the extent that a person will be quite unable to repent in the short or even the medium term. Some never get round to doing so. It is plain, then, that repenting for a significant fault or act of selfishness will often be a process that will go on over some time and take much effort as the sinner works on him/herself, so as to master his/her feelings and elicit the humility and courage to admit he/she was wrong and acted in a selfish and damaging manner.

In other situations there are further reasons making repentance much more difficult than we might expect or hope. Here we find ourselves repeating the same sins over and over, despite saying verbally that we are sorry and making perhaps many purposes of amendment, as we used to call them, i.e. resolutions in confession to avoid a particular sin in future. In this situation it is our habits of sin that we are talking about, habits that we often find resist our best efforts at conversion. Frequently, we have been puzzled as to why this should be the case and at a loss to find an answer.[1]

Contemporary psychology can help us here. It indicates that many of our sinful habits are rooted in our emotional life and in particular in the emotional wounds we picked up during our early years. These habits of sin will not be removed unless and until we heal the wounds that give rise to them by some process of emotional therapy. For example, a habit of aggressiveness or badly managed anger often has its roots in one's lack of self-confidence. One, then, easily feels under threat and so can readily go on the attack in an aggressive way. Similarly with jealousy, attention-seeking, domineering behaviour, etc. A related situation can come about in regard to masturbation or sexual fantasies ('bad' thoughts), where stress or anxiety or loneliness or sexual frustration can be the root from which these habits or symptoms spring.

Given this understanding of our habits of sin, we can readily see that such presumed remedies as saying more prayers, doing extra penances or simply gritting one's teeth, won't do much good. And why? Because they miss the real point, which is emotional healing or relief of stress, etc. It follows, then, that if we are really serious about repenting in these areas of our lives, we have to take the only available remedy, namely, emotional growth or relief of stress, so that moral growth may follow.

---

1. See pp 81-2 above in chapter 3 on sin for the main points made in the following paragraphs on repentance.

Other sins or sinful attitudes or tendencies may arise from some faulty values or priorities and so be not at all amenable to being repented of or uprooted. Here we need to become aware of these distortions of the Christian value system, as a necessary beginning to the process of conversion. Then we can set about the re-ordering that is needed to restore our value system and our priorities to what they should be. An example might be a husband or wife neglecting his/her family in an effort to further his/her career. Or a priest might make himself so busy running from one appointment to another that he allows himself no quality time to listen deeply to those who need an empathetic ear, or even to himself in tranquil contemplation – or even to God.

Perhaps it is in our relationships above all that our sinfulness expresses itself most often and most damagingly. If repentance is to come here quickly and effectively, one needs to develop the personal or emotional qualities of self-awareness and empathy. These will enable us to be sensitive to what may hurt others and to take steps to avoid such sinful activity in the future.

All this underlines the point that one's level of emotional or personal maturity relates very closely to one's level of moral maturity. If the former is low, that will lower one's level of moral maturity and prevent one from being converted from sin as fully and as quickly as one should.

We may add here that in relation to religious or spiritual matters a similar point can be made. Many spiritual difficulties are rooted in psychological or emotional ones and the former will not be resolved unless and until the latter are. E.g. strong feelings of anger and/or rejection towards one's father and/or mother that have been buried since childhood may well make relating to God as Father or Mother difficult or even impossible. More positively, the more we are in touch with ourselves and the more mature we are emotionally and personally, the better placed we are to engage in the search for God in the depths of our being and the more likely we will be to establish a deep and truly personal relationship with God in prayer and in our Christian lives generally.

It will be clear from what has been said about repentance here that repenting of our sinfulness and sins is often enough a process of considerable difficulty, not the relatively easy and quick thing that the legal model of sin led many of us to believe. In consequence, we may need to re-adjust our expectations of repentance in our own lives and, even in the context of the sacrament of reconciliation, be prepared for the long and often difficult process that true and full repentance or conversion may turn out to involve.

Forgiveness in daily life

It will be worthwhile at this point in our consideration of the sacrament of reconciliation to reflect briefly on the reality of forgiveness as it occurs in our ordinary relationships in daily life. Understanding it better will aid us in appreciating what is involved in the sacrament, where, as in ordinary life, reconciliation requires both repentance/sorrow and forgiveness/pardon, if it is to become a reality.

If we enquire about what forgiveness means or how it can be described, we may say that it means behaving in a particular relationship after an offence or hurt as if that offence or hurt had never happened. When one can do that, one will have forgiven the other fully. But experience teaches us that, like repentance, forgiveness in this sense can be very difficult and take a long time to accomplish, particularly after a significant offence of any sort.

The reason is that, here too, as in regard to being sorry for a sin, our feelings are involved. Forgiving is, then, not just an intellectual exercise but a personal one that engages one's emotions and so one's deeper self. Frequently when we are offended or hurt by another, we get angry and feel hurt, resentful and perhaps bitter. One can even be seething with rage and indignation and in no mood for entertaining thoughts of forgiving. It will be clear here that the core requirement for forgiving will have to be the letting go of all these strong feelings. One must somehow defuse one's anger and rage and retrieve the feelings that one had for the other(s) before the hurt took place. Needless to say, this is often far from easy or quick.

The obvious question here is, how does one let go of these feelings so as to forgive the other? The equally obvious answer is that there is no easy or instant way to do this. It is bound to be a painful struggle and to take some time. In fact, not infrequently a person may find it impossible to forgive in the short term or even at all, because of the depth of the hurt and the strength of the feelings accompanying it. This may well happen in cases like adultery, the murder of a close relative or some grave insult. In some instances, however, one who does not forgive may be motivated, perhaps unconsciously, by motives like wallowing in self-pity or enjoying the feelings of self-righteousness and moral superiority over the sinner. Also one may nurse one's anger and resentment as a means of protecting oneself from more painful feelings like sadness, loneliness, emptiness or even depression. Or not forgiving may enable one to control the other in ways that would not otherwise be possible, or maybe it could provide an excuse for remaining at a distance from that person, because deep down one really fears closeness.

If one continues to refuse forgiveness and so continues to nurse one's anger, hurt and resentment, the psychologists say one may be on course to bury these strong feelings. That can lead to the development of a deep sadness or even depression as one turns these feelings in on oneself, while they continue to retain their energy and power to do damage. It is possible that with time these buried feelings may give rise to physical effects in the form of symptoms of bodily ailments like skin disease, fever, ulcers, heart problems or even cancer. This is confirmed by some evidence from people in the Charismatic Movement who say that they find in their healing ministry that such refusal to forgive can block the healing process in relation to such physical ailments.[2]

This is not surprising, seeing that these ailments may well have been brought on in the first place by the refusal to forgive the offence one had suffered. On the other hand, the evidence is that forgiving and letting go one's deeply hurt feelings facilitates the healing of the kind of ailments mentioned above. This means that forgiving can be beneficial, not merely to the relationship that has been broken or damaged by the offence, but to the person who has been offended. Thus, it is in her/his own interests to forgive the other by letting go of the hurt feelings aroused by the offence. This should be an incentive to forgive in cases where there are physical symptoms that may be connected with not forgiving.

Other motives for forgiving would be the sense of relief and of shedding a burden that forgiveness brings, and the ending of the preoccupation with the hurt and the offender that often accompanies the refusal to forgive. Of course the biggest incentive

2. See Francis McNutt OP, *Healing* (Bantam Books, New York, 1974), chapter 12.

here should be the restoration of the broken or damaged relationship with the other person, assuming that that person repents.

It will be important also on occasion to ensure that one forgives oneself, which for some is more difficult than forgiving other people. In these cases one may be angry with oneself for failing or sinning, and disappointed with oneself over not fulfilling one's own expectations of oneself. Not forgiving oneself can, then, be a form of self-punishment. And this is particularly likely to happen when the person in question is somewhat low in self-esteem and may well feel he/she does not deserve forgiveness. This makes it all the more important and necessary to forgive oneself by letting go one's hurt feelings.

Occasionally one may find it hard to forgive God, whom one may see as the one who causes or at least permits some tragedy, illness, loss or injustice one has suffered. This may be understandable but it is, nevertheless, necessary that one let go one's anger and hurt feelings against God and forgive.

It will be important, in this context also, to ensure that one has the correct image or concept of God, not that of a punishing God but that of a forgiving God. If one has the former image, it may happen that one becomes oneself a person who is inclined to punish others as one imagines God does. One must rather try to be a forgiving person as God is forgiving.

It needs to be said too that the old advice that we are often given or may even give ourselves, 'forgive and forget', is faulty in its concern with forgetting. Forgetting is no part of forgiveness and is neither necessary nor at times possible. In fact it may be undesirable, since remembering may be important on occasion, so that one may forgive fully or recall from experience what it is like to forgive, so as to empathise with those who are struggling to forgive oneself.

Finally, if one is a forgiving person and knows from experience its great benefits for one's relationships and for oneself, then one will probably be inclined to seek forgiveness more eagerly and readily in the sacrament of reconciliation. Being able to forgive oneself for failure and sin will also be important as it will tend to facilitate one in repenting of those sins, growing in virtue and also accepting the forgiveness of the church and God in the sacrament. As has been mentioned above, being forgiving will often involve one in dealing with strong feelings of anger, hurt and desire for revenge. If one is able to deal well with these feelings and let them go, then the chances are that one will have some real degree of emotional maturity and competence. That should help one to work towards healing any emotional wounds one may have and so to repent more deeply and more effectively.

Reconciliation in our relationships

Our discussions of repentance and forgiveness lead us naturally to reflection on reconciliation, because these realities are the two essential ingredients that are required in order that reconciliation come about in any broken relationship. When the guilty party says 'I'm sorry' and the offended party says 'I forgive', then they are reconciled. So reconciliation is achieved when repentance meets forgiveness. But both these need to be expressed in some way, so that both parties to the dispute or falling out can come to know the attitude of the other. If, however, either party does not do her/his part, so that either repentance or forgiveness is missing, then there can be no reconciliation. So, if I'm sorry and you don't forgive, or vice versa, we are not reconciled. Our relationship can only be restored if and when both elements are present at the same time.

As already indicated, experience in our relationships should teach us that the process of reconciliation is often very difficult and may well take time and a lot of effort. Even then it may not be achieved. But when reconciliation is achieved, it provides us with a great sense of relief and joy that our relationship is restored. The prospect of such a happy outcome can often be a spur to us to undertake the difficult task of being reconciled with another, emboldening us to say, 'I'm sorry' or 'I forgive' or both. If we have experience of such reconciliation, then we may well be more at home in approaching the sacrament and more eager to celebrate it as, through it, we seek reconciliation with the church and with God.

Rituals of reconciliation

In ordinary life and relationships there are many well established and familiar rituals or gestures that we use to mark and celebrate a reconciliation that has been achieved. These have been devised by our society as a means to express outwardly and together what reconciliation means and thus to seal and confirm it. These are symbolic ways of saying 'We are reconciled; our relationship has been restored and we are happy about this.' Examples are a handshake, an embrace, a kiss, a drink or a meal together, sexual intercourse in marriage.

These are for the most part personal rituals of reconciliation. They take place in personal relationships between individuals and, of course, have great importance in that context. There are also group or communal rituals of many sorts which groups or communities use to express and confirm specific meanings and values within their communal life or with other groups or communities. Examples are saluting the national flag, playing the national anthem, signing treaties, having state visits, officially opening new premises or projects, etc. Some of these may relate to settling differences or solving problems and so may be said to be in the area we are referring to when we use the word reconciliation. Churches and religious communities also make use of rituals of this sort in their communal life and they carry significant meanings and values for the members. In the Catholic Church we are familiar with the sacraments, which are the main symbolic rites or rituals the church uses or celebrates to express and realise certain significant meanings and values for the church and its members. One of these sacraments or symbolic rites or rituals is that of reconciliation. That is the one we are interested in here and have explored and explained in the foregoing pages.

The sacrament, spiritual direction and counselling
In recent years spiritual direction and counselling have been clearly distinguished from the sacrament of reconciliation in both theory and practice. So nowadays spiritual direction is freely available, quite apart from the sacrament, and often by non-ordained people, while counselling is even more clearly seen as a distinct area requiring its own very valuable skills. The experience is too that both spiritual direction and counselling have grown in importance and are being more and more availed of, while the sacrament is in decline. This is in part understandable, since in the past confession was frequently a place where people sought spiritual direction and where counselling in an informal way often took place. This is less the case today and that may be a factor in the decline of the sacrament. The sacrament nowadays focuses more clearly on the individual penitent's need for conversion and reconciliation and so is seen as quite distinct from spiritual direction. Yet the two areas undoubtedly overlap and so no complete separation between them is either possible or desir-

able. Similarly in relation to counselling. There may well be links as we indicated earlier in discussing our habits of sin. Some priests can provide a lot of help even in confession as far as counselling goes; others are not good at it and so should steer clear of it both outside and especially inside the confessional.

The benefits of going to confession
These have been touched on earlier but a few extra points may be added here.

Rite 1: Because it is the most personal form of the sacrament, this rite confronts the penitent very directly with admitting and repenting of his/her serious (and maybe also non-serious) sins to another human person. This is difficult but can be very beneficial in the task of conversion. In addition, this rite allows one to get helpful spiritual advice from an experienced and wise Christian. All this takes courage and humility and can be very good for the soul. Receiving forgiveness from the church's representative will often be a consoling, encouraging and enriching experience. Knowing that this is not just the priest's, but also God's and the church's forgiveness, adds depth and significance to it and to the reconciliation it achieves. Being honest with oneself, admitting one has done wrong and taking responsibility for that, as well as sharing one's sense of guilt and shame, is healthy and can be beneficial emotionally and spiritually. All these benefits of Rite 1 will be especially apparent in our experience when we have serious sin or sins to confess. When we have only venial sin or sins, they will probably be sensed in a rather muted way.

Rite 3: As well as increasing one's sense of solidarity in sin and conversion, this form of the sacrament has frequently been experienced as a stepping stone to a deeper and more comprehensive confession and reconciliation in Rite 1. Rite 3 may well have less personal impact on the penitent as he/she will often be making a routine confession and very likely one with only venial sin. Still it can provide a sense of reconciliation with the church and God after a period of feeling alienated. That is an important value, especially for those feeling excluded or on the margins of the church.

Rite 2: This can combine to some extent the benefits of Rites 1 and 3, even if it is likely that it may do so in an imperfect and partial way. It can possibly become a Lent and Advent routine, but properly celebrated it can give a sense both of real conversion and heartfelt reconciliation with the church and God.

The spirituality of the sacrament of reconciliation
We have grown up with a very individualistic view of confession
and its spirituality. It has been very much a way of getting one's
sins forgiven, one's guilt wiped out and one's relationship with
God restored. This understanding is still very much with and in
us, both priests and people, and will not be easily reformed. Still,
we must try to make our own the much more adequate understanding and spirituality of the sacrament that has emerged since
Vatican II and which we have outlined earlier. Central to it is the
recovery of the ecclesial and social dimensions of sin, conversion
and the sacrament.

Since sin wounds other people and the church as a community
of grace and salvation, the sacrament of reconciliation has to be
seen as the ritual or liturgical action of the church by which the
repentant serious sinner's conversion and the church's and
God's forgiveness are symbolised and made present and effective. Thus, the sinner is reconciled with the church and with God.
Reconciliation with the church is the symbol or sacrament of the
penitent's reconciliation with God. For the penitent the focus is
on conversion from sin to God and the neighbour, and from the
confessor's viewpoint the main concern is the restoration of the
broken (or damaged) relationship of the sinner with the church
and with God. God is a forgiving and merciful Father and so the
sinner comes in a spirit of repentance and gratitude, comparing
his/her life with the example and commandments of Jesus and
aiming to grow into the likeness of Christ.

All this can be expressed also in terms of God's grace, working
through the church, calling the sinner to repentance, enabling
him/her to repent and reconciling him/her with the church and
with God through the forgiveness given in the priest's absolution.

Promoting the sacrament pastorally in our day
This is an extremely difficult issue; there are no quick fixes and
people disagree deeply on how to go about the matter, since they
differ widely on what the problem and its causes are. Most
would agree that wider issues about the church, renewal and
conversion are relevant and unavoidable here, as well as the
whole matter of the moral quality of society itself. So only a few
general but tentative points will be made.

1. A fuller development of our understanding of social sin
and social conversion, along with greater efforts to bring about
social reconciliation in all its forms at all levels of society, is needed.

2. Intensified efforts to make the church a more reconciled and reconciling community at all levels and in every way are urgently required.

3. Efforts to overcome the deep-set individualism of today and to develop a deeper and fuller social and ecclesial sense of belonging are called for, if the sacrament of reconciliation is to make sense to contemporary Catholics.

4. We need to promote conversion of heart, lifestyle and structures at all levels in the church. The sacrament would find its natural place in that setting.

5. More rituals of reconciliation need to be developed to celebrate reconciliation in its various forms in the church, e.g. the suggested new Order of Penitents for lapsed Catholics.

6. A better theological and liturgical understanding of the sacrament of reconciliation is needed among priests and people.

7. A more widespread use of Rite 3 is possible and desirable.

Further Reading

Dallen, James, *The Reconciling Community: The Rite of Penance* (Pueblo Publishing Company, New York, 1986);

Dallen, James, 'History and the Reform of Penance' in Robert J Kennedy, Editor, *Reconciling Embrace: Foundations for the Future of Sacramental Reconciliation,* (Liturgy Training Publications, Archdiocese of Chicago, Chicago, 1998), pp 79-90;

Dallen, James, 'Reconciliation, Sacrament of', in Peter E Fink, Editor, *The New Dictionary of Sacramental Worship* (Gill & Macmillan, Dublin, 1990), pp 1052-1064;

Favazza, Joseph A., *The Order of Penitents: Historical Roots and Pastoral Future* (Liturgical Press, Collegeville, USA, 1988);

Gula, Richard M., *To Walk Together Again: The Sacrament of Reconciliation* (Paulist Press, New York, 1984);

Hellwig, Monica K., *Sign of Reconciliation and Conversion: The Sacrament for our Times* (Michael Glazier Inc., Delaware, USA, 1982);

Huels, John M., *Disputed Questions in the Liturgy Today* (Liturgy Training Publications, Archdiocese of Chicago. Chicago, 1988), pp 75-90 (on General Absolution);

John Paul II, *Reconciliatio et Penitentiu* (CTS, 1984);

Kennedy, Robert J., Editor, *Reconciliation: The Continuing Agenda* (Liturgical Press, Collegeville, USA, 1987);

Orsy, Ladislas, *The Evolving Church and the Sacrament of Penance* (Dimension Books, Denville, New Jersey, USA, 1978);

Sofield, Loughlan, Juliano, Carroll, & Hammett, Rosine, *Design for Wholeness: Dealing with Anger, Learning to Forgive, Building Self-Esteem* (Ave Maria Press, Notre Dame, Indiana, USA, 1990).

CHAPTER 6

A Christian Understanding of Sexuality

In all the centuries of our existence there is perhaps nothing which we humans have found it harder to deal with and manage well than our sexuality. There is probably no area of our lives where we have achieved such little success as a race, and often enough as individuals, in understanding and integrating into our personality, relationships and life generally such an important and basic dimension of our being. For us human beings our sexuality has always been something of a puzzle and a mystery, and more often than not we have adopted extreme attitudes and practices in relation to it, either repressing it as too powerful and dangerous to be given any freedom, or allowing it free rein as a source of profound pleasure or a kind of game to play.

Today people generally, and Christians in particular, are realising the inadequacy of these approaches and they experience the urgent need to find and elaborate a more balanced understanding of our sexuality and a more life-enhancing use of it in our relationships and in our lives in general. Such an understanding and practice will need to avoid the extremes of the past just mentioned, while at the same time respecting fully the central message of the Christian gospel about, and the contemporary experience of, human sexuality. In this way we will be enabled to provide a realistic and Christian account of what we as sexual beings are and of how, as such, we should live and act in our personal relationships and in our community living.

The traditional Christian approach to the sexual dimension of human persons and human life has tended to focus its attention from the beginning on sexual behaviour and activity and thus to elaborate a sexual ethic. In the process it has given very little explicit thought to the deeper issue of the human person as sexual, i.e. to human sexuality as such. There was, of course, in that sexual ethic an implicit, unworked out understanding of and attitude towards human sexuality and this, we now see, was often very negative and even hostile. In the contemporary approach, it is seen as essential to focus first on this more general but also more basic level of our sexual existence, namely, our sexuality itself. We need to understand that sexuality well and, above all, positively, as the church in Vatican II requires, if we are to be in a position to discuss reasonably and maturely the relation of sexuality to morality, and in doing so to develop a balanced and realistic sexual morality for today's church and its members, married, single and celibate.

In accordance with this outlook, we will concern ourselves in this chapter largely with working out a realistic and Christian view of human sexuality itself. This will involve reflecting on various dimensions of the sexual life, including its affective and genital aspects, growth in this area of life, the purposes of sexuality and a brief look at chastity as the correct moral attitude and way of living as sexual beings. What we are attempting is to a great extent uncontentious and is generally agreed in contemporary Christian thinking. The difficulties today arise in the area of sexual morality itself, in connection with the moral judgments on specific sexual actions like contraception and homosexual activity. But, as is to be expected, these difficulties and disagreements have roots in our understanding of sexuality. Hence, a lot of what we will be saying will have significant implications for sexual morality and so will have added importance.

THE NATURE OF HUMAN SEXUALITY

The negative tradition

It is well known that, for many centuries and indeed right down to Vatican II itself (1962-5), the Christian Church had a very negative and pessimistic attitude to human sexuality. This is clear in numerous statements of Christian writers over the centuries and even among the Fathers of the Church, St Augustine and St Jerome being prime examples. It is not necessary, however, to quote particular statements in the present context. For our purposes it will be adequate to mention briefly the main expressions of this negative attitude to sexuality and how it persisted for hundreds of years and, in the process, coloured profoundly the Christian attitude to and teaching on sexuality and everything connected with it, e.g. sexual morality, sexual sin, marriage, celibacy / virginity and, of course, women.

Basic in this conception of sexuality was the teaching that the fall of our first parents had a significant negative impact on our sexual nature, bringing sin and concupiscence (the rebellion of our sexual appetite against our will) very much into play in our sexual activity and especially in sexual intercourse. While sexuality, sexual intercourse and marriage were all defended as good, because divinely created and God-given, the tendency was to say that sexual intercourse in marriage is justified only by the motive of procreation, that marriage is sin-infected and that sexual passion must be severely controlled and strictly limited to marriage. Sexual pleasure is wrong, if sought outside marriage or if it is the motive of sex within marriage. Celibacy/virginity is a superior state of life to marriage and perfect continence in marriage is urged on spouses, since sexual pleasure is somehow tainted with sin. In marriage sin is almost inevitable. Women are often seen as temptresses for men, as secondary to men and as having value mostly as receptacles for the male seed in the process of human reproduction.

Sexual sins came, in time, to be divided into those in accordance with nature (adultery, fornication, rape, incest) and those contrary to nature (masturbation, homosexual acts, contraception), the latter being more sinful than the former, because contrary to nature. Here nature is understood in a biological sense and the purpose of sexual intercourse is seen as primarily procreation. At times in this tradition, all sexual sins were considered mortal but later the view prevailed that the matter in sexual sin is always grave, though a particular sin might be venial, because of reduced responsibility on the part of the agent. In practice, it often seemed that sexual sins were the most serious of all and indeed, in the context of confession particularly, they often appeared to penitents and priests as the only real sins. Such were the negativity and exaggeration in regard to these matters!

With the Second Vatican Council a new era dawned in regard to the church's attitude to and understanding of human sexuality. To this we now turn.

The contemporary positive understanding of sexuality
An obvious fact of our experience is that we are sexual beings, sexed persons, men or women. Clearly too our sexuality is a basic dimension of our humanity, permeating our whole personality and influencing all our personal activities as human beings. Thus our sexuality is far more than a biological appetite or a mechanism for reproduction.

To describe what sexuality is we may say that it is that aspect of our nature as persons which gives us the characteristics of body and psyche that make us men or women, male or female persons. As such, our sexuality plays a major role in our personality development, in our growth towards psychosexual maturity, in our relationships with other people and in our insertion or socialisation into our society and culture.Thus sexuality has biological or physical aspects, but psychological, emotional, relational, social and even spiritual ones as well. That this sexual dimension of our humanity is a powerful force is obvious from our experience of relationships with the other sex, men with women and women with men. We can see it also by simply observing the massive attention and publicity, both positive and negative, that sexual relationships and other sexual matters get in Western society nowadays, and the huge sums of money that are regularly involved. At the same time we must remember that sexuality is only one dimension of the human personality and of human relationships. So, while it is always sexual persons who are involved in all our human activities, many of these activities and many of our relationships are, strictly speaking, non-sexual, e.g. prayer, work, sport, business contacts, parent-child relationships, etc.

Of course sexuality as such does not exist. It is an abstraction. What exists are men and women, sexual persons who are either male or female. Still, we can speak about sexuality as a dimension of these persons and their relationships. We take for granted here that men and women are equal as persons, having the same dignity and basic human rights and duties. That equality is still, however, to some extent an aspiration in society and in the church. Though great progress has been made, it has not yet become a full reality or been fully realised in the communal and institutional living of the human community or the Christian community. Our first concern here, however, will be the differences between men and women. They differ as sexual persons in their sexuality, not just biologically but also psychologically, emotionally, intellectually, socially, spiritually and instinctually. Some reflections on these differences will be of value and interest at this point.

Feminine and masculine sexuality
These labels refer to the sets of characteristics of personality and character that women and men tend to have in our and many

other cultures. They point to the social or cultural constructs that have emerged in society to describe the personality, qualities and modes of activity of men and women. In other words, we are saying that feminine and masculine sexuality are largely cultural stereotypes arising from social and cultural conditioning. This means that these stereotypes are the result of the way a culture shapes and forms the personalities of women and men, so that each has a typical or characteristic set of emotional, psychological and relational traits. Certain qualities are, then, referred to as typically feminine and others as typically masculine. In recent times authors speak of these stereotypes as indicating the 'gender' differences between men and women, while the physical or biological differences are spoken of as the 'sex' differences between females and males.

Given that these stereotypes or gender differences are, to a significant extent, the product of culture, it is clear that they are not necessarily innate or natural; they are not simply the way nature or God planned things. Rather they are quite changeable and indeed vary from society to society. They can be liberating or oppressive in whole or in part and so may need to be changed or improved. In Western society today, these gender differences or cultural stereotypes are changing and perhaps even breaking down. This provides an opportunity for both women and men to free themselves from the restrictions and oppressive aspects of these stereotypes and so to develop their personalities by acquiring at least some of the qualities and traits usually associated with the other sex.

We may summarise feminine and masculine sexuality, or the gender differences between women and men in our society, in the following manner. Women are taken to be emotional, intuitive, warm and caring, affectionate, gentle and tender, talkative and good at personal relationships, passive and self-sacrificing, moody and changeable, sensitive and submissive. On the other hand, men are credited with what are usually held to be masculine qualities: unemotional and cool, logical and rational, detached and emotionally uncommunicative, aggressive and competitive, good at taking initiatives and giving leadership, career-oriented rather than relationship-oriented, strong and assertive, dominant and bossy. These two sets of qualities are seen as complementary rather than opposed, thus giving rise to the common observation that men and women complement each other and so can form better and deeper relationships with each other than those between two men or two women. It is important to add that it is generally agreed also that men have a so-called feminine side or dimension, and women a so-called masculine one. This means that each has some of the characteristics of the other sex, though in a way that is weaker than and subordinate to their own dominant gender or type of sexuality as just described.

It would seem correct to say in this context that both men and women should see it as a major goal and indeed duty of their lives to develop to the full both aspects of their personality, the feminine and the masculine. Then they would be more fully integrated and mature human beings and would move beyond the stereotypes we have been talking about to a level or degree of personality and character growth and development, where the feminine and the masculine are both developed and integrated in a significant way, so that a high degree of psychosexual maturity is attained. Men would still be masculine and women feminine, but each would have a more balanced and a more mature personality and character and, hence, would be more capable of loving and be closer to being the best and fullest person he/she could be.

Gender differences and social roles
A significant consequence of the gender differences we have been discussing is that certain social roles have come to be regarded as masculine, or suitable for men only, and others as feminine and so suitable for women only. Examples are: for men leadership roles in the home, in society and in the church; for women caring and nurturing roles like rearing children in the home, nursing, housekeeping, teaching. This has long meant that men are regarded as superior to women in political and social life and women are seen as secondary and subordinate to men in terms of social status and responsibility in the public domain generally.

There is today, in the Western world at least, a vigorous debate about this inequality of women in terms of social roles. While all agree that men and women are equal as persons, it is not agreed that certain social roles are, as it were, natural to and so suitable for men alone, while others are for women alone. The equal-but-different school, which accepts this last point that certain social roles are natural to men and others to women, has a not insignificant number of adherents, including, it seems clear, the Pope and other official teachers in the church.[1]

But this position, which is referred to by some as 'ontological complementarity', is rejected by many, especially women theologians, as sexist and the product of a patriarchal society. While it verbally recognises the equality of woman, it also makes her different and this difference determines her destiny and her subordination. Thus it colludes in the oppression of women and seems to many to be an element in the argumentation that rules out the ordination of women to the priesthood.[2]

Instead of it, some say that all gender differences are culturally based and conditioned and so women are just as suitable for, and likely to be just as competent in, all social roles as men are. Another school of thought, which may be designated as moderately feminist, holds that some of the differences between the sexes are biologically based, though most are not. Which is which is not fully clear, however. Even so, women must be seen as equally competent with men for most social roles. Finally, what is often referred to as the transformative model of man-woman relationships and roles is critical of all the above viewpoints, primarily because they neglect the need to transform society, if true equality in terms of social roles is to be reached for all people and not just for the privileged classes as is the case in the West in our day. This position is well expressed, some feel, by the phrase 'equal and different', where equality is primary and difference is valued and celebrated and not used as a principle of exclusion or domination. The goal for all men and women is to become as fully human as possible, but social transformation is also essential, if sexism, injustice and the domination of women in society and the church are to be overcome and true equality is to become a reality for all. Such is the liberating vision of the reign of God in which the personal and the public or social are joined.[3]

1. Kevin T Kelly, *New Directions in Sexual Ethics: Moral Theology and the Challenge of AIDS* (Geoffrey Chapman, London & Washington, 1998), pp 50-4.
2. Kelly, p 51-3.
3. Anne E Carr, *Transforming Grace: Christian Tradition and Women's Experience* (Harper & Row Publishers, San Francisco, 1990), pp 123-8; Dermot A. Lane, 'The Equality of All in Christ', *Doctrine and Life*, February 1994, pp 77-80. See also Gareth Moore OP, *The Body in Context: Sex and Catholicism* (Continuum, London & New York, 2001), chapter 7.

Men and women need each other
Despite what has been said about the negative implications of the idea of complementarity between women and men, it remains true that the human person, male and female, has a deep need for relationships with others, both men and women, not just to enable him/her to grow and mature as a person but specifically to develop and flourish as a sexual person, as a man or as a woman. In other words, we are relational beings, and particularly as sexual beings we need relationships with the other sex as well as with our own to enable us to establish our sexual identity as men or women, to learn how to love others in a truly human and not just in a so-called masculine or feminine way, and also then to be ready to enter a significant sexual relationship, leading perhaps to marriage, if one so chooses, or to live as a mature single or celibate person.

Affective sexuality
While in the past sexuality was for a very long time understood as merely for procreation, we find in today's world the opposite tendency: to regard sexuality, sexual relationships and especially sexual intercourse as largely or even completely for fun and pleasure. Both these views overlook what is frequently referred to today as the affective or relational dimension of sexuality, a dimension that is foundational to a correct understanding of sexuality and of how to live as a sexual person.

To say that our sexuality has an affective or relational dimension is to say that it is closely linked to the human capacity and need for affection, tenderness, warmth, love and true personal relationships. In fact our capacity for loving and for being loved is grounded in our sexuality. And our need for affection and love in significant personal relationships can be met only by the warm and affective caring and loving of persons who have succeeded in developing their sexuality and emotional life so as to be capable of such deep caring and loving.

It is clear from this that having a healthy and mature sexuality is essential for being truly caring and loving in any form of personal relationship, and not just between boyfriends and girlfriends and spouses in marriage, e.g. parents and children, family members, friends, nurses and patients, etc. So our affective sexuality involves our capacity for caring and loving and requires it, in order to be mature and to work well in our personal relationships with others. If, therefore, we have a negative view of our sexuality and have repressed it or left it undeveloped, then our capacity for warm and caring relationships will be limited or even negligable. But if we have a positive attitude to our sexuality and have worked to develop it, then there is a good chance we will establish good, caring relationships at a variety of levels.

Deeply involved in this affective sexuality and capacity for warm relationships is our emotional life. We cannot have a developed affective sexuality or a worthwhile capacity for caring for and loving others, unless we have reached a significant level of emotional maturity. If we are emotionally immature and undeveloped, our sexuality in terms of affection and caring will be very limited and immature, and so we will find it very difficult to make and keep worthwhile personal relationships.Really loving others will probably be beyond us.

We may note that, in our society, in line with the cultural stereotypes that we mentioned earlier, it will generally be the case that women will have a more developed affective sexuality than men, i.e. a better capacity for love and affection, and so will be likely to make and keep better personal relationships than men. This is, however, changing and needs to change as the stereotypes break down and a fuller humanity becomes more possible for both men and women.

Affective and genital sexuality
These two dimensions of our sexuality are meant to be closely related in the fully sexual relationship we call marriage. When they are, then the relationship will be more inclined to flourish and be truly happy. Experience shows that genital sexual expression is best and most pleasurable and fulfilling when it takes place in a loving relationship. There genital sex will be an expression of the affection between the partners and will help to deepen that affection and love. In other words, genital sexuality works best and is most satisfying when it is an expression or a symbol of affective sexuality. If, however, people separate affective and genital sexuality, so that genital sex takes place without any noteworthy level of affection between the parties, then it is likely that such sexual activity, while it will very probably be pleasurable, will not achieve a lot as regards deepening the relationship or giving the parties a sense of being truly loved or truly loving, much less of true personal fulfilment.

It is generally recognised that our need for love and affection is a deeper or higher and more powerful need on the scale of basic human needs than the need for physical sex. Hence, when we feel adequately cared for and loved, our need for genital sex tends to become less imperious and more amenable to rational decision. Then also genital sex is more easily placed at the service of love in a marital relationship and becomes more enjoyable and fulfilling. If, however, our higher need for love and affection goes unrecognised and unfulfilled, then it may well happen that our physical sexual need may assert itself more powerfully. If in this context one seeks to assuage this need by genital sex, one will be likely to find that, apart from some momentary intense pleasure, one will experience little in the way of deep personal satisfaction and affirmation as a person. Sex without love may give pleasure, but it doesn't go very far to meet one's need for love and affection.

Not infrequently also people mistake what their needs really are. One may imagine or feel that what one needs is genital sex, when in fact what is really absent from one's life is love and affection. The result may well be that such a person will engage in genital sex in his/her search for a warm and loving relationship. And of course the inevitable outcome will be deep dissatisfaction and emptiness for oneself and very probably also for one's partner. In other words, genital sexuality is no substitute for affective sexuality; sex won't really fill the gap, if true love is absent. We may add that the less developed one's affective sexuality is, the more one tends to become preoccupied with genital sexuality in one's relationships, often in futile and/or destructive ways.

It will be clear from all that has been said here that the key to using our genital sexuality well and in an enriching manner is to develop our affective sexuality as fully as possible. That means becoming a warm and loving person and establishing warm and loving relationships. Within the one of these that becomes a marital relationship, genital sex can, then, find its place and bring enrichment and joy to both partners as it deepens and strengthens their relationship. If, however, one's affective sexuality remains undeveloped, then one will find that achieving fulfilment and happiness as a person and as a partner will prove exceedingly elusive, even if one engages in genital sex.

It needs to be asserted here also that, if one succeeds in developing one's affective sexuality significantly through good and wholesome personal relationships with both sexes, then one can achieve true fulfilment and happiness as a person without ever engaging in genital sex. In other words, one can be fulfilled and happy as a single or celibate person, provided one is successful in becoming a warm and loving person with significant personal relationships. Mature affective sexuality is the foundation of true personal fulfilment and happiness, whether genital sexuality is part of one's life or not, that is, whether one is married, single or celibate.

Finally, it hardly needs to be stated that it is much easier to engage in genital sexual activity than to develop one's affective sexuality and express it appropriately in loving relationships. But taking this easier way can't be a substitute for affective sexuality and its expression, and may even be a cop out from or an evasion of the task of working to make oneself more caring and loving. So in the area of our sexuality, the priority belongs to our affectivity. When this leads in practice to real growth in warmth and affection in one's personality, then true personal fulfilment and happiness are on the cards for the person in question, whether one has chosen to marry, stay single or commit oneself to the celibate way of life.

Sexual pleasure
The Christian tradition has not dealt very well with pleasure of any sort and least of all with sexual pleasure. As a result there has been a very negative understanding and moral assessment of pleasure in the Christian church.[4] However, as St Thomas Aquinas said, human beings cannot live long without delight or pleasure.

Life has many pleasures and delights that are attached to or involved in many activities and experiences, ranging from enjoying a good meal or good music through the delight and joy of success in business or sport, to the deeper pleasures of personal growth and true friendship and love. It is important to note here that we don't normally desire pleasure or set out to get it. Rather we get pleasure from doing things we want to do. It is because we want to do particular activities that we find them pleasant or pleasure-giving. In general, then, we do not desire to get pleasure so much as to do things that we know or believe will be pleasant.

As experience shows, whether an activity gives pleasure often

4. See Moore, 43-50, 64-67.

depends on who we do it with. Doing a particular activity with someone you like makes it pleasurable, e.g., playing a game, going for a walk, having a meal, having sex. These, then, are joint pleasures and are forms of the pleasure of being together.

The deep joys and pleasures of good friendships and loving relationships are among the most enriching and uplifting life has to offer. They are joint pleasures and depend for their quality and depth on the fact that it is people who are friends, who love each other, who are engaging in them. But people in these friendships and relationships cannot be said to be seeking only pleasure. Rather they want to be with one they love or are friends with in a particular way and this is the source of their shared pleasure.

All this applies to sexual activities and the pleasures that accompany them. As already indicated, warm love and affection provide the essential context or foundation needed in order that sexual activity bring pleasure and joy in a life-enhancing and authentic manner. Note here that there are many types of sexual pleasure in addition to that of orgasm, e.g., touching and being touched, kissing and being kissed, movement of one's body with or against another's, the pleasure of giving pleasure, etc.

One can, of course, spoil these friendships and relationships and the pleasures that accompany them, if one refuses to give and seeks only to get or take, that is, if one behaves selfishly and considers only what suits oneself. But here too it is the activity, what one does, that causes the problem rather than the pleasure involved.

In relation to morality, then, it may be said that a pleasure will be good and truly enriching, if the activity to which it is attached is itself morally right. Or, to put it somewhat better, if an action is loving and morally appropriate, then the pleasure that accompanies it will be good, life-enhancing and so to be fully enjoyed.[5]

Psychosexual development

The word 'psychosexual' here indicates that our sexuality is a dimension, not just of our body, but of our psyche and indeed our whole personality. Hence, the development of our sexuality is part of our growth as persons. We may then describe psychosexual development as the growth process through which our

5. See Moore, pp 50-63; also Evelyn Eaton Whitehead and James D. Whitehead, *A Sense of Sexuality: Christian Love and Intimacy*, (Image Books, Doubleday, New York and London, 1989), chapter 6.

capacity to love comes to fruition or through which we grow towards maturity in our relational and sexual lives. This growth
process has three obvious phases or stages: childhood, adolescence and adulthood. A brief look at adolescence and adulthood
is all that is possible here.[6]

Adolescent psychosexual development
Here we are talking about the normal process of psychosexual
growth that every person needs to go through at this stage of life,
if he/she is to reach adulthood in the full sense. It is an essential
stage on the journey towards adult psychosexual maturity and if
it is not well negotiated, then trouble lies ahead in one's relational and sexual life, whether one marries or not. If it is traversed in
a balanced way, one will have attained the psychosexual maturity appropriate to one's age and so will be ready to move on to
early adulthood and the growth and challenges it brings.

The main personal challenge or task of this adolescent phase
of one's growth as a sexual person is to form a sense of one's own
identity as a person, a sense of one's unique self.[7] This is another
step towards adult personal integration and involves many elements, especially from the viewpoint of psychosexual development. Three of these may be mentioned briefly at this point.

Sexual fantasising is an important feature of adolescent life. It
focuses on the other sex and on relationships with them. Such
fantasising should not be seen as necessarily unhealthy or
wrong. Rather it is a way of thinking imaginatively about the
other sex and relationships with them and as such can help one
to see more clearly what such relationships would involve and
how they should be conducted. It can also mean one is trying to
picture in one's imagination what being in such relationships
would feel like for oneself or even for the other person involved.
It is important to note here that fantasising about something, sexual or otherwise, or imagining oneself doing something, sexual
or otherwise, is not the same as wanting or planning to do these

6. For psychosexual development during childhood, see Fran Ferder &
John Heagle, *Your Sexual Self: Paths to Authentic Intimacy* (Ave Maria
Press, Notre Dame, Indiana, USA, 1992), chapters 4 & 5.
7. See Erik H Erikson, *Identity and the Life Cycle* (W. W. Norton & Co.,
New York & London, 1980), pp 94-100. Also Eugene C Kennedy, *What a
Modern Catholic believes about Sex And Marriage* (Thomas More Press,
Chicago,1975), pp 31-2.

things. This adolescent fantasy life is, then, a kind of imaginative rehearsal for real relationships with the other sex. As such, it is important that healthy sexual fantasies do take place as an element in the process of psychosexual development in adolescence.

Another feature of adolescent sexual life is preoccupation with the bodily changes that are taking place during that phase of the life cycle, especially at the onset of puberty. This focuses the adolescent's interest on his/her bodily development, on the accompanying sexual feelings and on the other sex. Masturbation frequently arises in this context and it is widely held by the experts nowadays to be something that, psychologically, is to be expected at this stage of psychosexual development.[8]

A third feature of adolescence is exploring relationships with individual members of the other sex, boy-girl or girl-boy relationships. Romantic interest and sexual desire have thus entered the young person's life and falling in and out of love will be par for the course at this point. All this is serious emotional business for the adolescent and constitutes an essential process of learning about sexual intimacy and love and discovering oneself emotionally and sexually. These relationships do not have any direct connection with marriage but are part of the process the adolescent has to engage in of forming her/his personal and sexual identity and laying the foundations for adult sexual loving.

Important moral questions arise in the context of adolescent psychosexual development, especially about unhealthy sexual fantasies, masturbation, physical sexual intimacies and sexual intercourse. These are addressed in sexual ethics. It will be essential, when doing sexual ethics, to keep in mind the fact that adolescence is a time of great psychosexual change and growth, that the young person is not yet sexually or emotionally an adult and, hence, that the criteria for judging his/her sexual activities morally ought to be ones appropriate to the stage of the life cycle at which the young person has arrived.

Psychosexual development in adulthood
We have tended to think that, once we have reached adulthood chronologically speaking, there is no more maturing or growing to be done emotionally and psychosexually. Today, however, we have learned that that view simply does not hold and that in fact

8. See Moore, p 22; Whitehead & Whitehead, chapter 8.

adulthood is a stage of life when growth is quite normal and is very necessary and very important. We may and should continue to mature in our adult years, because they too have their stages and phases, and negotiating these well is a basic requisite for good relationships and true happiness in the adult phase of life.

In early or young adulthood the task to be undertaken is to develop the emotional and psychosexual capacity for intimacy. Here intimacy means the ability to give and receive affection and love in equal, authentic and enduring relationships and friendships. In other words, to be able to be intimate means having the capacity to care and be cared for, to love and to be loved in an adult manner or, to use a relatively new word, to be able to practise mutuality in relationship. The intimacy in question here is, clearly, not necessarily marital intimacy but is possible and indeed required in all significant relationships among adults, whether one is married, single or celibate. The main signs or requirements of such intimacy are accurate self-knowledge, empathy, trust, equality and emotional openness.[9]

A point made by some psychologists today is worth noting at this stage. One's decision about a profession or job or vocation is one that most people make and are quite capable of making in late adolescence. This applies not just to secular professions or careers but also to a religious one like priesthood or religious life. However, in our Western culture today the choice or decision to marry or not is as a general rule a decision that most people are capable of making maturely only in their mid-20s to mid-30s. This is the time when they will most likely have acquired the capacity for intimacy, a capacity that is vital for married life.

Now this clearly implies that the choice of a celibate lifestyle can also only be maturely made at the same time that one becomes ready to marry, because only then will one have acquired the capacity for intimacy, which is as essential for celibate as for married living. But in the present seminary system candidates for the priesthood and religious life tend to make their choice for celibacy in their late teens, when they enter the seminary, that is, at the same time as they opt to become priests or religious.It seems obvious that opting for celibacy at such an age is much too early and quite unwise. The reason is that one's choice of the celibate state comes before the maturing process or struggle needed to

9. Ferder & Heagle, chapter 7; Erikson, pp 100-3.

resolve one's intimacy needs has really got under way. Hence, one is not ready to make a choice for or against celibacy, no more than one is ready to choose to marry. Not surprisingly then, the young celibate may well have problems with celibacy and especially with relationships with women/men some years after he/she leaves the sheltered environment of the seminary or novitiate. Experience confirms this. Many young priests especially, whether they leave the priesthood or not, have experienced problems with their intimacy needs and level of psychosexual maturity rather than with the priesthood itself. The obvious question that arises here is: Does it not seem that connecting the decision to become a priest or religious and the decision to become a celibate, so that both decisions are in effect taken at the same time (late adolescence), is unwise and indeed mistaken and needs to be changed?[10]

When one moves on to mid-life the task to be faced is different from that in young adulthood. Now the challenge is to become a truly generative person, that is, a creative, caring and responsible adult, especially in relation to younger people, whether one's own children, younger colleagues or clients or some project, plan or institution. Generous concern for others, often in some leadership position, is a sign of mid-life maturity. Such life-enhancing care and relationships at all levels indicate that psychosexually one has made the transition to mid-life effectively and fruitfully.[11]

Finally, the last stage of one's life cycle should bring one a sense of integrity, a feeling that one has completed one's life journey successfully, and has integrated one's personality well over the years by developing and using one's talents and opportunities appropriately and reaching a good level of personal maturity, especially from the psychosexual point of view. Of course, this integration is ever ongoing and never complete and problems continue to be encountered. Relationships remain central at this

10. See Kenneth R Mitchell, 'Priestly Celibacy from a Psychological Perspective', in Mary Anne Huddleston, IHM, (Ed), *Celibate Loving: Encounters in Three Dimensions* (Paulist Press, New York, 1986), pp 91-108.
11. Ferder & Heagle, pp 106-111; E. E. Whitehead & J. D. Whitehead, *Christian Life Patterns: The Psychological Challenges and Religious Invitations of Adult Life* (Image Books, Doubleday, New York & London, 1982), chapter 5; Bill Cosgrave & Ita Moynihan, 'The Mid-Life Transition', *The Furrow*, April 1995, pp 212-5; Erikson, 103-4.

stage of the life cycle and will continue to be life-giving as one reaches psychosexual maturity.[12]

The social dimension of sexuality

Sexuality is clearly an intra- and inter-personal reality. But equally clearly sexuality, sexual relationships and sexual activity are very important in and for society: marriages take place, children are born and families are established, etc. Few things are more important for any society. Because of these vital matters and other associated concerns, every society feels called to work out and enforce a sexual morality. This aims to regulate sexual relationships and sexual activity for the common good of the society and will contain values, principles and rules that serve as guides and directions for the members of that society in regard to what is to be judged as right and wrong in the sexual area of life. The members of the society are morally bound to accept and abide by this sexual morality. As a rule they do accept it, even though at times they violate one or more of the rules. In addition to this sexual ethic, societies also support some values, norms and arrangements in the area of sexuality by laws, conventions and rituals. Thus there may be a law enforcing monogamy, forbidding or allowing divorce, regulating artificial human reproduction and allowing or forbidding abortion. Rituals are established in relation to courtship, engagement and getting married, while conventions or customs are also to be found in every society in these matters.

We find the same things in the Christian churches, and the Catholic Church in particular has a very clear and definite sexual morality and also many laws, conventions and rituals surrounding sexual activity and especially marriage.

All this makes it abundantly clear that sexuality has a very significant social dimension. All accept this and what it involves, even though there may be tension from time to time between a particular moral rule or church or state law or regulation on sexual matters and the views and even practices of individual members of society or the church. Examples today are living together without being married, taking a second partner while the first one is alive, practising contraception.

---

12. Ferder & Heagle, pp 125-9; Erikson, 104-5.

The purposes of sexuality

To describe sexuality and to discuss its nature and characteristics in the way that we have just done leads one very quickly to ask questions like: what is the meaning of this dimension of our nature?, what is its purpose?, what is it for?, why are we sexed persons, male and female? Over the centuries and today a variety of answers have been and are given to these questions, depending to a large extent on one's understanding of the human person and of the meaning and purpose of human life itself. Here we will presuppose the basic Christian view of the human person and in that context go on to enquire about the meanings and purposes of human sexuality.

Reflecting on the Christian tradition and on our experience, it seems clear that there are two main or central purposes or meanings of human sexuality.

a) To draw us into relationship with the other sex: We experience our sexuality as a deep-rooted and powerful force within us urging and drawing us to go out of ourselves towards people of the other sex. We feel ourselves attracted to the other sex, men to women and women to men. This natural attraction is really a call from within ourselves, from our sexual nature as men or women, to relate to the other sex, not just physically or genitally but personally or in a personal way. Our sexuality invites and pushes us to give ourselves to members of the other sex in personal relationships, in love, and therein to find fulfilment and completion as a sexual person and in doing so to enable the other to find them too. We see, then, that our sexuality, not merely indicates to us that we are not self-sufficient, but it also directs us towards the place where, in a very special way, that insufficiency and lack can be filled up or met, namely, in relationships with the other sex.

Here, then, we discover the first purpose or meaning of our sexuality. It is intended by nature and by God to urge us at every level of our personality and being to establish personal relationships with members of the other sex, to give ourselves to them in love and thus to find fulfilment and happiness. Thus, it is clear that sexuality functions as a powerful antidote to loneliness and isolation. It is an insistent reminder that no man or woman is an island and that it is neither intended nor good that he/she should try to be so. On the contrary, both men and women are meant to be with others, especially those of the other sex, in friendship and love, there to grow as persons, reach maturity and achieve true happiness. Sexuality is, then, the creator's ingenious way of calling people constantly out of themselves and into relationships with others, above all, those of the other sex. In other words, it is our God-given energy for relationships of care and love, especially between women and men. In short, then, the first purpose and meaning of sexuality in human life is to facilitate and promote love between men and women.

In this context it can be said that sexuality and sexual activity are a means of communication between men and women. Through sexual activity, verbal and physical, a couple can communicate with each other, express and nourish their love and so strengthen and deepen their relationship. In other words, sexual activity is a kind of language of love in man-woman relationships. This way of describing sexual activity is intended to highlight the fact that sexuality aids personal communication between men and women, helps to build up their relationship and brings them closer together in true love.[13]

It is important to recall here that, while all love is sexual in the broad sense that it is always sexual persons who love, love is more than sexuality. Our sexuality is only one dimension of our humanity and so there is love that is not sexual in any ordinary sense. This is a fact of common experience, as we mentioned earlier.

(b) To make procreation possible: This is a purpose or meaning of sexuality that is even more obvious than the one we have been discussing, and it has usually been seen as the main and, for long spells, the only valid reason for engaging in sexual intercourse or even getting married. When sexuality achieves its purpose of bringing a man and a woman together in a relationship of love, then it may happen that that relationship will develop into the exclusive and lifelong one that we call marriage. If and when it does, then sexuality can and very likely will achieve its second and ultimate purpose of bringing new life into the world in the form of children. This is obviously a basic and essential purpose that gives further meaning and significance to sexuality in human life. In fact, since begetting a new person is perhaps the supreme achievement of a married couple, we may say that procreation is in a real sense the supreme achievement of sexuality in human life. In saying this, we do not intend, however, to com-

---

13. But see Moore's cautionary comments on this point, pp 105-8.

pare the purposes of sexuality, since to do so is neither necessary nor helpful and is frequently misleading.

While it is clear that procreation is an essential purpose of human sexuality as such, it is not so in relation to a particular married couple. For them actual procreation need not necessarily take place nor, at least in some cases, need it be an intention of the couple as, for example, in the case of a sterile couple, an older couple or a couple for whom having (further) children is ruled out for good and serious reasons. In relation to an individual person, he/she can choose to remain single or to be celibate, thus ruling procreation out of his/her life. This does not, however, prevent such a person from achieving the first purpose of his/her sexuality, namely, establishing good wholesome relationships of friendship and love with members of both sexes and so attaining maturity and happiness in this area of life.

In the light of this discussion of the meanings or purposes of human sexuality, a further descriptive point about our sexuality needs to be made here. For us humans our sexuality is both a gift and a task, a blessing and a challenge.

It is a gift because it is given to us by nature and ultimately by God to help us to love better. It does this by giving our personality its warmth, affectivity and empathy, thus facilitating and helping us in establishing personal relationships with others. It also gives us our sexual instinct and attraction and so makes relating to the other sex more absorbing and rewarding. Thus our sexuality fosters creative personal growth towards integration or maturity and contributes very significantly towards our happiness as individual persons. In addition, our sexuality plays an essential role in the process of procreation. It is, therefore, one of the greatest gifts or blessings human life has to offer. We need to appreciate it as such, all the more because Christian history has signally failed to do so and modern Western society trivialises and debases sexuality very profoundly.

On the other hand, experience clearly signals that our sexuality provides us with a big task or challenge. Our sexuality is frequently immature and can run wild in our relationships, being understood as a call to merely physical contacts or relationships with members of the other sex. To put it at the service of affection and love in these relationships is very difficult and demanding and requires a sustained effort, especially from men. Achieving a reasonable degree of sexual (and that includes emotional) maturity is a long and arduous process, whether one is married, single or celibate. In fact, the latter two can have added difficulties, stemming often enough from too little contact and real relationship with members of the other sex. It is not much of an exaggeration to say that, if one can attain a good level of sexual maturity, then one is well on the way to becoming a mature person in all areas of one's life as a person in relationship and in community.

It will be important to keep in mind both the gift and task aspects of our sexuality, so as to avoid an unbalanced view of one's life as a sexual person. One can become over-pessimistic or over-optimistic in regard to one's sexuality. We need to steer a middle course, appreciating the gift, while not under-estimating the task.

The differences between men and women and morality[14]
As will be obvious from what has been said already, contemporary thinking about human sexuality, and how that sexuality is realised in men and women, cannot fail to have a significant impact on the relationships between the sexes. And this will extend also to the moral dimension of those relationships. A quick look at this latter aspect of sexuality will be important here. We may do so by means of a brief discussion of the different emphases or priorities we tend to find in the approach to relationships and to life generally among men and women.

Due to the dynamics of their development as masculine persons, and especially in and through their relationship with their mother, the identity of males tends to be defined in terms of difference and separation. This results in men tending to place more emphasis on being separate, different and independent in relation to other people. In addition, men tend to be more preoccupied with power and, in consequence, they focus more on competing rights, the danger of being oppressed by others, the importance of fairness and fair rules and procedures. This orientation or sense of priorities tends to direct men towards what has been called an ethic of justice, so that in their moral concerns issues of justice are inclined to predominate. Another aspect of male psychology that is significant here is the fact that men have a tendency to see and organise their world in an hierarchical fashion. They often see life as a contest in which one has to struggle to keep one's status and independence. Men are more conscious of

---

14. Maureen Gaffney, 'Psychological Authenticity', *Doctrine and Life*, October 2000, pp 473-482. This article has a valuable bibliography.

who is the boss and who is taking the orders. In this context men tend to develop group structures in which roles and rules are clearly delineated, and by this means aggression and competition are limited and controlled.

In regard to women things look rather different. Because girls do not need to differentiate and separate themselves from their mother as boys do, their identity tends to be defined in terms of sameness and connection rather than in terms of difference and separation. So in regard to relationships with others, women tend to place more emphasis on being the same as, connected to and close to others. And rather than being preoccupied with power, women's focus tends to be on care in relationships and all that is involved in that: being responsive to individual need, attending to others' problems, being sensitive to the danger of abandonment and isolation and doing all possible to find solutions that embrace all who are involved in the situation, that is, solutions that are inclusive. This orientation or sense of priorities in women tends to express itself in what some call an ethic of care. In other words, women in their moral concerns give priority to issues of care and responsibility for caring for others. In addition, women do not tend to see life or to organise themselves in an hierarchical fashion. Rather they tend to form close intimate friendships with a few other women and in that context conversation is not so much for the sake of giving or getting information as for binding themselves together, keeping close and nourishing their relationships. In such groups women tend to establish relationships that are equal, close and supportive, in which there is little concern for status, being dominant or aggressive, where conflict is avoided or at least toned down, and where challenge is a rare event. Issues of power are dealt with more subtly than in the case of men, not so much by conflict as by suggestion and evasion.

Now all this about the personal development and social relationships of men and women cannot fail to have important consequences in relation to the approach of the sexes to the moral life and its various elements and aspects. As we have already noted, men tend towards an ethic of justice and women towards an ethic of care. One element of this is that a man, in approaching a moral choice, especially a difficult one, tends to begin from a position of being responsible to himself first and then he considers other people and their claims and needs. In other words, he thinks of his own rights first and then looks at how they may be in conflict with others' rights. Women tend to reverse this order of concern and care and do all they can to arrive at an inclusive response or choice.

Now in society over the centuries, so dominant has the male perspective been that this male approach has been taken as normative and women's approach has been judged to be that of a less morally developed person. In other words, moral maturity has been judged by a male standard and thus priority has been given to an ethic of justice. This is at best one-sided and partial. There is need now for the individual, society and the church to attend to both the ethic of justice and the ethic of care. This will require a broadening of the idea of psychological and moral development so as to include both justice and care considerations. Necessary always will be respect for moral principles, but also a much higher place needs to be given to empathy, the psychological and emotional capacity to put oneself in other people's positions and sense their needs and rights in a personal way. Then one will be better placed to exercise a caring responsibility in relation to the people involved in any particular situation, and not just concern oneself with rights and rules.

In short then, it is clear that both the ethic of justice perspective and that of care are necessary for the individual, society and the church, if people are to grow to full moral maturity, if truly human moral choices are to be made and if society and the church are to evolve an ethos and an ethic that are fully humanising and fully in line with the basic values of the gospel.

The virtue of chastity

In the previous pages we have been considering human sexuality in its nature and purposes. These are objective realities in human existence, which we discover and have to face up to in our daily lives, but we do not invent or create them. Now we move from this objective realm to that of the personal or subjective. Our focus is now on the individual's basic moral attitude to sexuality and this is usually called the virtue of chastity.

Part of the negative tradition that was widespread in the past in society and in the church in relation to sexuality was a negative attitude to chastity. In the context of the time this is not surprising. This conception of chastity saw it as that virtue which controls or regulates our sexual faculty and its activities. Chastity seeks to moderate and restrain our sexual appetite and drives, especially our appetite for sexual pleasure. Today we see that this is a one-sided, male and control-dominated approach and it needs to be developed so as to present a positive and more adequate understanding of this important virtue, in line with our positive and fuller understanding of sexuality.

Chastity may, perhaps, be described in the following terms. It is that basic moral attitude and capacity (i.e. virtue) which accepts and appreciates one's own and others' sexuality in all its aspects; which seeks to integrate one's own sexuality into one's personality, relationships and life generally and put it at the service of love in those relationships; and which, therefore, seeks to order one's sexual activity in such a way that it will promote the welfare of oneself and of the others in those relationships. There are, then, three central elements in the virtue of chastity:

(i) Appreciation of sexuality and all it involves, implying a good knowledge and understanding of the values and ideals at stake in it. It should be clear here that, unless one has a positive and balanced view of sexuality, such as has been outlined above, one will have grave difficulty in practising chastity fully and in growing significantly in this virtue, even though one may be successful in the negative sense of avoiding notable selfish sexual behaviour.

(ii) Integration of one's sexuality into one's personality and life. This demands a dedicated effort to come to terms with one's sexual nature, accept it as a fundamental dimension of one's personality and put it at the service of friendship and love in all one's relationships, especially those with the other sex, whether one chooses to marry, to remain single or to live a celibate life. Involved here will be the necessity of growth in one's emotional life, so that one is in touch with one's emotions, has achieved a good level of emotional maturity and so can express one's emotions and especially the positive ones well, while also ordering them so as to avoid destructive words, attitudes and activities.

(iii) Control of one's sexuality and more particularly of one's instincts and desires, one's thoughts, words and deeds. This requires self-discipline so as to ensure truly loving sexual behaviour in all one's relationships and the avoidance of selfishness at all times. This element of the virtue of chastity was the one that was almost exclusively emphasised in the older approach that we have criticised earlier. It is now clear that that approach was inadequate because it was partial and negative.

From what has been said, it will be clear that chastity, like every other virtue, represents a middle way between two extreme attitudes to sexuality. On the one hand, there is repression, which found expression at times in the theology and practice of the church in the past, but is now giving way to a more accepting and optimistic understanding of our sexual nature. On the other hand, there is the extreme of sexual permissiveness or licence, an error into which some contemporary advocates of sexual freedom fall. But chastity, properly understood, seeks to find the golden mean between these two poles. As we have tried to show, chastity, as it is understood in the church today, seeks to appreciate sexuality as an aid to our friendship and love-relationships, especially with the other sex, but at the same time is realistic enough to recognise the task and struggle doing this involves for most of us, whatever our state in life.

The person who is chaste in the sense described here is the one who is truly loving and human. She/he is the one who is aware of and appreciates what it is to be a sexual person and who has learned with time and effort to put his/her sexuality at the service of friendship and love and of his/her whole humanity in his/her personal relationships. As a result she/he is now capable of much greater openness towards others, much greater commitment to and love of them than the unchaste person, and is incapable of abusing them for her/his own selfish sexual interests. The more chaste a person is, then, the more loving he/she is and the more capable of establishing and maintaining good sexual relationships with others, without having them damaged or even destroyed by disordered and unruly sexual instincts and desires, expressing themselves in selfish attitudes and activities. We can say, in fact, that one's chastity is the measure of one's capacity as a woman or as a man to love others as men and women.

It can be seen from this that chastity has nothing to do with aloofness, coldness or indifference to people of the other sex. On the contrary, the truly chaste person is the truly loving person, who is warm and affectionate and capable of responding sensitively to others, both men and women, without fear of tenderness or love, on the one hand, or of being overcome by sexual passion, on the other.

If one wishes to judge how chaste one really is, one will find a good practical guideline in the depth and quality of one's relationships or friendships with other people and especially with members of the other sex. Remaining at a 'safe' distance from the other sex is not a sign of chastity but is rather evidence of one variety of unchastity, a variety which is no less wrong and damaging, because it tended to be praised as virtuous in the past or is less noticed than its opposite. This holds for married, single and celibate people.

We may note too that chastity is not a virtue which is acquired once and for all at some stage of one's life. It is not a static thing that one has and with luck holds on to. Rather, like every virtue, it presents us with a continuing and life-long challenge or task to become more chaste, to grow in our appreciation, integration and ordering of our sexuality and so to attain full maturity in Christ as our life's journey ends.

It is only in the light of the faulty understanding of the past that one needs to make the point that chastity is a virtue for everyone, married, single or celibate. Everyone is called to be chaste and to seek the ideal of perfect chastity. All are on the road towards that lofty goal but the path to be taken will differ in some respects, depending on whether one is living in marriage, celibacy or the single life. For all, however, it will involve the three central elements of chastity that we outlined earlier, namely, appreciation, integration and control of their sexuality in the way appropriate to their state in life. Thus these three kinds of chastity have the same standing and value and no one is superior to the others. They are equal but different ways in which the sexual person puts his/her sexuality at the service of love in his/her personal relationships. Whichever state of life one chooses, only the truly chaste person can live a really loving and fruitful life, a life which will be at the same time joyful and happy for her/him and for those in relationship with her/him.

Further Reading:
Cahill, Lisa Sowle, *Between the Sexes: Foundations for a Christian Ethics of Sexuality* (Paulist Press, New York, 1985), chapter 5;
Cahill, Lisa Sowle, *Sex, Gender and Christian Ethics* (Cambridge University Press, England, 1996), chapters 4-6;
Carr, Anne E., *Transforming Grace: Christian Tradition and Women's Experience* (Harper & Row Publishers, San Francisco, USA, 1990), chapter 6;
Coleman, Gerald C., *Human Sexuality: An All-Embracing Gift* (Alba House, New York, 1992), chapters 1 & 2;

Cosgrave, William, 'A Christian Understanding of Sexuality', *The Furrow,* June 1979, pp 361-371. This chapter is a revised and significantly expanded version of this article.

Dominian, Jack, *The Growth of Love and Sex* (Darton, Longman & Todd, London,1982), chapters 1-7;

Dominian, Jack, *Proposals for a New Sexual Ethic* (Darton, Longman & Todd, London, 1977), chapters 1-4;

Erikson, Erik H., *Identity and the Life Cycle* (W. W. Norton, & Company, New York 1980), chapter 2;

Ferder, Fran & Heagle, John, *Your Sexual Self: Pathway to Authentic Intimacy* (Ave Maria Press, Notre Dame, Indiana, USA,1992), chapters 6-8;

Genovesi, Vincent J., *In Pursuit of Love: Catholic Morality and Human Sexuality* (Gill & Macmillan, Dublin, 1987), chapter 4;

Goergen , Donald, *The Sexual Celibate* (SPCK, London, 1974), chapters 2 & 3;

Kelly, Kevin T ., *New Directions in Sexual Ethics: Moral Theology and the Challenge of AIDS* (Geoffrey Chapman, London & Washington, 1998), chapters 3 & 7;

Kennedy, Eugene C., *What a Modern Catholic Believes about Sex and Marriage* (Thomas More Press, Chicago, 1975), pp 31-3;

Kosnik, Anthony, et al., *Human Sexuality: New Directions in American Catholic Thought* (Paulist Press, New York, 1977), chapters 4 & 5, and pp 99-102;

Lane, Dermot A., 'The Equality of All in Christ', *Doctrine and Life,* February,1994, pp 77-80;

Moore, Gareth OP, *The Body in Context: Sex and Catholicism*, (Continuum, London & New York, 2001), chapters 4-7.

Whitehead, Evelyn Eaton & James D., *A Sense of Sexuality: Christian Love and Intimacy* (Image Books, Doubleday, New York, 1989), Parts 1 & 2.

CHAPTER 7

Understanding Marriage Today

Few will deny that marriage is a vitally important relationship and institution in human society and in the church. It is a central reality in nearly everyone's life as the vast majority of people are born into and grow up in a marriage, most people get married and live their lives in marriage, and almost everyone has close relationships with married people and their families. In addition, the health and stability of marriage and the family contribute immensely to the welfare and stability of society, while, if marriage is experiencing trouble and is subject to threats and instability, then society itself comes under threat and may find its very foundations being shaken.

All this explains why in societies at all times and places, and in the Christian church too, close attention has constantly been paid to the welfare of the institution of marriage and much effort has gone into supporting and strengthening it. Today extra special efforts are called for as new and serious threats to the stability of marriage as an institution, and to individual marriage relationships, emerge in society and the church and wreak their not unexpected havoc, e.g. marriage breakdown, divorce, cohabitation apart from marriage, abortion, extra-marital pregnancies, sexual affairs by married partners, etc. These practices, which seem to be becoming ever more widespread in the Western world at least, present major difficulties to society and the church today and no easy or quick solutions are in sight.

In the context of these difficulties for society and the church in our day, it will be important, by way of providing a solid foundation on which to base one's response, to develop our understanding or theology of marriage itself. We will do this here by, first of all, outlining and contrasting two models or ways of understanding marriage that have been and are prominent in the Catholic Church, the legal model and the relationship or personalist model. Then we will devote our attention to a number of specific problems about marriage that are current and much discussed among Catholic scholars nowadays, namely, the question of indissolubility and that of the marriage in church of baptised unbelievers.

The legal model of marriage
In the context of the Catholic Church's legal understanding of the Christian moral life in general, it is no surprise that the church's official teaching on marriage came to be expressed in largely legal terms. This legal understanding or model of the Christian life and of marriage held sway in the church for many centuries before Vatican II (1962-5). In relation to marriage it goes back to the twelfth century and by about 1350 marriage was commonly thought of as essentially a legal contract between the spouses. Philosophers, theologians and canonists had by then come to this view and so the legal model of marriage was firmly in place in the teaching and practice of the church from around the middle of the fourteenth century. As time went on it came to be spelled out more fully and more clearly and received perhaps its fullest expression at the official level of church teaching in the 1917 Code of Canon Law. A brief summary of the core elements of this understanding and of the legal regulations governing marriage will provide us with a basic outline of the legal model of marriage, while also clarifying some of its main presuppositions and implications.

While the 1917 Code contains no definition of marriage, it is clear that it views marriage as essentially a contract, speaking, as it does, of the contract itself of marriage. Since this contract between baptised persons has the dignity of a sacrament, it is impossible for a valid contract of marriage involving such people to exist without it being by that very fact a sacrament. So here the contract and the sacrament are inseparable. If we ask, what is this contract concerned with or what is its object, the answer in the Code is that it is a contract by which each party gives and accepts a perpetual and exclusive right over the body of the other for acts which are themselves suitable for the generation of children. This contract of marriage is created by the consent of the parties lawfully expressed, since consent makes marriage. If we now ask, what are the purposes or ends for which marriage was created and is entered into, the Code's answer is familiar: the primary end of marriage is the procreation and education of children; its secondary end is mutual help and the remedying of concupis-cence. If we enquire about the essential properties of marriage, we are told that they are unity (or monogamy) and indissolubility and that this indissolubility acquires a unique firmness in Christian marriage by reason of that marriage's sacramental character.

Here the hand of history shows itself and makes what looks like an absolute statement in relation to indissolubility less than it appears. Marriage is by its nature indissoluble and once entered into cannot be voided as long as the parties live. But this is not understood as ruling out two practices that the church has been making use of for centuries. The first is dissolving non-consummated Christian marriages, where consummation is un-derstood in physical terms as the first act of sexual intercourse after the marriage takes place. Such consummation is taken as sealing the contract and rendering it unbreakable. If the marriage is not so consummated then, in line with a papal decision in the twelfth century, that marriage is dissolved if and when one of the parties makes solemn religious vows and enters religious life. This is based on the conviction that religious life with its celibate lifestyle is a superior state to marriage. In the 1917 Code such a dissolution of a non-consummated marriage can be given for any just reason and not only because one of the parties enters the reli-gious life.

The second practice concerns the dissolution of non-sacra-mental marriages, i.e. marriages in which at least one of the par-ties is not baptised. Here the pauline and petrine privileges are invoked and on this basis the Pope dissolves these valid mar-riages in favour of the faith, i.e. in cases where the Catholic party wishes to marry another partner, perhaps a non-Catholic or even a non-Christian one.

It is clear from this, then, that the only form of marriage that is absolutely indissoluble is a consummated marriage of two bap-tised people, i.e. a consummated sacramental marriage. All other marriages – and that is the vast majority of marriages in the world – are open to papal dissolution.

This legal understanding of marriage involves as a basic ele-ment the concept of the bond of marriage. As the 1983 Code of Canon Law says (Canon 1134), 'From a valid marriage there arises between the spouses a bond which of its nature is permanent and exclusive.' This bond is superior to every other interpersonal bond (Paul VI) and is understood as an ontological reality which does not depend for its continued existence on the will of the spouses alone. It is a separate reality from the relationship of the couple and is a reality which, not merely should not be broken but, in fact, cannot be broken or terminated. So, even if the relationship of love between the partners dies and becomes non-existent, the marital bond still continues in existence. As Paul VI said in 1976, once the couple's marital consent has created its juridical effect, which is the marital bond, this consent becomes irrevocable and loses any power to destroy what it has created. Thus the marriage bond becomes irrevocable and is guaranteed by the fidelity of God.[1]

Evaluation of this legal understanding of marriage
It will be obvious that the positive and negative points which we noted in Chapter 1 in relation to the legal model of morality in general will apply in their own way to the legal model of marriage, and they don't need to be repeated here. There are, however, a number of specific issues which Catholic scholars today discuss and make suggestions about, and which it will be important to outline in the present context. This we will do in due course. But first we need to focus our attention on the conception of marriage that the church teaches today in the wake of the pastoral constitution on the church in the modern world (*Gaudium et Spes*, 1965), nn. 47-52 of the Second Vatican Council (1962-5), and the encyclical letter of Paul VI, *Humanae Vitae*, nn. 7-9 (1968). The understanding of marriage that emerges from these official documents may be referred to as the relationship or personalist model of marriage. It has been more fully elaborated by theologians and official church documents in the years since Paul VI issued his letter. We will here set forth the main lines of this way of understanding marriage.

---

1. *Code of Canon Law 1917*, Canons 1012-3, 1081, 1110, 1118-27; *Catechism of the Catholic Church* (Geoffrey Chapman, London 1994), n. 1638-1640; Theodore Mackin SJ, *What is Marriage?* (Paulist Press, New York, 1982), pp 186-9, chapter 8; Theodore Mackin SJ, *Divorce and Remarriage* (Paulist Press, New York, 1984), chapter 16; Timothy J. Buckley CSsR, *What binds Marriage?: Roman Catholic Theology in Practice* (Geoffrey Chapman, London, 1997), chapter 2.

The relationship model of marriage

Our exposition will take place in two main steps or stages. We will look first at what may be called the human reality that we call marriage. Then we will dwell rather briefly on the explicitly Christian religious dimension or aspect of that reality.

The human reality of Marriage

The complex reality that marriage is, especially in the Western world today, may best be described by outlining the three closely related fundamental elements or facets of that reality.

(a) The essence of marriage

In our culture and in the Christian church today the basic fact about marriage is that it is a relationship between a man and a woman. Relationship is the very heart or essence of marriage. Marriage is really two people relating to one another in a special way, so that the relationship between them is of decisive importance. From the point of view of the spouses, the marital relationship is the marriage. Now, this marital relationship is clearly a personal relationship, i.e. it is a relationship between persons as persons and not a business or formal relationship. What is centrally important in this kind of relationship is not what kind of work the partners do nor how much money they have nor the level of their academic attainment. Rather what makes all the difference is what they are as persons, what they are from the viewpoint of personality, character and level of personal maturity, and how they relate to each other at the personal level.

We may put this another way and say with Vatican II that marriage is a community of love between a man and a woman. It is a love relationship in which the partners come together in deep trust, profound sharing and complete openness, giving and receiving what they are and have as persons, so that they become two-in-one, while yet remaining individual persons. In its innermost nature, then, marriage is a relationship of love and the key to its success is the ability of the partners to love each other deeply and in a lasting way. To put this in other words again, we may say that marriage has the character of friendship. Thus it involves the whole person, intellect, will and emotions; it is based on mutually attractive qualities and is nourished by shared values, interests and activities. There will be a deep emotional affinity between the partners and their relationship will be characterised by personal warmth, security, support and enrichment. And of course such a relationship will be a matter of free choice by those involved.

Two other words frequently used to describe marriage today are partnership and covenant. Both are helpful and valuable but are limited in their suitability. While partnership is a much better word than contract, and it emphasises the equality of the spouses as regards both rights and duties, it is, nevertherless, a rather cold word for the warm loving reality that marriage is. In addition, from its use in other contexts it may well suggest a partial and temporary arrangement. The word 'covenant' is a biblical one and helps bring out the care, love and fidelity that are central to marriage. It is, however, rather unfamiliar to most people and so may be less illuminating than one would wish.

An obvious fact about marriage is that it is a sexual relationship in the fullest sense. The couple's sexuality is involved in a very direct, explicit and full way and, as such, that sexuality plays a very big part in drawing the partners together, in deepening their relationship and in maintaining it at an intense level. Very obviouly too this sexual dimension of marriage usually bears fruit in new life, i.e. in the birth of children. Thus sexuality in marriage achieves its two fundamental purposes: it promotes love between men and women and it leads to the procreation of new human persons. In a word, it fosters both love and life.

Now the more one's sexuality is involved in a relationship, the more is the person involved. The more sexual it is the more personal it is. Hence, we can say that marriage is the fullest personal relationship that we know of in human life. We can even speak of it as a total relationship or total love as *Humanae Vitae* (HV) n. 9 does. All this makes marriage unique in human life, it being significantly different from other personal relationships but also having a lot in common with them.

(b) The basic qualities of marriage

Here we describe briefly some qualities or aspects of marriage that are also essential, though some of them do not seem to be as basic as the ones discussed in the previous section.

Creative: We are referring here to the experience of many that true love enables the partners to grow as persons so as to love themselves and each other more deeply. When truly loved, one begins to value and appreciate oneself more, one's emotional scars begin to heal and one begins to realise one's potential and become a better and fuller person. In this sense, married love is creative of better persons and this creativity is a source of great joy and happiness. When such growth takes place in the married partners, their relationship too will be strengthened and deepened. That will tend to make it a lasting relationship and so help to ensure that it is lifelong and truly indissoluble.

Exclusive: Every relationship of true friendship or love has an element of exclusiveness about it, i.e. it exists between two particular individuals and them only, and hence others are excluded from it at that particular level. This is especially true of sexual love and, above all, of married love. So, to say that marriage is exclusive means that it is by its nature a relationship between one man and one woman and that all others are excluded from it at the deep level it has attained. In other words, marriage is by its nature monogamous. This exclusiveness of marriage has the advantage that it facilitates the development of the equality of the spouses and the depth of their relationship. But it also gives rise to the obligation of lasting fidelity.

Permanent: The deep sexual love that we find in marriage clamours for permanence. It does not want to be limited by time but yearns to go on and on. So we say that marriage is by its nature lifelong or permanent. We can speak too of an obligation on the partners to make their marriage lifelong; they are called to lasting fidelity till death ends their relationship. To put this in other words, we can speak of marriage as indissoluble, as an unbreakable union of husband and wife. We have already noted that this is the teaching of the church and we will focus on some aspects of it later.

Growing: Today we are very aware that the human person is not a static being but is called to grow to his/her full potential as a person. This is true of one's relationships also and in particular of marriage. So we can say that marriage is, by its nature, a relationship that should grow and deepen as time goes on. Indeed the partners are obliged to ensure that this happens. As it does, so love grows and with it happiness and fulfilment for the partners.

Procreative: We have mentioned this aspect of marriage earlier and referred to it as the fruitfulness of married love. So we must say that marriage of its nature is procreative. In relation to an individual marriage, however, the most we can say is that it should be open to procreation, since it happens that some marriages are, unfortunately, sterile. So actual procreation is integral to a marriage rather than essential to it. Clearly, procreativeness is one form of creativity in marriage but only one. So it must not be exaggerated, in particular at the expense of the creative quality of marriage we mentioned earlier.

Social: While marriage is obviously a personal relationship, it also has an essential social dimension. Married couples exist in society and are linked with other individuals and other married couples by many bonds. They are supported by these in many ways and influenced by them significantly, while the support and the influence go the other way too. As well as speaking of marriage as a personal relationship, we must also recognise that it is an institution in society. This means that society, convinced of the importance of marriage for the welfare of society, supports, strengthens and regulates marriages by many rules, rituals and customs, e.g. marriage begins with a formal ceremony or ritual; it has the character of a contract from the legal point of view; sexual intercourse with another person's marriage partner is disapproved of, etc. This institutional aspect of marriage is not at all opposed to its personal dimension, but there can be tensions between them.

Gift and task: Here we are referring to the experience of many in marriage that being married is a source of great love, joy and enrichment for the partners. One feels blessed to be married; the whole reality seems a kind of gift that is bestowed on one by one's partner and the love the partners share. In the Christian view, this gift comes ultimately from God through one's partner in marriage. On the other hand, marriage is regularly experienced as a big responsibility, a challenge which the couple has to meet in equal, if different, ways. In fact it can be said to be a task to be undertaken by the spouses that can be very demanding, e.g. full commitment, lasting fidelity. Both these aspects of marriage need to be given their proper weight or an unbalanced outlook on one's marriage may result.

(c) The purposes or ends of marriage

This traditional language was used, as we noted earlier, to refer to procreation as the primary purpose or end of marriage, and mutual love and the remedy of concupiscence as its secondary purpose or end. In Vatican II, however, noteworthy development has taken place in this context. As we saw above, love is not so much a purpose of marriage as its very heart or essence, and procreation is referred to in conciliar teaching as the fruitfulness of marriage, a description that seems more accurate. And the language of primary and secondary in this regard has been left aside by the Council Fathers. This does not resolve all the problems that can arise in regard to these two dimensions of marriage, problems that centre around the question of responsible procreation. This is once again the problem of contraception and its associated issues, but these cannot be treated here.

The Christian meaning of Marriage

We have up to now been reflecting on the human reality that we know as marriage in our experience in western society and in the church in our day. Now we move on to look at how our Christian faith illuminates and enriches this reality. In other words, we are attempting to understand the explicitly Christian religious dimension of marriage. We need to attend to two major elements of this religious dimension at this point.

Marriage as a vocation

In the Christian view of things, the whole of human life is seen as a gift from God. God is the ultimate donor or source of all the gifts and blessings of life. But our experience also teaches us that every gift involves a call of some sort; an obligation goes with and arises from every gift we get. This is a call to appreciate, accept and make use of the gift as God wishes those things to be done. Now another word for call here is vocation. So, we can say that human life itself involves a call or vocation from God to live it well, to live as a human being should. This is how we see human life in the Christian vision. Continuing this line of thinking, we can and should say that marriage for the Christian is a call or vocation from God through the church. This means that married people are called to marry each other and to live in marriage as truly Christian spouses. God wants them to be spouses to each other and to love each other all their days as husband and wife should.

From this fact that marriage is a vocation for the Christian, we can discern certain implications. Firstly, this fact enhances the dignity of marriage and of married people, giving the marital union greater meaning and depth and providing added motivation and inspiration for the spouses to live in a truly Christian manner. It reminds us that to love another person is to love God and doing this is to fulfil the greatest commandment of the Christian gospel. Secondly, to call marriage a vocation enables us to see that it is a grace-filled reality. God is in the marital union, and in and through that union God loves and graces the couple in profound ways. Thirdly, to speak of marriage as a vocation prompts the thought that there are other vocations in the Christian life for the sexual person. These are consecrated celibacy and the single life. It is the privilege and the responsibility of every Christian person to choose freely between these different ways of life, remembering that in doing so she/he is choosing between vocations or Christian ways of life that are of equal standing and are equally good, Christian and grace-filled. Finally, we may remind ourselves here that, just as the human person is more than her/his sexuality, so she/he is more than her/his marriage. Hence, it is a common experience that people, while being married, take on other vocations in the area of their career, e.g. being a doctor, teacher, farmer, office worker, etc. The same is true in regard to celibacy and the single life.

Marriage as a sacrament

The Council of Trent in the sixteenth century defined marriage as a sacrament, and that remains the teaching of the church today. The word sacrament here refers both to the wedding ceremony and to the marriage relationship of the two Christians who live in wedlock. The wedding ceremony or ritual is, therefore, understood to be a sign or symbol and source of grace for the married partners. It symbolises and realises or makes present the love of the spouses for each other, and their love and that of the church for Christ. In addition, this ritual is a symbol of the love of Christ for them and for the church too. The marriage relationship is to be understood as a kind of continuing sacrament. The state of being married is a lasting sign or symbol of God's love for all people and of Christ's love for the church. And in so far as there is real love in the marriage relationship, it makes that divine love present and active in the lives of husband and wife. So we may say that the marriage relationship is also a sign and source of grace and so is truly sacramental, using this word in a somewhat extended but, nevertheless, real sense.

ISSUES IN CHURCH TEACHING ON MARRIAGE IN OUR DAY

From our discussion of the two models of marriage in the foregoing pages, it will be clear that the official teaching of the church today incorporates important elements of both models. Church teaching on marriage itself is substantially an exposition of

Vatican II's understanding of marriage and so is very much in the relational or personalist mode. On the other hand, aspects of marriage like indissolubility continue to be articulated for the most part in terms of the medieval legal model. It is not very surprising, then, that quite a significant number of contemporary Catholic theologians and canonists have turned their attention to the issue of how these two models or approaches to our understanding of marriage and its various aspects fit together in the church's official teaching. In relation to annulment there seems to be a noteworthy influence by the relational model of marriage on the older interpretation as is evident in, say, the grounds for annulment now recognised in the 1983 *Code of Canon Law,* e.g. in c. 1095, nn. 2 & 3. In relation to indissolubility theologians and other scholars feel called to enquire about how it might be understood in relational or personalist terms and how that would impact on the legal understanding. We also find concerns being raised about whether the contemporary phenomenon of the absence of Christian faith in some Catholics as they marry in church has any impact on the sacramentality of their marriage.

Given this context we will here discuss three topics, two of which relate to the indissolubility or permanence of marriage, while the third has to do with the question of weak or absent faith in Catholics who come for marriage in church.

The Principle of Economy

This principle of economy (*oikonomia* in Greek) is used in the Orthodox Churches to refer to the basis on which these churches grant or allow a departure from strict conformity with a canonical norm or law in particular cases. It closely resembles the use of dispensation in the Catholic Church. This principle is invoked to resolve a number of practical situations of which one is broken marriages. Thus the Orthodox churches, while they teach a doctrine of absolute indissolubility of marriage and disapprove of divorce and remarriage, recognise at the same time that, because of human sin and weakness, a marriage may break down irretrievably. Hence, in certain circumstances (cf Mt 19:9), by economy, these churches allow or tolerate divorce and remarriage. The Orthodox churches accept that marriages are being dissolved in daily life by, e.g. sin and ignorance, passion and selfishness, lack of faith and lack of love. But they as churches do not dissolve any marriages or grant any divorces. They acknowledge and tolerate such dissolutions and divorces and then, to the lonely and abandoned, they sorrowfully grant the right to take another spouse. There is, however, as a rule a strong penitential aspect to the liturgy of such a second marriage because of the way the first one ended.[2]

It is important to remember here that in the Orthodox churches the doctrine of indissolubility is interpreted differently from in the Catholic Church. Their teaching on indissolubility has not been given the precise legal or juridical formulation that it has in the Catholic Church. Hence, it functions as a kind of guiding principle rather than providing explicit and detailed legislation in relation to practical cases of marriage breakdown. In consequence, the principle of economy can be invoked in a way that dispensation can not be in the Catholic Church.

Among theologians, canonists and pastors in the Catholic Church today there is a growing interest in this Orthodox principle and practice of economy in relation to marriage and its breakdown. The Council of Trent was careful not to condemn this practice and the 1980 Synod of Bishops in Rome recommended that it be carefully considered for the light it might shed on Catholic pastoral practice. At present a significant number of the Catholic Church's experts are of the view that this Orthodox principle and practice might provide some illumination and direction for the Catholic Church in our day in relation to at least some of the difficulties it is experiencing over the issue of marriage breakdowns, second unions and remarriage.[3]

New thinking on indissolubility
Among Catholic scholars today several important points are discussed and some suggestions are made in connection with the understanding of indissolubility in marriage. Significant here is the personalist or relational teaching of Vatican II on marriage

2. See John Garvey, 'Second Marriages in Orthodox Tradition', *Doctrine and Life*, October 2000, 464-466.
3. See Symeon Lash, 'Economy' in Alan Richardson & John Bowden (Editors), *A New Dictionary of Christian Theology* (SCM Press, London, 1983), pp 171-2; Timothy J. Buckley CSsR, *What Binds Marriage: Roman Catholic Theology in Practice* (Geoffrey Chapman, London, 1997), pp 125-6, 172-7; Richard P. McBrien, Editor, *HarperCollins Encyclopedia of Catholicism* (Harper Collins, New York, 1995), p 451; Charles E. Curran, *New Perspectives in Moral Theology* (Fides Publishers Inc, Notre Dame, Indiana, 1974),pp 269-271; Charles E. Curran, *Ongoing Revision: Studies in Moral Theology* (Fides Publishers Inc, Notre Dame, Indiana, 1975), pp 85-6.

which we have already outlined, and the implications of that, as some scholars see it, for the church's legal and institutional understanding of marriage as indissoluble. It will be interesting and stimulating to outline rather briefly some of the thinking on this area that Catholic theologians and others have been doing in recent times. We will advert also to the response of the church's magisterium to these ideas on indissolubility.[4]

The word 'indissolubility'

This is clearly a legal word indicating the quality of a Christian marriage by which it cannot be broken or dissolved. It is a word taken from the area of law dealing with contracts and it makes the point in the present context that the contract that marriage is cannot be dissolved or put asunder. This indissolubility is an essential property of the institution of marriage which each couple enters and it is something neither the couple nor any human power can interfere with or remove from any marriage. In terms of the relational or personalist model of marriage, indissolubility would more naturally be referred to as the permanence or lifelongness of marriage, a property which is, of course, essential to marriage. From the viewpoint of a couple in marriage this permanence is assured when it is the fruit of lifelong fidelity.[5]

The consummation of marriage

In the church's teaching since the twelfth century, consummation has been understood in a physical sense. This understanding fitted well into the legal model of marriage and indissolubility.

4. See Kevin T Kelly, *Divorce and Second Marriage: Facing the Challenge* (Geoffrey Chapman, London, 1982, 1996), chapters 1 & 2; Philip Keane, *Sexual Morality: A Catholic Perspective* (Paulist Press, New York, 1977), pp 140-8; Margaret Farley, 'Divorce, Remarriage and Pastoral Practice' in Charles E. Curran (Editor), *Moral Theology: Challenges for the Future* (Essays in Honor of Richard A. McCormick SJ.) (Paulist Press, New York, 1990), pp 213-239; Richard A. McCormick SJ, *Notes on Moral Theology 1965 through 1980* (University of America Press, Washington, DC, USA, 1981), pp 332-347, 372-381, 544-561; Charles E. Curran, *New Perspectives in Moral Theology*, chapter 7; Charles E. Curran, *Ongoing Revision: Studies in Moral Theology*, chapter 3; Ladislas Orsy SJ, *Marriage in Canon Law: Texts and Comments, Reflections and Questions* (Dominican Publications, Dublin, 1986), pp 202-6, 270-2, 265-8; Theodore Mackin SJ, *Divorce and Remarriage* (Paulist Press, New York, 1984), chapters 17 & 18; William Cosgrave, 'Rethinking the Indissolubility of Marriage', *The Furrow*, January 1980, pp 8-23.
5. Kevin T Kelly, *Divorce and Second Marriage*, pp 15, 17.

The contract of marriage was considered consummated when the partners engaged in sexual intercourse after marriage. A single act of sexual intercourse was sufficient to seal the contract and achieve consummation. And when a marriage of two baptised Christians was thus consummated, it was and is held to be absolutely indissoluble. In the 1983 *Code of Canon Law* this teaching is complemented by the phrase 'in a human manner' (c. 1061, par. 1) and this is interpreted as meaning free and voluntary.[6]

If we ask how consummation in this sense makes a marriage absolutely indissoluble, thus limiting the church's power to dissolve marriage, then it must be responded that no consensus has been reached on this point among theologians and canonists and so the search for a satisfactory explanation must continue.[7]

Some are suggesting also, in the light of the personalist theology of Vatican II, that a purely physical concept of consummation is hardly adequate and hence a more personal or spiritual understanding of this reality must be sought, thus broadening the definition of consummation. The International Theological Commission, which is based in the Vatican, admitted this possibility in 1977 and its secretary at that time expressed the opinion that 'the consummation theory of the medieval canonists may well turn out to be too inadequate to be tenable any longer.'[8]

As yet, however, little progress has been made in working out an acceptable theory of consummation in personalist or relational terms. At the same time, developments in the area of marriage annulment may well point towards an eventual recognition of this broader concept of consummation. In relation to annulment (c. 1095, n. 3) the 1983 Code lays it down that, if a person does not have the capacity to assume the essential obligations of marriage, the marriage of that person can and should be declared invalid. These obligations surely include the capacity to make and maintain a marital relationship, i.e. the intimate partnership of married life and love which Vatican II talks about. Here is a powerful personalist emphasis that in due course could be extended to the idea of consummation.[9]

6. See John P. Beal, 'The Separation of Spouses' (cc. 1141-1155) in John P. Beal, James A. Coriden & Thomas J. Green, Editors, *New Commentary on the Code of Canon Law* (Paulist Press, New York, 2000), p 1364.
7. See Orsy, *Marriage in Canon Law*, p 266.
8. Quoted by Beal, p 1365; see Orsy, 266-8.
9. Orsy, p 268.

Consummation in this relational or personalist sense would refer to a relationship that has so deepened and strengthened that the husband and wife experience themselves as a couple, as two in one flesh. Then their marriage is completed or consummated so as to be unbreakable.[10]

The bond of marriage

Church teaching and church law speak frequently of the bond of marriage. It is a central concept in the church's understanding of marriage in its legal norms and pastoral practice. In the light of the Second Vatican Council's understanding of marriage, and the prominence of the relational model of marriage in church thinking and practice today, it will be interesting and illuminating to look briefly at what some theologians and canonists are saying and suggesting in relation to a more personalist understanding of the bond of marriage.

In the New Testament and the patristic writers, remarriage after divorce was viewed as immoral, a grave sin. Augustine moved this prohibition from the level of immorality to that of ontology, stating that the bond of marriage remained after the first marriage ended in divorce and it is this bond that makes a second marriage not just immoral but actually impossible. In later centuries, the principle was established that the bond of marriage between Christians could be sundered only by death and was, therefore, indissoluble, and absolutely so in the case of a consummated marriage between two baptised persons. This position represents the church's official teaching since the twelfth century down to the present.[11]

In this understanding the bond of marriage is seen as an ontological reality which comes into existence with the consent of the marriage partners and then no longer depends for its continued existence on the will of the spouses alone. Here marriage is essentially a bond, which of its nature is exclusive and perpetual. The bond itself is the essence of marriage.[12]

Some contemporary theologians and canonists raise questions about this understanding of the bond, basing themselves largely on the shift from a contract-centred theology to a

10. Kelly, 34-36.
11. Beal, p 1360; Timothy J. Buckley CSsR, *What Binds Marriage: Roman Catholic Theology in Practice,* chapter 2, especially at pp 43 ff.
12. Buckley, p 54; Mackin, *Divorce and Remarriage,* pp 493-4; Mackin, *What is Marriage?,* pp 318-350.

covenant- or love-centred one. The main issue here centres on how this bond can exist and persist irrespective of what happens to the relationship of the couple. Can the essence of marriage be a juridical reality or bond in such a way that it excludes the love and intimate partnership of the spouses from that essence? Can this juridical essence exist apart from and independently of the wills of the partners, and have the juridical effect of so binding them to each other that they may not marry again, however dead their marital relationship may be?[13]

For these scholars it is difficult to envisage the marriage bond as a reality separate from the relationship of the couple, either in a juridical or an ontological sense. It seems to them better to view the bond of marriage as a relationship between the spouses, a relationship or bond that is, of course, institutionalised in the social framework or institution we know as marriage. This bond is one of mutual respect and love that unites the partners as persons in an interpersonal union, and grounds their obligation to nourish their marital relationship as much as possible.[14]

This more personalist or relational interpretation of the marriage bond seems to be very much in line with what Vatican II says about marriage, and something of a consensus seems to have emerged in regard to it. Still, it has not yet had a significant impact on church teaching or law and so the search for a fully satisfactory understanding of the bond of marriage must continue.

Marriage as indissoluble

In the light of the preceding observations we are in a better position to deal with the central issue of the indissolubility of marriage itself. There has been quite a bit of discussion about this among Catholic theologians in recent decades, and among some at least elements of a convergence of opinion can be found. Some of the main ideas put forward will be summarised here.

In the context of the personalist or relational model or understanding of marriage, the indissolubility or permanence of marriage is no longer viewed as something that is given from the beginning and is achieved once one enters the institution of marriage, so as to persist no matter what happens to the marital relationship of the couple. Rather, among these authors the tendency is to understand indissolubility as indeed an essential property of marriage but one that flows from the very nature of the spouses'

13. Mackin, *Divorce and Remarriage,* 520.
14. Orsy, pp 271-2.

relationship and love for each other. As such indissolubility is variously understood as a moral obligation involving the task of making one's marriage permanent, an absolute precept binding the partners to make their marriage lifelong, or a moral ideal that the couple are bound to strive for by a most serious obligation. So, in these views, indissolubility is something to be realised in the course of a marriage and, when it is, it is the fruit of lifelong love. Another word for this permanence is lifelong fidelity.[15]

Others again, viewing marriage as a commitment, see indissolubility as part of what one commits oneself to. This commitment is made not only by each partner to the other, but both partners also commit themselves to God and to the church and to society. In addition, this marital commitment is made to marriage as an institution or framework of life. In this context, permanence can serve the good of children, of society and of the church.[16]

A central assertion, or at least presumption, of these authors in discussing permanence or indissolubility is that a marriage can break down irretrievably and so can simply cease to exist as a marital relationship. In a word, a marriage can die. Here the focus is clearly on marriage as a personal relationship. While this relationship is institutionalised as a contract, it remains the heart of marriage and can, as experience shows, disintegrate and break down totally for a variety of reasons. When it does, then the marriage has simply, if sadly, gone out of existence, even though significant effects and consequences of it will very likely remain for the partners. These effects and consequences are not just the children and the experience of being married partners, but also the personal, social, emotional and even ontological (in their very being as persons) changes that their marriage relationship has brought to both husband and wife.

This assertion that a marriage can die and so cease to exist would seem to be the crucial point in the understanding of permanence or indissolubility among these theologians. Since their primary emphasis is on the personal relationship as the central reality or essence of marriage, it is not really surprising that, recognising the fact that is obvious from widespread experience,

15. Kelly, 15-24; Richard McCormick SJ, *Notes on Moral Theology 1965 through 1980,* pp 372-381, 544-561; Curran, *New Perspectives in Moral Theology,* pp 251-176; Curran, *Ongoing Revision: Studies on Moral Theology,* chapter 3, especially at pp 75-106; Keane, 142-8.
16. Farley, 226-234.

namely, that the love or relationship between the partners in a marriage can disappear and die, they conclude that this is the end or death of the marriage also. It follows that, when a marriage has thus died, then the obligation of indissolubility or the duty to make the marriage permanent ceases, because it is now impossible to fulfil it, and/or because the marriage no longer serves love, and/or the marriage obligation can in the circumstances yield to a more weighty obligation.[17]

Now in relation to these marriages which have died and gone out of existence, it can be said that they never reached the state of achieving indissolubility; they were never consummated in the personal sense. Rather they declined and died. They were thus dissoluble and in fact did dissolve themselves over time. So the church could declare them so dissolved, though it would not dissolve them or any marriages as it does at present and for many centuries past.[18]

In this view, then, the church's teaching that a consummated marriage of two Christians is absolutely indissoluble remains true and certain. Only non-consummated marriages can dissolve and die.

In the light of this thinking about marriage and its permanence, these theologians go on to discuss the possibility and the morality of a second marriage in the wake of the first dissolved one. Such a marriage may be morally right, they say, because, when a marriage, which is not consummated in the personal sense, disintegrates and dies, then to enter a second marriage is not being unfaithful to the first one, since that marriage no longer exists. And so one cannot speak of the second marriage as adulterous. It follows then that from the moral point of view such a second marriage can be acceptable, as can second marriages, in the church's present teaching, after a non-consummated one has been dissolved by the church.[19]

The second marriage we are talking about is seen as justified by some theologians for different reasons, e.g. there are proportionate reasons for it, or whatever obligations remain for the spouses from the first marriage do not rule out a second one.[20]

If we ask now whether the second marriages we are talking

17. Farley, 229f.
18. Kelly, 38
19. Kelly, 38.
20. Farley, 229ff.

about here can be sacramental, the answer tends to be in the affirmative, though the theologians we are discussing tend to add that maybe such marriages should not be put fully on a par with the first marriage from the sacramental point of view.[21]

The official church response to these suggestions
Since quite a bit of the above theologising had been published in the early 1970s, the Vatican intervened on three occasions in that decade to reassert the traditional or medieval teaching of the church on the indissolubility of marriage, and especially the indissolubility of consummated sacramental marriages. The Signatura (1975), Paul VI (1976) and the International Theological Commission (1978) combined in their firm rejection of the idea that a marriage can die and cease to exist without any binding remainder. On the contrary, since marriage is essentially a juridical relationship, a bond, it continues to subsist independently of any subsequent change of will by the contracting parties and does not cease to exist if, later, love between the spouses ceases or if the intimate communion of life and marital love disappears. They firmly rejected the idea that with the failure of some subjective element, such as marital love, the marriage itself no longer exists as a 'juridical reality'. The essence of marriage is the juridical bond and as such love, intimacy, the sharing of life, etc, do not belong to this essence. Hence, these subjective elements of a marriage may go out of existence without affecting the juridical essence of that marriage. In fact this juridical essence of marriage is indestructable and so consummated sacramental marriages are absolutely indissoluble.

This position on the indissolubility of marriage is grounded in an ontological argument. When a couple marry, they make a total gift of themselves to each other and, once made, this total gift cannot be revoked by the partners or indeed by anyone. It transcends any change of mind by the partners. It is final. And because of this, it makes another commitment to marriage impossible. Hence, the consummated marriage of two baptised persons has an indissolubility that is indestructable, absolute.[22]

With these three authoritative statements, the question of the indissolubility of marriage was effectively closed as far as the magisterium was concerned. Still, a number of theologians con-

21. Kelly, 40-1.
22. Farley, 225, 231-2.

tinued to reflect on the issue and the problems involved, rehearsing again the arguments we have already recounted, critiquing the reasoning in the official positions just now summarised and presenting what they considered to be the implications of the personalist or relational understanding of marriage taught so authoritatively by the Second Vatican Council.

Concluding comments

To conclude this section on indissolubility, two comments seem warranted. Firstly, the recent popes, some bishops, theologians and canonists were, it would seem, anxious, pastorally speaking, that the new theories of indissolubility that were emerging in Catholic theology and legal studies would reduce the indissolubility of marriage to a mere moral ideal, or at best a serious moral obligation, and so open the way to an unwarranted and uncontrollable amount of second marriages. In addition, if love, the sharing of life, marital intimacy, etc, were introduced into the very essence of marriage, then, they feared, it would be virtually impossible to verify the presence or absence of these subjective elements of marriage in court or legally speaking. This would result in the validity of numerous marriages being called into question in a way that would be exceedingly difficult to resolve. Hence, the firm rejection of the new thinking on indissolubility in all its central assertions as we have outlined above.

On the other hand, secondly, the argumentation presented in the Vatican's statements in defence of the traditional understanding of the absolute indissolubility of some marriages seems far from convincing, especially in light of the contemporary experience of marriage. To claim that love and the intimate sharing of life and love in marriage are not part of the essence of marriage, and can disappear from a marriage without the validity or essence of that marriage being affected, is very difficult to accept and makes little sense nowadays to vast numbers of good Catholics, as well as to quite a few pastors, theologians, canonists and, presumably also, some bishops. It has been argued that it is quite unnecessary so to exclude love, etc, since love, understood as Christ's love for his people as distinct from infatuation, sexual attraction or an emotional high, could be written into the definition of marriage, along the lines of Vatican II in its *Constitution on the Church in the Modern World*, without making legal verifiability any more difficult than it is in regard to consent to marry.[23]

23. Mackin, *What is Marriage?* 341-2.

The juridical reality or bond that survives the total break-down of a marriage relationship is also difficult to comprehend and relate to experience. Here it would seem that juridical categories are substituted for the real human relationship and the only effect is that the spouses are not bound to each other but are bound not to marry another partner.[24]

The ontological argument, while appealing, is also subjected to criticism which calls in question our ability to forge bonds that are completely indestructable.[25]

In view of these two sets of observations it would seem that, while the official position on the indissolubility or permanence of marriage is still firmly in place, the issue of how to understand this indissolubility will continue to be investigated among some of the church's scholars, as they try to bring the insights of the relational or personalist understanding of marriage to bear more fully on the traditional teaching and its expression in the church's law on marriage. No quick developments are to be anticipated, but the search for a deeper understanding will and should continue. What is certain is that the wisdom we need must come from a communal effort in which the issues we have discussed in the preceding pages are kept open, and the evidence continually re-examined.

The issues in the debate about the marriage of baptised non-believers

The main problem in this area arises at the pastoral level in some Western countries where baptised people who have lost their Christian faith come to request a church wedding. Not merely are such people not churchgoers, they are in fact also alienated from the church and no longer Christian believers. This places the priest in a dilemma as he has to decide whether he should marry them or not. Such a decision is not easy to make, since it raises major theological questions which need to be answered in order that a decision be arrived at. For some years now this problem has been the subject of quite widespread discussion and debate among Catholic theologians, canonists and pastors, and it continues to be a matter of controversy at the present time.[26]

---

24. Mackin, *Divorce and Remarriage,* pp 519-520; Mackin, *What is Marriage?* pp 332-350.
25. Farley, 233.
26. See Ladislas Orsy SJ, 'Faith, Sacrament, Contract and Christian Marriage: Disputed Questions', *Theological Studies* (TS),1982, pp 379-398;

Experts identify two pivotal questions that must be addressed in this area of discussion: a) Is faith necessary to participate in/receive the sacrament of marriage? and b) Can the marriage contract be separated from the sacrament in a marriage of two baptised people? Here we will summarise briefly the discussion about each of these issues.

Is faith necessary to participate in/receive the sacrament of marriage?
There seems to be agreement generally that Christian faith is necessary for the validity of any sacrament and, hence, for the sacrament of marriage too. So, no faith, no sacrament and, in particular, no sacrament of marriage. But it is by no means agreed what sort of faith or how much faith is required here in order that marriage be a valid sacrament. There seem to be two main viewpoints.

Some say it must be a rather explicit faith, involving a surrender of the person to God and Christ and a profession of faith in at least the principal Christian mysteries, what one might refer to as a comprehensive 'yes' to Christian and salvific realities. And it must be an active Christian faith.[27]

These writers express this point in another way when they say that the virtue of faith which is infused in baptism is not sufficient here. This infused virtue must blossom out in a personal act of faith and it is this act of faith, however minimal, which makes one a Christian believer.[28]

This same assertion is articulated in yet other words by saying that when personal faith is absent, so too is a right sacramental intention, and without this intention, the sacrament is not valid.

Susan Wood SCL, 'The Marriage of Baptised NonBelievers: Faith, Contract and Sacrament', *Theological Studies*, 1987, pp 279-301; Michael G. Lawler & William P Roberts, Editors, *Christian Marriage and Family: Contemporary Theological and Pastoral Perspectives* (The Liturgical Press, Collegeville, Minnesota, USA, 1996), chapter 3; Ladislas Orsy SJ, *Marriage and Canon Law: Texts and Comments, Reflections and Questions* (Dominican Publications, Dublin, 1986), pp 268-270; Denis F. O'Callaghan, 'Faith and the Sacrament of Marriage', *Irish Theological Quarterly*, 1986: 3, pp 161-179; John McAreavey, 'Faith and the Validity of Marriage', *Irish Theological Quarterly*, 1993: 3, pp 177-187.
27. Orsy, *Theological Studies* (1982), pp 385-7; Lawler, 'Faith, Contract and Sacrament in Christian Marriage: A Theological Approach' in Lawler, & Roberts, pp 42-7; Wood, 294.
28. Lawler, p 49; Orsy, *TS*, 383, n. 7.

So, no personal act of faith, no right intention to marry and, hence, no sacrament of marriage.[29]

Taking a second different viewpoint, other theologians and canonists settle for less in the matter of faith. They say that all that is required is the state of believers that baptism confers and not necessarily interior active faith in the form of an act of faith. In other words, what is needed to celebrate a valid Christian marriage is not personal faith but the baptismal character.[30]

Others put this differently and say that in the lives of baptised couples we can presume faith, however implicit or tacit or inchoate.[31]

If such faith is present, a person will have the right intention in regard to marrying. So, in the view of these writers, the conclusion is that the present law of the church should remain and so any baptised person, believer or non-believer, may marry validly in the church.

We may note that in *Familiaris Consortio* (1981), Pope John Paul II refused to make distinctions between levels of faith. He does, however, lay down a minimum standard or lower limit below which a couple cannot be admitted to the celebration of marriage: explicit and formal rejection of what the church intends to do when the marriage of baptised persons is celebrated.[32]

So the Pope refuses to take sides in the theological discussion we are concerned with, leaving it to develop over time. At the same time, speaking in terms of the intention to marry, he refers to couples, who marry for non-religious reasons, implicitly consenting, by virtue of their baptism, to what the church intends to do when she celebrates marriage. This seems to lean towards the second viewpoint mentioned above but without closing off the debate, a point borne out by the subsequent continuation of the discussion.

Can the marriage contract of two baptised people
be separated from the sacrament?
On first acquaintance one might think that this question is quite

---

29. Lawler, p 48; International Theological Commission (1977), 'Propositions on the Doctrine of Christian Marriage', nn. 2:3, quoted in Orsy, *TS*, p 385.
30. Wood, p 294-5.
31. Dermot Lane, quoted in McAreavey, p 181.
32. See O'Callaghan, pp 163-4.

separate from the previous one, so that the answer to it wouldn't be closely connected to the answer given to the issue we have just been discussing. In reality, however, this is not the case. The present issue is very much linked with the previous one, so that the answer to the first one provides the context and the foundation for one's answer to the question now under consideration. This close link will soon become clear as we proceed to discuss the present issue. There seem to be two basic positions on this question, in line with the two stances taken on the issue of faith and the validity of the sacrament of marriage above.

First position: contract and sacrament can be separated

Since many baptised people who are, nevertheless, non-believers, come for marriage in the church, at least in some countries of the Western world, one soon finds oneself pushed beyond the pastoral issue to the deeper theological questions underlying this problem. One such question that theologians and canonists raise in an effort to resolve the difficulty is this: might it be possible that such baptised non-believers could celebrate a marriage in church that is a true and valid marriage in the eyes of the church, but not a sacramental one? Now in order that this be possible at all, it would be necessary to separate the sacrament from the contract or covenant of marriage, in such a way that the latter could exist for baptised people without the former (the sacrament) becoming a reality for them in their marriage. If such separation is not possible, then we have no option but to carry on as at present by celebrating a sacramental marriage or, simply, refusing to marry such people.

A significant number of church scholars are not happy with being limited to these two options by the statement in the 1983 *Code of Canon Law* in canon 1055, par. 2: a valid marriage contract cannot exist between baptised persons without its being by that very fact a sacrament. Hence, these scholars tend to the view that sacrament and contract can be separated. Their reasoning goes along the following lines.

First of all, they tend to the view that personal faith expressing itself in an act of faith is necessary in order that the marriage of two baptised people be a valid sacramental marriage. Without this kind of faith, they say, the marriage such a couple enters can't be a sacrament. This is the first position outlined above in relation to the necessity of faith for the celebration of a sacrament and of marriage in particular. The next step is to question the principle from the Code. This principle dates back only to the 1917 *Code of Canon Law,* where it was first enunciated in the following terms: Christ the Lord raised the matrimonial contract between baptised persons to the dignity of a sacrament (canon 1012, par. 1). However, it was not precisely the contract of marriage that Christ raised to the dignity of a sacrament, but marriage itself. This latter is what the Council of Trent also taught, and the late nineteenth-century popes held that marriage among believers (not among the baptised) is always a sacrament.[33]

Putting these points together, this position concludes that the contract and the sacrament can be, and in fact are, separated in the case that is being discussed, that of baptised unbelievers.

In this way, these authors claim, the discussion of this problem is re-opened after it had been prematurely and illegitimately closed by the 1917 Code. In fact the 1980 Synod of Bishops echoes this, when in one of its propositions it says that 'We must investigate further if this statement applies to those who have lost the faith: A valid marriage between baptised persons is always a sacrament'.[34]

This position which we are outlining, has important pastoral consequences. The first is that the church would need to find some way of recognising the natural marriage of baptised unbelievers, which is, in this view, non-sacramental. Such a marriage has the human reality of marriage but it does not participate in the sacramental mystery.[35] Clearly, baptised unbelievers have the capacity to create a natural marriage and it is hard to see how this capacity could be cancelled out by baptism.[36] It would seem, in fact, that the church's practice of granting a *sanatio in radice* in the case of canonically invalid marriages, without the need for renewal of consent and even without the knowledge of the parties, implies the existence of a union which can't be far removed from being a natural marriage.[37]

The other important pastoral consequence of this position, which posits the separability of contract and sacrament in the marriage of two baptised persons, is that, since these marriages of baptised unbelievers are not sacramental, they are open to

33. Lawler, pp 49-53.
34. Lawler, p 54.
35. Orsy, *Marriage in Canon Law,* p 269.
36. Orsy, *TS,* 395; Wood, 290-1.
37. Orsy, *Marriage in Canon Law,* pp 269-70.

being dissolved in accordance with the church's long-standing practice.[38]

Second position: Contract and sacrament cannot be separated

The proponents of this position, which is the one at present enshrined in church law and pastoral practice, include the Vatican based and controlled International Theological Commission. These theologians, canonists and pastors recognise the problem of baptised unbelievers, but basically continue to uphold the present law and pastoral practice of the church in relation to the marriages of baptised people. Such marriages are all sacramental, since contract and sacrament are inseparable. The writers who adopt this position tend strongly to take the view which favours the necessity only of implicit faith or the baptismal character in order that a marriage of two baptised persons be valid.

In the light of this position, they see no need nor possibility of separating the contract from the sacrament in marriage. Hence, they continue to insist that the valid marriage of non-believers who are baptised cannot in any way be recognised by the church as a non-sacramental conjugal society, even though such a couple still have the natural right to marry and to form a relationship that resembles marriage. But if it is to be called a marriage, then it cannot be other than a sacrament as well.[39]

One author adds to this by asserting that for the baptised there can be no return to the natural order, because such an order does not exist. It is an ecclesial impossibility to offer an alternative form of marriage to a sacramental one to a person who has been baptised. So, the only thing that could prevent the marriage of baptised persons, even non-believers, from being a sacrament would be an explicit, direct intention against the sacrament. Such an intention would make the marriage invalid and so prevent the sacrament from coming into existence.[40]

To this position on the impossibility of baptised people marrying non-sacramentally, the reply is made that this view consigns all baptised unbelievers to a limbo. They would be the only ones in the immense human family who would have no right to marry: not naturally, because they are baptised; not sacramentally,

---

38. Lawlor, p 55.
39. International Theological Commission, 3:5, as quoted in Orsy, *TS*, 391-2.
40. Wood, p 300.

because they have no faith. Such a position does not make sense.[41]

Further Reading

Buckley, Timothy J. CSsR, *What Binds Marriage? Roman Catholic Theology in Practice* (Geoffrey Chapman, London, 1997);

Curran, Charles E., *New Pespectives in Moral Theology* (Fides Publishers Inc, Notre Dame, Indiana, USA, 1974), chapter 7;

Curran, Charles E., *Ongoing Revision: Studies in Moral Theology* (Fides Publishers Inc, Notre Dame, Indiana, USA, 1975), chapter 3;

Farley, Margaret A., 'Divorce, Remarriage and Pastoral Practice' in Curran, Charles E., Editor, *Moral Theology: Challenges for the Future (Essays in Honour of Richard A. McCormick SJ)* (Paulist Press, New York, 1990), pp 213-239;

Kelly, Kevin T., *Divorce and Second Marriage: Facing the Challenge* (Geoffrey Chapman, London, 1982, 1996), chapters 1, 2 & Appendix 2;

Kelly, Kevin T., *New Directions in Sexual Ethics: Moral Theology and the Challenge of AIDS* (Geoffrey Chapman, London & Washington, 1998);

Mackin, Theodore SJ, *Marriage in the Catholic Church: What is Marriage?* (Paulist Press, New York, 1982); *Divorce and Remarriage* (Paulist Press, New York, 1984);

McAreavey, John, 'Faith and the Validity of Marriage', *Irish Theological Quarterly,* 1993: 3, pp 177-187;

McBrien, Richard P., Editor, 'Economy, principle of', *HarperCollins Encyclopedia of Catholicism* (HarperCollins, New York, 1995), p 451;

McCormick, Richard A. SJ, *Notes on Moral Theology 1965 through 1980* (University Press of America, Washington, DC, USA, 1981), pp 332-347, 372-381, 544-561;

O'Callaghan, Denis F., 'Faith and the Sacrament of Marriage', *Irish Theological Quarterly,* 1986: 3, pp 161-179;

Orsy, Ladislas SJ, *Marriage in Canon Law: Texts and Comments; Reflections and Questions* (Dominican Publications, Dublin, 1988), chapters 8 & 9, pp 260-294;

Orsy, Ladislas SJ, 'Faith, Sacrament, Contract, and Christian Marriage: Disputed Questions', *Theological Studies,* September 1982, pp 379-398;

Paul VI, *The Regulation of Births,* 1968, nn. 7-9;

Vatican Council II, *The Church in the Modern World,* nn. 47-52;

Wood, Susan SCL, 'The Marriage of Baptised NonBelievers: Faith, Contract, and Sacrament', *Theological Studies,* June 1987, pp 279-301.

---

41. Orsy, *TS,* p 391.

CHAPTER 8

Divorce, Remarriage and the Eucharist

In the church today and for some years now, one issue that has provoked a great deal of discussion and argument at the theological, canonical and pastoral levels is the question of whether Catholics living in second relationships, after their marriage has broken down, and possibly also after divorce, may go to communion. Most often the issue concerns Catholics who are divorced and remarried, but it involves also those who are living in second non-marital relationships. In essence, the debate concerns the official teaching of the church on this matter, a teaching which is seen by many theologians, canonists and pastors as over-rigid and lacking in compassion towards many, though not all, of those in the situation we have described. In this chapter we intend to outline the issues in the discussion, indicate the official teaching of the church and present some of the suggestions put forward by theologians and others as contributions to the debate.

The official church position
Before Vatican II the generally accepted view about the issue of whether divorced and remarried Catholics could receive communion was negative. They were considered as living in an adulterous union, in sin, and, hence, were excluded from the sacraments of penance and the eucharist. Moreover, their situation was intolerable, because it could be a source of scandal to the faithful. If they wanted to go to communion, then they had to separate or live as brother and sister, i.e. without a sexual relationship. Discussion arose about a possible 'good faith' solution by which a Catholic could receive the eucharist, if he/she had entered a second marriage in good faith, believing that the first marriage was invalid, though it could not be proved to be so. This case came to be distinguished from other cases where the first marriage was, presumably, valid but had broken down and one of the partners had remarried. In time this good faith solution

came to be referred to as the internal forum solution, because a solution was offered in the internal forum, i.e. in confession or in private counselling, that was not in line with the requirements of the external forum, i.e. the law of the church. Some suggested that this internal forum solution be extended to cases where the first marriage was only doubtfully (as opposed to certainly) invalid.

In 1981 the Pope reiterated the earlier position just outlined and formulated more precisely what was and still is the official teaching of the church. John Paul II proclaimed that all divorced and remarried Catholics and all those living in an invalid second union were to be excluded from the eucharist. He gave two reasons for this conclusion: a) They may not receive communion because their situation is an objective contradiction of the unity which the eucharist signifies; and b) their going to communion would cause error and confusion among the faithful, i.e. it would give rise to scandal.

Note here that the Pope avoids the phrase 'living in sin' and speaks only of irregular unions which constitute an objective contradiction of the union of love between Christ and his church which is signified by the eucharist. This is a significant advance and means that the Pope recognised that some people in second unions might not be in serious sin, even though their marriage was invalid in the eyes of the church. They might have repented, be living good Christian lives and be morally bound to remain in their present relationship. In addition, outsiders are in a very poor position to judge the sinfulness of another person and, hence, they should not presume to do so by using phrases like 'living in sin' or its equivalents. The upshot of this line of thinking is that today, at all levels of the church, the phrase 'living in sin' is and should be no longer used in reference to Catholics in irregular marital relationships. We are on safe ground when we speak of them as being in irregular unions or even irregular marital unions or relationships, thus leaving the judgment of the partners' personal sinfulness to God and avoiding the presumption that they are in serious sin.

Reactions to this official teaching
In response to John Paul's statement excluding all Catholics living in irregular marital relationships from communion, there was a widespread and strong reaction among theologians,

canonists and pastors around the world. Even before 1981 there were suggestions that such a total ban was excessive and lacked the compassion of Christ. Now these views were articulated in more detail and on a wider scale. We may summarise the general trend or tenor of these responses in the following way.

a) Criticism of the official position and its arguments

The first step consisted of critical comments on the papal view and on the argumentation used to support it.

i. The teaching that a couple in an irregular union may receive the eucharist only if they live as brother and sister, is deeply flawed. In the first place it is quite unrealistic in today's world, since for most couples it will be impossible, totally unappealing and almost certainly very damaging to their relationship. In addition, this solution to the problem is quite ineffective as far as avoiding scandal goes. How is anyone to know that a particular couple are living as brother and sister? Despite this, church teaching accepts this position as opening the way to receiving the eucharist. But even more basically, one has to ask, why is the sexual element of the second relationship singled out for exclusion, when in fact what is really contrary to the first marriage and its indissolubility is the whole second relationship and not just the sexual part of it? It would seem that the papal viewpoint here is founded on the pre-Vatican II legal understanding of marriage as a contract in which each partner is given a lifelong right to sexual union with the other. If a person leaves this marital relationship (by divorce or otherwise) and enters a second relationship, then he/she violates the legal right of his/her marriage partner to sexual intercourse. And if he/she is to receive communion, then this violation must be corrected by abstention from sex, i.e. by a brother and sister arrangement.

However, in Vatican II's understanding of marriage as a covenant or community of love, this approach makes little sense, since sexual intercourse is not so much a right as an expression of the deep and fully personal relationship between the partners. If, then, the partnership disintegrates, no right to sexual union exists and, consequently, a second sexual relationship does not violate such a right and so cannot be condemned on that ground. It follows that a brother and sister situation should not be required of people in a second relationship.

ii. The argument that living in a second invalid marital relationship is an objective contradiction of the eucharist as a sign of unity is not very convincing. This is a new argument, replacing the one about living in sin, and was first articulated in the 1970s. It is, however, an argument that, onesidedly, stresses one aspect of the eucharist to the neglect of an equally important second aspect of it. It sees going to communion as a sign of full unity in faith with the church and views a second invalid union as such a serious form of public separation from or disunity with the church that it bars one from going to communion completely. However, the church sees the eucharist, not just as a sign of full unity but also as a means or a help to that unity. This is why in exceptional cases the church allows non-Catholic Christians to receive the eucharist and even commends that practice. Would this not also apply to Catholics living in second invalid marriages and be a basis for at least some of them approaching the eucharist even if only in exceptional cases? We may add that we Christians need the eucharist, not because we are holy, but because we are sinful. It is spiritual nourishment that can help us sinners to deepen our unity with Christ and the church.

iii. In relation to the teaching that people in irregular unions going to communion will give scandal, serious problems are also raised by theologians and pastors. Scandal here must be taken to mean, not surprise and upset, but rather error and confusion in relation to one's faith, so that the practice in question is an obstacle to the faith of other believers. If, then, scandal is caused, there should be evidence of it; it could be documented. But no such evidence is provided in official church teaching and, hence, one cannot say convincingly that scandal is actually caused in these cases. We may add that it is just as likely that scandal will be caused by a hardline total exclusion from communion of all people who live in irregular second unions as by allowing some of them to receive the eucharist. Such a harsh practice is far from the compassion and forgiveness of Christ. Finally, as already alluded to, the church permits and even commends the brother and sister arrangement but seems not to be concerned about any scandal that might arise in such cases, since people won't know that such a couple are living in this way and yet they go to communion. How come, then, that church officials are so worried about possible scandal in other cases where people in irregular unions approach the Lord's table?

There is no doubt that the criticisms which we have just outlined are significant and leave one with the feeling that the official church stance on this issue of communion for Catholics in irregular second unions is far from fully convincing. In fact one could be pardoned for suspecting that a reasonable case could be made for saying that some divorced and remarried Catholics could feel morally justified in approaching the altar for communion at least occasionally. Many theologians and pastors are of this mind too and they make their case along the following lines.

b) Accepting that receiving communion is morally right for some in irregular unions

i. The German bishops' initiative

We may begin with a brief look at the 1993 initiative of three German bishops, two of whom are outstanding theologians,[1] while the third is vice-president of the German episcopal conference. They do not question the church's official position on this issue but they do assert that the papal norm cannot cover all situations and so we need to exercise pastoral flexibility in particular cases. Distinguishing between spouses who are innocent parties to a marital breakdown and those who are guilty of destroying a valid marriage, and between those who believe their first marriage was invalid and those whose first marriage was valid, the three bishops ask whether these different situations can lead to some divorced and remarried people coming to communion. Stressing the importance of a well informed conscience, the bishops demand that those living in an invalid union and wishing to receive the eucharist should always consult a priest. This is to ensure that such a couple's conscience is well informed. Then such a couple should be able to judge for themselves their position before God and decide whether or not to go to communion. This is not *carte blanche* for all couples in second invalid unons but recognises that, under carefully defined conditions, some of them may arrive at a conscientious decision to receive the sacraments.

In 1994 the Vatican rejected this pastoral initiative from the three German bishops and re-affirmed the earlier norm. The three bishops in reply reasserted their position, saying they did not question the general norm but were of the view that there does exist room, beneath the threshold of the binding teaching,

1. One of these two, Walter Kasper, has since been elevated to the position of Cardinal (2001) and also to the Presidency of the Vatican's Council for Promoting Christian Unity. The other, Karl Lehmann, has also been made a Cardinal (2001).

for pastoral flexibility in complex individual cases, a flexibility which is, of course, to be used responsibly.

ii. Conditions for the admission of some in irregular unions to the eucharist

Assuming here the criticisms made in the previous section, we move on to discuss the positive proposals of many theologians and pastors on this issue. Their basic conclusion is that at least some of the Catholics living in invalid second unions should be considered in a position where it is right for them to receive the eucharist at least occasionally.

The theologians and pastors we are speaking about begin by insisting that we must avoid both indiscriminate exclusion of these people from communion and also indiscriminate re-admission of them. Hence, we must distinguish between different cases, in particular treating differently innocent and guilty parties and also those who believe their first marriage was invalid and those who accept they were validly married in the first place.

Reception of the eucharist must in all cases be seen as justified only under certain conditions. As we list and explain these, it will be important to note that they are conditions for the making of a correct moral decision, not a canonical or legal one. In consequence, legal terminology is not helpful here and will be avoided. These conditions laid down by the theologians and pastors we are talking about may be summarised in the following way:

a) The first marriage must be irretrievably broken down and without any real possibility of being restored.

b) If necessary, repentance for one's part in the breakdown of that first marriage should be demonstrated.

c) All duties in justice towards one's first spouse and the children of the first marriage must be fulfilled to the extent that that is possible.

d) The second union or marital relationship must be stable and the couple doing their best to live good Christian lives in what is to all appearances a good marriage. Part of this will be that they believe and experience their present relationship as what God wants them to do.

e) The desire for the eucharist must be motivated by genuine faith and the wish to express that faith in and with one's local Christian community, thus getting help and support as one continues one's Christian pilgrimage in the church.

The theologians and pastors who advocate this approach to

the reception of the eucharist by Catholics in second relationships do not generally think it necessary that a priest intervene to
judge if the conditions are met. Many couples will be well informed themselves and so will be able to make their own moral
decision in this matter, though in line with the German bishops
cited above, it may seem to some that consulting a priest will be a
big help in ensuring that the couple's consciences are well
formed and informed. It may be added that others besides a
priest could fulfil this consultative role, e.g. a spiritual director, a
retreat master or mistress, or some other pastoral minister.

Recent Official Statement
Most recently, in July 2000, the Pontifical Council for Legislative
Texts, after consultation with the Congregation for the Doctrine
of the Faith and the Congregation for Divine Worship, again reiterated the official Vatican position. In presenting its commentary on canon 915 of the *Code of Canon Law*, which states in part
that those 'who obstinately persist in manifest grave sin are not
to be admitted to Holy Communion', the Pontifical Council rejects the assertion of what it refers to as 'some authors' that this
canon does not apply to the divorced and remarried. The Council
goes further and says that the prohibition in canon 915 is derived
from divine law and transcends the domain of positive ecclesiastical law. Any interpretation of this canon which sets aside its
substantial content is clearly misleading.[2]

It is to be noted here that, apart from who the authors referred
to might be, the Pontifical Council goes beyond what the Pope
said in 1981, as mentioned earlier, and clearly means to assert
that divorced and remarried couples can be in manifest grave
sin. This looks like a move in the direction of the earlier position
that these couples are 'living in sin'. The problems with such a
view were outlined above in discussing John Paul II's position
and they still stand. However, the Pontifical Council does not say
that divorced and remarried couples actually are in grave sin but
only that they could be. That is, of course, possible, but it should
not be presumed and may well not be the case. The Pope's position
must be preferred here as it is morally more correct and pastorally
more sensitive.

---

2. See *The Tablet*, 15 July 2000, p 967.

Conclusion

It would seem that in pastoral practice many pastors judge the approach which allows some couples in irregular unions to go to communion to be right and in line with the compassionate and forgiving attitude of Jesus himself to sinners. Consequently, many of these pastors adopt this viewpoint in their pastoral ministry and are not unhappy with it, even though they know that the Vatican rejects it and insists on the total exclusion of Catholics living in irregular marital relationships from the reception of the eucharist.

This is the actual situation in the church today, though how one assesses it is another matter that one has to decide for oneself. It is certainly regrettable that the official position of the church's chief teaching authority does not commend itself more widely, and that, as a consequence, the church community is itself divided on this very important pastoral issue. It may be, however, that this widespread disagreement with the Vatican viewpoint is not simple disobedience or a well intentioned mistake, but rather an expression of the voice of the Spirit speaking from below, as it were, and pointing the whole church towards an insight into the solution of this urgent pastoral problem that has so far been resisted by the church's highest official teachers.

Further reading

Himes, Kenneth R. OFM & Coridan, James A., 'Pastoral Care of the Divorced and Remarried', *Theological Studies,* March 1996, pp 97-123.

Kelly, Kevin T., *Divorce and Remarriage: Facing the Challenge* (New and Expanded Edition) (London & New York: Geoffrey Chapman, 1982 & 1996), chapters 3 & 4 and Appendix 2.

CHAPTER 9

The Theology of Liberation

It seems safe to say that most people who take any real interest in the affairs of the Catholic Church will have heard something about this topic, at least under its shorter title 'liberation theology'. There are at least two reasons for this. Firstly, liberation theology has been a very widely known, high profile and influential theology throughout the whole Catholic world in the last thirty years, and not least in the Vatican itself. Secondly, it has stirred public controversy in and outside the Catholic Church almost from its beginnings in Latin America in the late 1960s, and in a way that again involved the Vatican, church people at all levels of the church and a sizeable number of politicians and commentators around the world.

Conflicts have been sharp, passions strong and often more heat than light has been generated with extreme, and in many cases, inaccurate views being expressed by both the enemies and the supporters of liberation theology. Countless books and articles have been written and endless lectures given about this new form of theology. Attitudes to it range over the whole spectrum from the extreme hostility of those who see it as a covert attempt to smuggle communism into the Catholic Church and other Christian churches in the name of Christianity, to the exaggerated claims of some of its more fervent, if less than fully objective, fans who consider it to be *the* way of doing theology in these post-conciliar times, the understanding of Christian spirituality we have been waiting for. Some claim it has been condemned by Cardinal Ratzinger in Rome, while others stress the affirming 1986 comments of John Paul II that liberation theology is not only opportune but useful and necessary.

In more recent years, however, we haven't been hearing as much about liberation theology as we did in the 1970s and 1980s. This may be a good thing. It may indicate perhaps that the main controversies are over and that liberation theology, albeit in a somewhat modified version, may now have come to be accepted more fully in the Catholic Church and elsewhere. In this it may be considered to be a bit like the Charismatic Movement which, after a lot of controversy in the 1970s, is now rarely heard of, but which is today quite helpful in the spiritual lives of many. On the other hand, it may be the case that liberation theology is fading, perhaps under pressure from Vatican-appointed conservative bishops. We shall see.

The present chapter cannot aim to give a full and comprehensive account of liberation theology or to do it, or indeed its critics, full justice. All we can hope to achieve is to present a rather brief overview or summary of this theology of liberation, taking a look, on the way, at its origins, its growth, its central concerns and emphases and some of the objections made by its critics and the responses of liberation theologians to them. Some comments on the present situation of liberation theology will also be made.

The name

The very name 'theology of liberation' is helpful in giving us a preliminary clue or pointer to the nature and concerns of this body of theological and spiritual reflection which has made such an impression in church circles and beyond in recent decades. The focus is on liberation from the poverty, oppression and social injustice which the poor suffer under in many countries in South America. To achieve this politico-economic liberation there is need for an analysis of society so as to enable us to understand more clearly and highlight more fully the evils that oppress the poor and keep them in their down-trodden and unjust situation at the base or lowest level of society. In the light of this analysis, the church and its members and others too are called to make an option for the poor in the sense of concerted and public action to change the structures of injustice and oppression that characterise many societies in Latin America. The word 'theology' in the title points to the fact that those who do liberation theology seek to understand their option for the poor and their work for liberation in the light of, and by the inspiration of, the Christian gospel. They begin, naturally, with the Bible and draw also on Christian tradition, the present teaching of the church and the resources of contemporary theological research and thinking. From this process of Christian reflection has emerged the theology of liberation.

To provide a summary description of it we may say that liberation theology is the Christian understanding of (human) liberation, worked out in a systematic and thorough manner, in the
light of the experience of oppression and injustice in Latin
American society, by those who are themselves involved in some
real way in the process of liberating those who are suffering the
oppression. Liberation theology is not, therefore, an ivory tower
study but a product of the church in Latin America which has
made its option for the poor and, in doing liberation theology, is
attempting to live out that option.

History
Our concern here is liberation theology in its original sense, i.e.
the theology that developed in the late 1960s and 70s in Latin
America and which we have just been describing in rather general
terms. There are, however, other forms of liberation theology,
most of which took their inspiration in some degree from the liberation theology we are considering. One author puts it this way:
'Liberation theology currently describes a diverse array of practical theologies – feminist, black, Hispanic, among many others –
each of which attempts to understand and articulate the
Christian faith from the perspective of its own group's particular
experience of the struggle to overcome oppression.[1]

Historians of the theology of liberation in Latin America list
many factors in the societies of that continent, and in the church
there, which contributed to the emergence of this new theological growth. In the 1950s and early 60s strong popular movements
seeking profound changes in the socio-economic structure of
their countries began to make their presence felt, in a context
where Latin American countries were feeling the oppression of a
capitalism that was deeply dependent on the economies of the
North and which excluded the great majority of their popul-
ations from any of the benefits of that capitalism. The socialist
revolution in Cuba gave great hope to many who found themselves suffering under this burden.[2]

1. Paul J. Wojda, 'Liberation theology' in Richard P. McBrien, General
Editor, *The HarperCollins Encyclopedia of Catholicism* (HarperCollins
Publishers, New York, 1995), 768.
2. Leonardo Boff & Clodovis Boff, *Liberation and Theology 1: Introducing
Liberation Theology* (Burns & Oates, Tunbridge Wells, Kent, 1987), 66-7;
Arthur F. McGovern SJ, *Liberation Theology and its Critics: Towards an
Assessment* (Orbis Books, New York, 1989), 6-7.

In the churches too a great wind of renewal began to blow in the early 1960s even before Vatican II. A new emphasis on the involvement of the laity emerged, the educational work of Paulo Freire in Brazil became influential, student movements and Christian Democratic political parties were formed, foreign missionaries arrived in great numbers and European theology, especially political theology, began to have a notable effect on the thinking of many theologians in Latin America in relation to society and social justice. Then came Vatican II which, together with some papal documents of that time, laid the foundation of liberation theology.[3]

Latin American thinkers and theologians were encouraged to reflect creatively on their situation in society, and in particular on the relationship between faith and poverty, the gospel and social justice, etc. Even as early as 1964 Gustavo Gutierrez, a Peruvian theologian, was speaking of theology as critical reflection on praxis, an approach which was further developed in the following years. But it was the Second General Conference of the Latin American Bishops (CELAM), meeting in Medellin, Columbia in 1968, which gave the newly developing theology its greatest impetus.[4]

The emphasis now shifted from development to liberation as people came to realise that the real problem in Latin America was not lack of development but the dependence of Latin American economies on the rich industrial nations of the North and especially the USA. What was needed, then, it was becoming clear, was liberation from that dependence. In this context the bishops and the Latin American theologians began to elaborate a theology or Christian understanding of this liberation. This found its fullest and most influential expression in Gutierrez's 1971 book, *A Theology of Liberation,* a work that has since become a classic and the basic text for liberation theology. Defining this new method of doing theology as critical reflection on Christian praxis in the light of the Word (of God), Gutierrez understands theology as focusing on the pressing social and political concerns of Latin America and on liberation from the poverty, oppression and dependency that so characterised the societies of that continent. Several biblical themes showing God and Jesus as liberating from sin and its consequences (oppression, injustice, etc.) are

3. Boff & Boff, 67-8; McGovern, 4-6.
4. Denis Carroll, *What is Liberation Theology?* (Mercier Press, 1987) 14-17.

then taken up and expounded. Gutierrez also challenges the church to become involved in the struggles of the poor, though of course that means it cannot avoid being political.[5]

Liberation Theology advanced very significantly from these early defining moments and gained widespread favour and influence.[6]

But opposition was not far away and it too became vociferous and powerful. Perhaps the sharpest clash took place in Chile where the bishops voiced major criticisms of a group set up in 1972 called Christians for Socialism (CFS) and banned clergy from joining it. This group had been severely critical of church teaching and called for radical, revolutionary Christianity. In this they were not representative of liberation theology generally but, as things turned out, the views of the Chilean bishops in relation to this group greatly affected church attitudes to liberation theology. In particular the 1984 Vatican instruction on liberation theology reflects almost point for point the charges made by the bishops of Chile against CFS. All the failings of that organisation's teaching were, it seems, attributed to liberation theology itself, though liberation theology was less marxist, less aggressive and less critical of the church's social teaching than CFS.[7]

Some saw this as a carefully orchestrated plan to discredit liberation theology.[8]

But, if it was, it didn't succeed, though it undoubtedly had significant negative effects on liberation theology and those associated with it.

Of great significance also in the development of liberation theology was the Third General Conference of CELAM in Puebla, Mexico in 1979 which was attended by John Paul II. The bishops made liberation a prominent theme in their final document, encouraged the base communities and stressed the preferential option for the poor. The Pope warned that the church's mission is not political and that Jesus should not be presented as a revolutionary.[9]

5. Gustavo Gutierrez, *A Theology of Liberation: History, Politics and Salvation* (Orbis Books, New York, 1973), chapter 1; see Boff & Boff, 68-70; McGovern, 7-11; Wojda, 768.
6. Boff & Boff, 73-5.
7. McGovern, 12-3.
8. McGovern, 13.
9. Third General Conference of Latin American Bishops, Puebla:

The 1984 Vatican Instruction on liberation theology, issued by Cardinal Ratzinger's Congregation for the Doctrine of the Faith (CDF), aimed to draw attention to the deviations and risks of deviations to be found in certain forms of liberation theology. This document seems to have been aimed at particular prominent liberation theologians and articulated three main criticisms of liberation theology: a) While acknowledging that liberation is an authentic biblical theme and a legitimate focus for theological reflection, the Instruction charged that liberation theology, or at least certain unspecified forms of it, reduces faith to politics. b) Liberation theology also adopts marxism uncritically and allows its theology to become captive to marxist ideology. c) Liberation theology attacks authority in the church, rejecting its social doctrine, opposing a church of the poor to the hierarchical church, and discrediting the hierarchy by presenting them as belonging to the class of oppressors.[10]

This Instruction was followed in 1986 by the CDF's own understanding of what a theology of liberation should include and be about.[11]

This latter document understands liberation largely in terms of personal and spiritual freedom and only indirectly concerns itself with liberation theology as such. In the same year John Paul II's letter to the Brazilian bishops spoke of liberation theology as not only opportune but also as useful and necessary. This elicited the comment from one episcopal official of CELAM that the problem with liberation theology had passed for Latin Americans. Perhaps! But later critical comments from the Pope and other high church officials, and especially the continuing Vatican policy of appointing conservative bishops, seem to indicate otherwise.[12]

It should be remembered too that there has been noteworthy development in liberation theology itself, especially in the 1980s. It has moved to a position where marxism is now scarcely men-

Evangelisation at present and in the future of Latin America: Conclusions (St Paul Publications, Slough, England & Catholic Institute for International Relations, London,1980), 4.

10. Sacred Congregation for the Doctrine of the Faith, *Instruction on Certain Aspects of the 'Theology of Liberation'* (Veritas, Dublin, 1984), VII-X. See McGovern, 15-7; Carroll, 82-6; Wojda, 769.

11. Congregation for the Doctrine of the Faith, *Instruction on Christian Freedom and Liberation* (Catholic Truth Society, London, 1986).

12. McGovern, 18-9; Carroll, 90-1.

tioned at all, where there is much more emphasis on spirituality and so on the personal dimension of the Christian life, alongside the social and political. This also focuses more attention on God's presence in the world, especially in the midst of suffering and among the poor. While liberation theologians are usually opposed to capitalism and tend to favour socialism, they seem more recently to confine themselves largely to advocating the ideals of socialism without spelling out what sort of structures and institutions a socialist society might or should set up. In addition, liberation theologians in more recent times do very little social analysis; they tend to be more theological and lean more towards political democracy.[13]

No doubt the fall of communism in 1989 and the failure of the Soviet experiment in socialism has had a notable impact on how liberation theology and its practicioners have looked on socialism in the last decade or so. This has contributed to the declining interest in and advocacy of socialism in Latin America and would seem to lend force to the observation of Gutierrez in 1988 that socialism is not an essential of liberation theology.[14]

We in the West have heard relatively little about liberation theology in the 1990s. This would seem to reflect the developments mentioned in the last paragraph and also the growing influence on this theology, and on the Latin American church generally, of the increasingly conservative hierarchies of Latin America. There is no doubt, however, that the poverty and oppression of the majority have been getting worse rather than better in Latin America in that decade. Thus, liberation theology remains as necessary as ever and will continue to make its contribution to understanding and doing justice well into the future, especially since the international context offers it a greater potential for growth and maturation and a challenge to consciously and critically respond to the urgent needs of the people.[15]

What is liberation theology?
We come now to the central issue we are concerned with in this chapter. It presents us with considerable difficulties, not just

13. McGovern, 86-9, 132-3, 180-6.
14. McGovern, 148.
15. Pablo Richard, 'Liberation Theology in the New International Context', *PASOS*, Costa Rica, 1992, 4. See also Francisco Chamberlain SJ, 'What Remains to be done in Liberation Theology', *LADOC*, Vol. XXVII, n. 5, May/June 1997, 1-6.

because this theology is relatively new but also because it is so different from the kind of theologising we in the West are used to doing and hearing about. The main difference lies more in the way these theologians of liberation approach their subject and the theological method they employ than in what they basically assert. But these two, the method and the content, are so closely related that how this theology is done cannot really be separated from what is being said; its method powerfully influences its content. In fact it is very difficult to understand liberation theology and what its chief concerns are without some understanding of the approach and method being used by the theologians of liberation. Hence, we need to begin with a discussion of the theological method of liberation theology, and that will put us in a favourable position to understand what it is really saying, what its central assertions are. In other words, we focus first on how liberation theologians go about their work and follow that with some consideration of what they are saying. But these two are by no means fully separable and it is not always clear where method ends and content begins.

Theological Method of Liberation Theology
While most of us are, understandably, much more concerned about what the church teaches and what we ourselves believe and live by, than about how the church or we ourselves arrive at those beliefs or conclusions, there is great interest in theological circles today in the methods we use in doing our theology. It is generally recognised in fact that these methods are very important in relation to the content of the church's, our own or any theology. So a few words on method will be helpful.

A method of doing theology is an instrument or tool which we use to help us to understand theological truth, in this case, the doctrines of our religious faith. It is usually a complex reality and will be vindicated by the kind of theology to which it conduces. A method generally includes such things as the starting point we select, the presuppositions we work with, the sources we use, the authorities we appeal to and how we understand, interpret and bring all these into play as we reflect systematically on our faith. Quite often we are only dimly aware of the method we are using and at times we are completely in ignorance of it and even of the fact that we are making use of any method in our theological thinking. But it will be obvious that the method we use has great importance, and having at least a modicum of clarity about it would seem to be essential.

When we come to study liberation theology, we are confronted immediately by this question of theological method and we soon come to realise its vital importance. Complex and closely linked to the content of liberation theology though it be, we will endeavour to set out here briefly the main elements of the method used by liberation theologians in their work of understanding and living out the Christian gospel in their situation in Latin America. Our exposition of this method of doing theology will already bring it home to us that liberation theology is in significant ways quite different from theology as we usually understand and do it. We will see that it is indeed a new way of doing theology rather than simply a new theology which sets out to teach new doctrines that are not already found in the church's teaching.[16]

1) The theologian's faith-commitment: an option for the poor

For liberation theology the first essential for doing any theology is commitment to the task of achieving true liberation in human society. Hence, the theologian can't be just a theoretician but is to be primarily a worker for justice who is in some real way actively involved in the struggle to bring about social liberation. Now, given this,(s)he can begin to reflect systematically on what (s)he is experiencing in that struggle and do so in the light of her/his religious faith. The product of this reflection will then be this theologian's liberation theology. In other words, to be a theologian of liberation one must first have made a basic choice or fundamental option to work for social justice. This choice is usually referred to or expressed in the well-known phrase 'an option for the poor', which is explained as follows.

Workers for justice in Latin American societies will be sharing the experience and the problems, not of the rich minority or of government officials, but rather that of the great majority of the people who are, in fact, poor, deprived and oppressed by the structures of their own society, which are maintained in existence by the rich and the government. Now, this oppressed majority is usually referred to simply as 'the poor', and a person who wishes

16. See Roger Haight SJ, *An Alternative Vision: An Interpretation of Liberation Theology* (Paulist Press, New York, 1985), chapter III; Also Roger Haight SJ, 'Liberation Theology' in Joseph A. Komonchak, Mary Collins & Dermot A. Lane, Editors, *The New Dictionary of Theology* (Gill & Macmillan, Dublin, 1987), 572-3.

to be a liberation theologian must commit him/herself to seeking justice for them. In other words, (s)he must make an option for the poor as a precondition for her/his theological reflections on their experience and their struggle for justice.

To do this realistically one must in some true sense share the situation and experience of the poor. This will involve identifying with them to the extent of living with them and showing solidarity with them in their struggle. In addition, one is called on to share the biblically based belief that, if social justice is to be won, it will be won only through the action of the poor themselves; they are the main agents of justice in their own society.

2) Praxis: the starting point of liberation theology

In the light of this it is easy to see why one author has described liberation theology as 'critical reflection on Christian praxis in the light of the word of God'.[17]

Here the word praxis doesn't just mean practice or action of any sort. It means rather the practical activity needed to transform or liberate society and make it free and just. It is called forth by the actual socio-economic and political reality of society, with its injustice and oppression, and it is inspired and informed by the word of God in the scriptures and the church's teaching. Engagement in this Christian praxis is the expression and the proof of one's option for the poor. So the option for the poor issues in this Christian praxis and the praxis or activity for liberation helps to make justice and freedom realities in society. Theology, then, comes in as a second step.[18] It does not produce this pastoral activity but the theologian sets out to reflect on it in a systematic way, so as to elaborate a theoretical understanding of this praxis. Praxis, then, provides the raw material for the theologian in the construction of her/his liberation theology. This theology in turn influences and shapes the liberative action that must continue to take place in order that true and full liberation may become a reality in society. Liberation theology, then, does not begin with the scriptures or the church's teaching, but with the experience in society of poverty, oppression and injustice and the practical attempt to achieve liberation from them. And as a critical reflection on this liberative action, theology furthers the process of liberation for the community by pointing up faults

17. Gustavo Gutierrez, *A Theology of Liberation,* chapter 1. See McGovern, 32-35.
18. Gutierrez, 11; Boff & Boff, 4-9.

and wrong actions and by throwing the light of the Christian gospel on the situation in society and the activity undertaken to change it. Theology is, then, a practical activity, which thinks deeply for the purpose of taking action that will transform society as it is at present and so build a better future.

It can be seen from this that liberation theology gives precedence to praxis over theory or theology, and so follows the principle of the primacy of praxis or transformative action over theory. This implies, not just that how one actually lives conditions powerfully how one thinks and the theory one holds, but also that the basic test of Christian truth is right living (orthopraxis) even more than right believing (orthodoxy). The measure of right theory is, in fact, the extent to which it issues in right practice or living.

From all this it can be seen that liberation theologians believe that to do theology in a detached, theoretical way, as Western or first world theologians have long done, is to go a long way towards falsifying that theology at its very root. In practice, doing theology in this detached manner generally amounts to a passive acceptance of the status quo in one's society and, hence, often enough to the condoning of grave injustice.[19]

What we have said here makes the point also that liberation theology is very much a theology of experience. This is experience in and of society and particularly of its negative and destructive aspects. As such, the theology of liberation illustrates particularly well the rediscovery of and the return to experience that characterises contemporary theology in the west and around the world.[20]

3) Liberation: the central theme

As the name implies, and as will be already abundantly clear, liberation is chosen in the theology we are discussing as its basic concept or theme. The reason for this choice is that the theologians who do liberation theology see this as the fundamental need of their society at this time and, consequently, as the primary goal of their striving and the chief object of their reflections as theologians. Earlier, the emphasis in Latin American society and in the church there had been on development in the economic, social and political areas of life. It was soon realised, however,

---

19. Dermot A. Lane, *Foundations for a Social Theology* (Gill & Macmillan, Dublin, 1984), 19-24.
20. See Dermot A. Lane, *The Experience of God* (Veritas, Dublin, 1981), chapter 1.

that the real root of Latin America's problems was economic dependency and political domination, and that the efforts made to achieve development were not having the desired effects, largely because they failed to criticise or seek to change the existing economic, social and political structures and arrangements between the rich northern countries and the poor southern ones. Latin American under-development seemed more and more to be the by-product of the development of other countries.[21]

In addition, it became clear also that the concentration of the ownership of land in the hands of a small wealthy elite, to the exclusion of the vast majority of the poor population, contributes greatly to the poverty and oppression of that majority.[22]

In this context, what is needed is liberation from the poverty, oppression and injustice that so beset Latin American society.

It will be important to understand clearly what the theologians of liberation mean here by liberation. They do, of course, refer to and call for economic, social and political liberation. But that is not all they mean. Since they are reflecting on society and its injustices in the light of their Christian faith, liberation is understood as freeing people to assume control of their own lives and to become fully human persons, free from all that prevents them from being in communion with self, with others and with God. The point is made also that all these aspects of human liberation are interconnected and, while they are distinct, they are not separable. In other words, liberation is about freeing people from personal and social immorality and sin.[23]

4) The vision that inspires: a new humanity

Another basic element in the theological method of liberation theology is its vision of the future, its ultimate goal or fulfilment. This is what it often refers to as a new humanity, the 'Utopia' we look forward to, when all oppression and injustice have been removed and justice and integral liberation have been achieved. This will be God's reign of perfect love and justice, God's kingdom finally and fully established. It is this vision, general and far from being realised though it is, which is the inspiration for the struggle for justice and liberation now going on and for the critical reflection on that struggle which we call the theology of liberation.

21. Gutierriez, 26, 82-8; McGovern, 135-8; Boff & Boff, 4-6.
22. McGovern, 168-176; Gutierrez, 84-8.
23. Carroll, 32-4; Gutierrez, 88-92.

5) The use of scripture in liberation theology

The theological method of liberation theology involves a particular way of understanding and applying scripture. It is a way that its users find relevant to and valuable in their economic, social and political situation in Latin America, and one that tends to support the theological emphases and social concerns that are foremost in liberation theology. The perspective from which the Bible is read by liberation theologians is that of the poor and oppressed people of Latin America. This is also the perspective from which it is read in and by the base Christian communities in Brazil and other countries on that continent. Hence, liberation theology stresses themes that speak to the poor and oppressed, e.g. God as liberator, especially in the Exodus event, the prophets' call to social justice, Jesus' option for and ministry to the poor and marginalised, the kingdom of God and the final vision of God's reign of justice, love and peace, etc. This emphasis is not, however, placed to the exclusion of everything else. Liberation theologians are very aware that, while these themes may not be the most important in the Bible, they are the most relevant to the poor in their situation of oppression and injustice.[24]

Liberation theology does not pretend to give a neutral or academically detached reading of the scriptures, nor one that is timeless or universally valid in all cases. But neither does it hide its own perspective from which it interprets the scriptural text. The important thing, these theologians see, is not so much interpreting the scriptural text as interpreting life according to the scriptures.[25]

Others might well interpret the same passages differently, but this does not necessarily involve distortion, since no one is fully free from concerns and interests, often unrecognised, which influence their interpretation of the Bible or at least parts of it. As we will see later, this approach to the Bible has been criticised by some in the church as being unfaithful to the Bible and the teaching of the church. In response to this, the incompleteness of some liberation themes is admitted, some emphases have changed and fidelity to God's word in its totality is stressed.[26]

---

24. Boff &Boff, 32-3; McGovern 62-3.
25. Boff & Boff, 34.
26. McGovern, 63.

6) Social analysis and liberation theology

In liberation theology the experience of life among the poor and oppressed people of Latin America, and their struggle for integral liberation through liberating praxis, constitute the primary source and object of theological reflection. Now, to understand this experience as fully as possible, and to facilitate the best liberating praxis, one must seek to understand the society which generates them. So one must engage in an analysis of Latin American society, and to do that one needs an instrument of social analysis that is thorough and scientific. In search of such an instrument, liberation workers and theologians turn, not to philosophy, as western theology has long done, but to the social sciences. In doing this their aim is to uncover the causes of poverty and oppression in their society. When they have done this, liberation theologians seek to understand the situation in the light of Christian revelation, and especially in the light of those biblical themes that are most relevant to the situation of the poor and oppressed. They then respond to the obligation they feel to engage in social and political action, that is, liberating praxis, which will overcome the evils they have become aware of and help towards achieving integral liberation. We will look at how this social analysis is done by the theologians of liberation, giving it significant attention because of the controversies that have surrounded it.

Dependency[27]

In its earliest years, liberation theology tended to accept and make use of what is called dependency theory. This form of social analysis was widespread and very popular in Latin America in the late 1960s and the 1970s and provided significant insights into the causes of poverty, oppression and injustice there. This theory holds that the real problem in Latin America that results in grinding poverty and continuing oppression is not backwardness or laziness among the population, but rather the continent's deep economic dependence on the capitalist countries of the northern hemisphere, especially the USA. Latin America's underdevelopment is due, therefore, not just to lack of economic progress at home, but to the deeper cause of its longstanding and continuing dependence on the North. But this is not all. In addition to the fact of this dependence, there is the reality that Latin America is not merely underdeveloped but it is kept in this state

---

27. McGovern, 135-8; Carroll, 40-6.

of underdevelopment by the dominant northern economies. So northern development and wealth are built on southern or third world underdevelopment. Not surprisingly, then, many Latin American economists, social analysts and liberation theologians too became strongly critical of the economic model of development, or of what came to be called developmentalism, because they had come to understand it as being built on, and in fact maintaining, the dependence of Latin America on the USA and the rich northern countries. It was in the light of this social analysis that the concept of liberation became prominent in Latin America generally, and among liberation theologians also, and took on the political significance it soon acquired, particularly in liberation theology. The core point being asserted in this change was that what Latin America really needed was to be liberated from its economic and political dependence on the first world. To do this it was seen as essential to move away from the model of development and all it involved, and work towards liberation at the economic, social and political levels.

It will be noticed that this dependency theory places all the blame for Latin American underdevelopment and poverty on external factors and attributes it all to the exploitation of the North. Soon, however, some liberation theologians began to express reservations about this view. While there could be no doubt about the fact that Latin America is dependent on the rich nations of the North, there seemed also to be causes beyond external ones. The poverty and oppression in Latin America couldn't all be attributed to the exploitation of the periphery by the centre. In addition, liberation theologians began to point out that this theory was only a theory and not an established fact and that it did not offer any help towards finding a way out of this dependency. So it was that liberation theologians began to see dependency theory as simplistic when viewed as a full explanation of Latin America's situation. There were, it became clear, many internal factors as well that played a part in maintaining the dependence and the poverty and oppression we are discussing. Chief among them were the rich elites in Latin American countries, who held on to their wealth and power and sought to increase them, while ensuring that the poor remained so. Relevant too is the doctrine of national security to which many governments in Latin America, mostly dictatorships, adhered in the 1970s and 80s with devastating consequences: human rights widely violated, thousands made to disappear, torture frequently practised by state agencies, thousands murdered by right-wing death squads – and the vast majority of these victims coming from the poor and oppressed classes at the base of society. Here were other methods used by the rich elites and those in positions of power to maintain their power and affluence, while the poor and powerless were kept firmly in their place at the margins of society.

It will be noticed that here there is emphasis on conflict between different classes within Latin American society rather than reference to external causes for poverty and oppression. This points to the movement away from dependency theory, which was more and more being seen as an inadequate tool for analysing society in Latin America and indicates a trend towards a more class-conscious analysis of the causes of poverty and oppression in the South.

Anti-capitalism and socialism in liberation theology
Liberation theology has from its beginning taken a very negative view of capitalism as the economic system that is the root cause of Latin America's economic and social problems. Latin American capitalism is dependent capitalism and so long as that capitalism remains in place the problems of that continent can't be solved. So capitalism must be overcome and replaced.[28]

Given this strong anti-capitalist position of liberation theology and of many others as well, it is not surprising that people came to look towards marxism, and especially marxist social analysis, as offering perhaps a more illuminating understanding of the problems of Latin America and to see in socialism a way out of the dependence and poverty that had for so long held Latin American society in their grip. So we need to turn our attention to marxist social analysis and how it is viewed and used by liberation theologians.

Marxist analysis in liberation theology
In its early days especially, liberation theology advocated the use of Marx's analysis of society as a tool or instrument with which to understand the economic, social and political problems besetting Latin American societies, but being careful at the same time to

---

28. McGovern, 138-140; Nicholas Lobkowitz, 'Historical Materialism', *Sacramentum Mundi* (Herder & Herder, New York & Burns & Oates, London, 1969), 3, 426-8.

distinguish this analysis from marxist ideology (its materialism, determinism and atheism) which liberation theologians were unanimous in rejecting.

Marxist social analysis states that economic factors are most decisive in shaping society and creating change over the course of time. The key to understanding these changes is to be found in the manner in which humans bring about economic production, i.e. the modes by which they produce goods. These modes depend on the natural resources, labour skills and tools available at a given time but, more importantly, they depend on how work is socially organised, that is, what Marx calls the relations of production. In capitalist society there are owners or capitalists and workers, and these form two social classes, capital and labour, with the capitalists being the dominant and wealthy class. It is important to note here that it is this socio-economic organisation of life in society at the material level which determines the general character of the social, political and spiritual processes of life generally. And of course it is the dominant class which is best served by the social, political and legal arrangements in any particular society, and whose interests are given preference in the state and its laws and in the cultural and religious ideas that prevail. This is a point that is given great prominence in liberation theology. Thus the economic system and the structures of society favour the capitalist class or the bourgeoisie, while the poor workers or the proletariat are placed in a position which ensures that they remain poor and oppressed. From this situation class struggle emerges and will inevitably lead to a social revolution (not necessarily violent). This will in part be due to the fact that capitalism contains the seeds of its own destruction, but also to the revolutionary praxis (that is, group action to transform society in accordance with the values of the workers) that would be necessary to bring socialism and the classless society it will lead to into existence.[29]

Engaging in social analysis as an aid to constructing a theology, especially a social theology, is now quite common in the Christian churches, but it is the use of this marxist analysis above all which has raised serious questions about liberation theology

---

29. McGovern, 123-4; Carroll, 40-46; Boff & Boff, 27-8. Marx did not specify what this revolutionary praxis might be or involve but Lenin did, when he spoke of the dictatorship of the proletariat, the possibility of violent revolution and the necessity of atheism. See McGovern, 123-4.

and made this element of its theological method a matter of great controversy, especially in the Catholic Church. Later we will discuss the criticisms of this use of marxist social analysis in liberation theology along with other criticisms that have been made of liberation theology.

7) The turn to politics

We saw earlier that as an expression of his/her option for the poor, the worker for liberation and, so, the liberation theologian, engages in social action for liberation and then reflects critically on this in the light of Christian revelation. The result of the reflection will be further action for liberation now shaped and inspired by biblical and Christian themes and values. Here we are talking about what we previously referred to as liberating praxis and, in the context of the social theology we are discussing, we may speak of it also as a turn to politics. Here politics is used in a very wide sense, referring not to party politics or even to the whole business of governing society, which is our non-party meaning of the word. For the theology of liberation politics is simply group action for social justice or social action for liberation or, again, liberating praxis. In this sense of the phrase, all in society can and should be involved in politics and this includes the church and its bishops, priests, religious and laity.

In this regard liberation theologians and other workers for liberation stress the point that one cannot be neutral or avoid taking sides. Doing nothing is really supporting the unjust status quo in Latin America. On the other hand, making an option for the poor involves a political commitment to working for justice in society. We may say, then, that the theology of liberation is a form of political theology in which social and political action for justice and liberation is the primary practical concern and aim. And as has already been noted, this liberative praxis also constitutes a very important element in the theological method of liberation theology.

The Theological Content of Liberation Theology

After our rather lengthy consideration of the method employed by liberation theologians in doing their theologising, and the various elements involved in that method, we are now in a position to move on to what will appear much less new and controversial, namely, what the liberation theologians have to say about the main Christian doctrines which are relevant to and important for the concerns of liberation theology. In other words, we turn from theological method to theological content. And as we noted earlier, method and content are here closely related, so that in speaking about method we have already spoken about the way liberation theology treats the central Christian beliefs, e.g. God, Christ, the church, etc. Hence, a rather brief treatment will be adequate at this point.

1) God and Christ

In the theology of liberation God is understood primarily as Liberator/Saviour of humanity from sin and all that involves. Abundant evidence for this model of God is to be found in the scriptures, especially in the Old Testament. The Exodus is characterised as the great liberating event of salvation history before Christ. God the Liberator is active in this event to free God's people, not just from spiritual bonds but from all oppressive forces, especially social, economic and political ones.[30]

Thus, God wills and is active in the world in the cause of integral liberation for humanity. God has made an option for the poor and calls all to work for this same liberation by also making this option for the poor who most need liberation. Such an option will require one to engage in political or community action for justice in society. The message of the prophets also is a denunciation of injustice in society, of the oppression of the poor by the rich and powerful, and constitutes a call to do justice, especially for the poor and the powerless. It is clear here that liberation theology sees God as present and active in human history, as working in and through human action for justice and as enabling us humans to take part in the struggle for justice and liberation.[31]

Christ is the sacrament of this God of Liberation. In Christ God has entered history fully to continue God's liberating work at a new level and a new intensity. Jesus is, then, the Liberator God incarnate giving us the gift of integral liberation and salvation and empowering us to work for and achieve that liberation as we make our option for the poor and commit ourselves to action for social justice. In doing christology, liberation theologians tend to start from below and focus on the humanity of Jesus and the words, life and historical journey of Jesus Christ. The central message of Jesus lies in his preaching of the kingdom of God. This is a social image and presents us with an ideal model or reli-

30. McGovern, 65-9.
31. Carroll, 50-54.

gious vision for human society. The full and final coming of the kingdom will involve the total transformation of this world, free from all that alienates human beings, free from pain, sin, divisions and death.[32]

Jesus made an option for the poor and a lot of his ministry was concerned with the weak, the excluded and the despised. This was Jesus' liberative praxis as he inaugurated the kingdom and, while he stressed the personal dimension of this ministry, for him the coming of the kingdom must have a socio-political form. His death was intrinsically connected to the mission and work of his life and resulted from the reaction of a system threatened by his liberative practice.[33]

Liberation theologians nowhere present Jesus as a revolutionary but as the liberator of the poor from poverty, oppression and injustice.

(2) Liberation and Christian salvation

The theology of liberation, anxious as it is to overcome any misconceived dualism between God and humanity, grace and nature, etc., sees the process of human liberation as intimately linked with the reality of Christian liberation/salvation, though they should not be identified with each other. As Gutierrez says, the growth of the kingdom is a process which occurs historically in liberation; the historical, political liberating event is the growth of the kingdom and is a salvific event, but it is not the coming of the kingdom, not all of salvation. Hence, Christians are called to work for salvation and the coming of the kingdom by immersing themselves in the process of human liberation in society. Whatever promotes this liberation is salvific; whatever oppresses human beings is of sin and the opposite of salvation. In other words, siding with humanity is siding with the Christian God, and love of that God is expressed in and through love of one's neighbours, especially those who are poor and oppressed.[34]

(3) The church and its mission in the world

In line with what has been said above, the theology of libera-

---

32. Leonardo Boff, *Jesus Christ Liberator, A Critical Christology for Our Time* (Maryknoll, New York, Orbis, 1978; original 1972), 44-47 as quoted in McGovern, 74; Haight, *An Alternative Vision*, 137.
33. Carroll, 55-8; McGovern 78.
34. Carroll, 31-4; Gutierrez, *A Theology of Liberation*, chapter 9, especially p 177.

tion highlights some particular models or images of the church. These models are given preference because they fit better with some fundamental presuppositions or principles of liberation theology about the church. We may list three main principles here.[35]

a) The church should be understood in relation to the world. It is not a self-enclosed community concerned only about its own welfare and growth. Rather it is in the world and for it. It has to be some sort of medium or link between God and human society, an instrument seeking to fulfil God's purposes for the world. Hence, the ideas of the church as sacrament of God and Christ and as the servant of human society and its members.[36]

b) The church is not the centre of the world. God and God's Holy Spirit are at the centre and are active everywhere in the world, both inside and outside the church. But the church is special in God's plan for humanity and so it is to be understood as the sacrament of God's presence and love in and for the world. As such the church is called to witness to God's love and justice in the world and to cooperate with them as fully as possible in and by its liberative praxis.

c) The church has a specific role to play in the world. Its mission has an essential social dimension by which it is to cooperate with others and work for the good of all. So the church is called to criticise situations of social injustice and to engage in evangelisation and liberative activity for the welfare of society and its members. In other words, the church in its mission must be committed to the building of a just social order; it must be an active promoter of social justice and integral liberation. Given these presuppositions about the church, liberation theology understands the church as basically the community of believers in Jesus as Lord and Saviour and tends to take a rather negative view in relation to the church as institution. On the other hand, a very positive view of the Base Christian Communities in Latin America characterises liberation theology. They are seen as a valid and important realisation of the church and, in fact, they constitute a new way of being church.[37]

The church has a mission to the world: it is the sacrament of God's and Christ's love for humanity and also the sacrament of

---

35. See Haight, *An Alternative Vision*, 163-6.
36. See Gutierrez, chapter 12.
37. McGovern, 214-8.

truly human living, showing by the quality of its own life what living in a truly human manner really is and involves. In consequence of this emphasis liberation theology stresses, in relation to the church, praxis, doing and bearing witness to the truth and functioning as servant of God and of humanity in its life, structures and activities.

A fuller development of this ecclesiology or understanding of the church and its mission highlights a relatively new model of the church. This is the church from, with and for the poor. Not just a church for the poor which is a well established idea but, more importantly, one that comes from the poor and is seen to be in solidarity with them. Such a model of the church presupposes a preferential option for the poor and implies that the church is of and with the poor. At the same time the church's mission is universal as it seeks to bring integral liberation/salvation to all.[38]

(4) *The spirituality of liberation*

Spirituality, though very difficult to define or describe, may be said to signify the whole way of life of the Christian, the manner in which the Christian lives in the church and in the world.[39]

There are two levels in this spirituality. Firstly, there is the actual living of one's Christian life from day to day. At this level there are as many spiritualities as there are Christians. A second level of spirituality refers to our understanding of this Christian living. All of us have some sort of understanding of the lives we lead, some view of the meaning of the life that is ours, but it is very often implicit and not reflected on. When that understanding is made explicit in a thorough manner, then we have a systematic conception or theory of our Christian life, of our Christian spirituality. These two levels or dimensions of Christian spirituality are two aspects of the one reality and can't really be separated. Together they constitute our Christian spirituality. In addition, they influence one another in a kind of circular fashion: in seeking to understand our Christian life more fully, we engage in critical reflection on it and that may lead us to modify some of the values, principles and practices that we have been living by and so to arrive at a somewhat different manner of living as Christians.[40]

---

38. Carroll, 61-7.
39. Haight, *An Alternative Vision*, 240-1; Gutierrez, 203-4. See also Chapter 11 below.
40. Haight, *An Alternative Vision*, 241-2.

In the 1980s writings on spirituality far outnumbered works in all the areas of liberation theology that had been contentious. In fact, spirituality was then the dominant theme of liberation theology.This spirituality involves both a call to follow Jesus in working for and with the poor, but also profound reflection on what all Christians can learn about God from the poor.[41]

Essentially liberation spirituality calls for a commitment to the process of liberating the poor and oppressed from all that weighs them down and keeps them from achieving integral liberation as persons in the church and in the world.This will involve a profound conversion to the neighbour, so that one engages in liberative praxis as the way of transforming society in favour of the poor and oppressed.

In presenting its spirituality in this manner, liberation theology can be said to be reacting against a one-sided view of four different aspects of the Christian life.[42]

a) Moving from an over-emphasis on the transcendent dimension of God, liberation spirituality stresses that God is immanent in our world and especially in our neighbours and it is only in and through these that God can be encountered today.

b) Reacting against a split between the spiritual and material or corporeal dimensions of the person or of human existence, liberation spirituality emphasises that the Christian life embraces the whole human being, body and soul and involves living a corporeal and bodily existence in the world according to the Spirit of God.

c) The spirituality of the liberation theologians seeks to find a correct balance between action and contemplation in the Christian life, in this way correcting an imbalance that tended to make contemplation the highest Christian ideal. Thus, this spirituality insists on the formula 'contemplation in action', that is, contemplation both within the context of Christian activity, stemming from it and leading back to it, and within activity itself.[43]

d) Finally, the tension between the personal and the social dimensions of human existence gets a lot of attention in liberation spirituality. Avoiding a one-sided focus on the individual's personal relationship with God that tends towards individualism

41. McGovern, 83.
42. Haight, 236-9.
43. Haight, 238; McGovern, 84, 86-7.

and privatisation, this spirituality re-emphasises the social aspect of the person and of our existence in the world. Thus, our relationships with God, with the self and with others in society must be governed by our Christian spirituality and it is towards all of these that our Christian love and compassion must be directed.

It will be clear from what has here been said that the spirituality of liberation theology is central to it and is carefully attended to and elaborated. It is a distinctive Christian spirituality and very much in line with the central emphases of liberation theology on the option for the poor and commitment to liberative praxis as basic to Christian living and theologising.

(5) Base Christian Communities

No consideration of the Latin American Church and of liberation theology in our day would be complete without some reference to the vital role played in both by what are called base (or basic) Christian (or ecclesial) communities (BCC), to which passing reference has already been made. There were said to be up to 70,000 such BCCs in Latin America in the 1970s and 80s but one has the impression that they have not prospered so well in the 1990s, or at least we haven't heard so much about them.

These communities are small groups of Christians from the base of society, the poor, which have been formed at the grassroots level of the church. They devote themselves to reflection on the Bible and its implications for themselves, to prayer and to planning activities to promote social justice and liberation in their local area. It is from these little groups that a great deal of the inspiration and action for justice and liberation has come in the Latin American church. They have been very influential in the development of liberation theology itself; they embody its spirit and can be considered as a general expression of it in practice.[44]

These BCCs are frequently spoken of as showing us a new way of being church. This assertion is made because BCCs involve some major shifts in how they as church work: a shift from clerical dominance to the active presence of lay people and religious women; a shift from an overly spiritualist approach to a broader one that incorporates human material needs as well; a shift from treating people as objects of evangelisation to respecting them as active subjects of their own spiritual development; a shift from a paternalistic role on the part of the institutional

44. McGovern, 199.

church to the model of a church of service; a shift from seeing church action as always coming from the top down to endorsing creativity coming from below; a shift from starting from theory to using experience and reality as the basis for reflection.[45]

The Latin American bishops at Puebla referred to BCCs as a 'reason for joy and hope' and as 'centres of evangelisation and moving forces of liberation', while the Vatican's Instruction on Christian Freedom and Liberation (1986) is also positive, if guarded, in their regard. BCCs have been most widespread and influential in Brazil but they have been significant elsewhere too.[46]

Evaluation of the Theology of Liberation
Making a balanced assessment of liberation theology is particularly difficult because of a number of factors. It is a quite new theology. It originated and developed in a society vastly different from those in the Western world in major respects. Its focus on the economic, social and political dimensions of life in society tends to evoke strong reactions from first world citizens and even South Americans and makes fair theological judgment more difficult than usual. The Latin American church is in many ways quite different from the churches of the West and has in recent decades chosen some priorities and emphases that we in the west may find hard to understand fully or sympathise with. Also the Latin American church has been and is sharply divided over liberation theology. Finally, the theology of liberation has itself developed in its thinking in significant ways over the decades since it began, while its progress has been negatively affected by attitudes in the institutional church towards it. These attitudes have been changing in the 1980s and especially in the 1990s as the Vatican policy of appointing bishops who are unsympathetic to it has become more pronounced and its effects more profound and far reaching.

In this context we will highlight some areas of agreement and some of disagreement.
Areas of agreement
There seems to be fairly general agreement that the theology of

---

45. McGovern 202-3, quoting Marcello Azevedo, *Basic Ecclesial Communities in Brazil*, 245-6.
46. McGovern, 208-212; See Niall O'Brien, 'Basic Christian Communities – A Six Year Parish Experiment', *The Furrow*, February 1984, 92-102.

liberation can and should be seen as a new way of doing theology. This means that its methodology is so significantly different from classical European theology, as we have seen, that it amounts to a methodological revolution. In other words, its whole approach to and manner of reflecting critically and systematically on our Christian faith and experience are basically new, at least in modern times, and this justifies us in referring to liberation theology as a new kind of theology or, more accurately, a new way of theologising. This newness in method may explain in part at least the caution of many including the Vatican in relation to liberation theology.

Turning to some elements within the theology of liberation, we find widespread ageement on the basic analysis of the economic, social and political problems in many Latin American countries: the situation is one of grave social and political oppression, injustice and poverty. The consequent obligation on Christians and others to work for social justice and liberation in these societies by social and political action or, in other words, the duty to make an option for the poor, is generally recognised also both inside and outside the church. Few would deny too that this obligation should be a top priority for the churches and all their members. All this is summed up and powerfully advocated in the documents of the Medellin and Puebla episcopal conferences. The strong condemnation there of all violence, especially institutional and revolutionary violence, is another topic on which liberation theologians are unanimous, despite there being some reluctance by one or two to make this an absolute judgment.

Finally, no claims are made that the theology of liberation is either definitive or perfect. All see it as open to criticism and improvement and, as has been noted, it has evolved in notable ways in the last two decades, in part at least as it has endeavoured to respond to its critics. It would be conceded also that some advocates of liberation theology have damaged their own cause by exaggerated or careless assertions, thus giving an opening for some extreme critics to make serious but rather unfair accusations. Today, however, liberation theologians are generally careful to avoid such statements and have clarified their positions in significant ways.

Areas of disagreement

The element of the theology of liberation that has caused the most controversy has been its use of marxist ideas and social analysis. The 1984 Vatican Instruction made this its major criticism of liberation theology, speaking of certain forms of liberation theology as using 'in an insufficiently critical manner, concepts borrowed from various currents of marxist thought'. This the document calls 'a deviation damaging to faith and Christian living', adding that 'if one tries to take only one part, say, the analysis, one ends up having to accept the entire (marxist) ideology'. Many critics in the church echo this viewpoint, the central criticism made against the theology of liberation.[47]

Supporters of liberation theology and many fair-minded commentators consider this criticism to be unjustified, because they see it as not well grounded and as simply not the case.

We should note, as we begin to consider this objection to liberation theology, that liberation theologians have never made a great deal of use of marxist analysis and most of the time they have talked about using it rather than use it themselves. In the 1980s and 90s there has been very little reference to marxism or its analysis in liberation theology, and so the importance given to marxist ideas in liberation theology has diminished siginificantly.[48]

It is clear that no liberation theologian accepts the materialist philosophy of marxism. In addition, these theologians believe that marxist analysis can be separated from the philosophical worldview of marxism, a point disputed by the 1984 Vatican Instruction. The liberationist position here is supported by the fact that no logical or intrinsic connection binds the analysis and worldview together. They came to be linked together historically by Engels, Lenin and Stalin.[49]

In addition, the church and its theologians have throughout history borrowed insights, concepts and methods to help articulate the faith and haven't been captured by the unacceptable systems of the thinkers in question. John Paul II himself borrows concepts from marxism. And even the critics of liberation theology admit that marxist analysis has been useful in pointing out structural injustices in Latin American society.[50]

47. See McGovern 151-2.
48. McGovern, 161, 164; Arthur F. McGovern SJ, *Marxism: An American Christian Perspective* (Orbis Books, Maryknoll, New York, 1981) 183-4.
49. McGovern, *Marxism: An American Christian Perspective*, 49-64; McGovern, *Liberation Theology and its Critics*, 161.
50. McGovern, *Liberation Theology and its Critics*, 161.

We can say, then, with reasonable certainty that liberation theologians have not used marxist analysis in an uncritical way and today are far from doing so. So, while the Vatican's criticism may well apply to the radical group in Chile called Christians for Socialism, a group against whom this criticism was first directed by the Chilean bishops, it is not well directed against liberation theologians, past or present.[51]

The criticism is also expressed that liberation theology, at least in some of its forms, takes an exclusively political view of the Bible and so reduces Christianity to a purely political form of salvation or liberation. This again is denied by the proponents of liberation theology. They assert that, while their main emphasis is political in the wide sense of social action for the transformation of society, it is by no means an exclusive emphasis. They clearly affirm the other dimensions of Christian salvation, including its personal dimension and, above all, its religious or transcendent aspect.[52]

Some charge liberation theologians with advocating violence or violent revolution. But this seems to be a baseless criticism as no statements to that effect have been found in the writings of these theologians. They do talk of social revolution and revolutionary change but these do not imply violence. On the other hand, liberation theologians point out that Latin American society is characterised by a great deal of institutional violence, i.e. oppressive regimes, laws and state practices that violate human rights and serve to maintain social injustice. This tends to provoke armed resistance as a counter measure.[53]

Likewise, liberation theology recognises that class struggle is a reality, a fact in Latin America and that there is much social conflict in that society, as John Paul II himself confirms. But no liberation theologian advocates class struggle as a remedy for social injustice.[54]

It is objected also that liberation theology appears to talk of and even to want to set up a 'people's church' as distinct from,

51. Carroll, 44-6, 69-71, 84-6; Rosino Gibellini, *The Liberation Theology Debate* (SCM Press, London, 1987), 46-7,
52. See Gutierrez, *The Power of the Poor in History* (SCM Press, London, 1983), chapter 1; McGovern, *Liberation Theology and its Critics,* chapter 4, especially 80-2; Carroll, 35-40.
53. McGovern, *Liberation Theology and its Critics,* 186-9.
54. McGovern, 187-8; Carroll, 75-7, Gibellini, 47.

and perhaps in opposition to, the church as institutional or hierarchical. Such a view misrepresents the mainstream of liberation
theology. Some statements of some liberation theologians might
suggest this division or opposition but, in so far as they do, they
need to be clarified and perhaps modified. Generally, however,
what is meant by this kind of language is not a revolt against the
hierarchy but a new emphasis on the Vatican II theme of the
church as the People of God, and a reference to that part of the
church which lives out the preferential option for the poor and
practises a liberating evangelisation.[55]

Here is a new way of being church, where the church is not
simply *for* the poor but is a church *of* the poor, where the poor
constitute its basis. The stress, then, is on the church as a servant
of the poor, especially in the context of the base ecclesial communities that are so widespread in Latin America.[56]

At the same time, to be true to itself the church of the poor
must retain a wider communion with the universal church and
the hierarchical church too. And, to remain relevant to the lives
of the poor at the base of society in Latin America, the church
universal and hierarchical needs the church of the poor and even
liberation theology.[57]

Conclusion

There is no doubt that the theology of liberation has been and is a
significant development in the church and has achieved much
since its beginning after Vatican II. It is clearly not a passing fad
and has been accepted in many of its main points by the highest
authorities in the church. It has become a source of worldwide interest, influence and inspiration inside and outside the Catholic
Church and in the process has developed and deepened its insights in many areas, e.g. spirituality, and in significant ways it
has overcome the main weaknesses that brought it so much
criticism early on.

One can, therefore, only be saddened by the turn of events in
the last decade or so whereby it seems that church authorities in
the Vatican and many in Latin America itself have turned against
liberation theology and all its activities and have even shown

55. Gibellini, 32.
56. McGovern, *Liberation Theology and its Critics,* chapter 11, Carroll, 61-7,
Gibellini, 31-2
57. McGovern, 220-3.

themselves hostile to all it stands for. Especially important here has been the appointment by the Vatican of many conservative, and in particular Opus Dei, bishops who have sought to undo as much as possible of what had been achieved by the movement for liberation and its theologians. One author[58] recently described the situation in El Salvador in forthright terms, saying that the decline of liberation theology there is indisputable and base communities are thin on the ground, with fewer than 3 per cent of Catholics attending them. Liberation theology is less coherent now in the post-war period and its adherents are greatly reduced in number. But it has not disappeared. 20 per cent of clergy favour its approach, while another 20 per cent oppose it. Liberationists still remain active implementing programmes and classes. While this author says that some of this decline has been self-inflicted, the main cause has been the hostility of the hierarchy. The strategy has not been to reform liberation theology but to undo and remove all traces of it. There have been frequent denunciations of it by bishops and many of them have withdrawn funding and support; priests have been strategically shifted and nuns expelled. Drastic changes have been made in the seminary curriculum, books have been banned. But it is the sermons that most register the change. All this amounts to a purge of liberation theology as the church in El Salvador has been re-romanised. Priorities about maintaining orthodoxy and reasserting church authority appear to outweigh social concerns.[59]

One has to assume that similar trends have been showing themselves in Brazil, Peru and other Latin American countries.

All this, combined with the worsening of economic and social conditions in most Latin American countries, has served to dim today the hopes expressed in liberation theology in its earliest years. While it is true that liberation theology has had a lower profile in the church outside Latin America in the 1990s than it had earlier, and has suffered a decline and renewed opposition within the continent, there is no doubt that its contribution to church life, the welfare of society and especially the poor remains very important. New theologians are needed to carry on the work of the first generation of theologians; new thinking is probably called for also and new ways of living out the option for the

---

58. Marianne Johnson,'The Hand of Opus Dei in El Salvador' *The Tablet*, 18 November 2000, 1552-3.
59. McGovern, *Liberation Theology and its Critics*, 231.

poor must be devised. Above all, however, a renewal of the spirit, attitudes and priorities of Vatican II at the level of the Vatican, many of the bishops and of the clergy, would see liberation theology and the practitioners of liberation re-invigorated. Then the option for the poor would be much more widely made and acted out of, and the poor themselves would take significant steps towards the integral liberation and salvation that the gospel and the theology of liberation both proclaim is the basic gift God wills them all to enjoy.

Further Reading

Boff, Leonardo & Boff, Clodivus, *Introducing Liberation Theology* (Liberation and Theology Series, 1) (Burns & Oates, Tunbridge Wells, Kent, & Orbis Books, Maryknoll, New York, 1987);

Carroll, Denis, *What is Liberation Theology?* (Mercier Press, Cork & Fowler Wright, Leominster, England, 1987);

Congregation for the Doctrine of the Faith, *Instruction on Certain Aspects of the Theology of Liberation* (Veritas, Dublin 1984);

Congregation for the Doctrine of the Faith, *Instruction on Christian Freedom and Liberation* (CTS, London, 1986);

Cosgrave, William, 'The Theology of Liberation', *The Furrow,* August 1986;

Gibellini, Rosino, *The Liberation Theology Debate,* (SCM Press, London, 1987);

Gutierrez, Gustavo, *A Theology of Liberation* (Orbis Books, Maryknoll, New York, 1973);

Gutierrez, Gustavo, *The Power of the Poor in History: Selected Writings* (SCM Press, London, 1983);

Haight, Roger, *An Alternative Vision: An Interpretation of Liberation Theology* (Paulist Press, New York, 1985);

Haight, Roger, 'Liberation Theology', in Joseph A. Komonchak, Mary Collins & Dermot A. Lane, Editors, *The New Dictionary of Theology* (Gill & Macmillan, Dublin, 1987), 570-6;

Lane, Dermot A., Editor, *Liberation Theology: An Irish Dialogue* (Gill & Macmillan, Dublin,1977);

McGovern Arthur F. SJ, *Liberation Theology and its Critics* (Orbis Books, New York, 1989);

McGovern, Arthur F. SJ, *Marxism: An American Christian Perspective* (Orbis Books, New York, 1981).

CHAPTER 10

Development in Church Teaching on Religious Freedom

In modern times the idea of religious freedom is being more and more widely recognised, accepted and respected by churches, societies and states, particularly in the Western world. In the Catholic Church this concept has figured prominently in official teaching, especially in the last hundred years or so.

In this chapter an attempt will be made to trace briefly the history of religious freedom in the teaching of the Catholic Church and also in that of the World Council of Churches. We will, then, illustrate the operation of that teaching of the Catholic Church before Vatican II and after it, in relation to specific socio-moral issues which have arisen in Irish society in the last fifty years. In the final section an examination will be made of how the teaching of Vatican II on religious freedom impacts on the Catholic citizen as he/she carries out the civic duty of voting in an election or a referendum.

Pre-Vatican II Catholic teaching
The issue of religious freedom has a long and difficult history in the Catholic Church and has been influenced by various historical, political, legal and theological developments. For our purposes here we may distinguish two stages in the evolution of church teaching on this topic prior to the Second Vatican Council (1962-5).

a) In the medieval period and down to the time of Pius IX (d. 1878) the essential teaching of the Catholic Church may be summarised as holding that the establishment of the Catholic Church as the official state religion was the only acceptable arrangement between church and state. Pius IX listed as error No 77 in his *Syllabus of Errors* (1864) the following statement: It is no longer expedient that the Catholic religion should be treated as the only religion of the state, all other forms of worship whatever being excluded.[1]

This pronouncement of Pius may be understood as summarising the main thrust of the position of the Catholic Church on religious freedom for many centuries down to 1864. From this it is quite clear that in that lengthy period the Catholic Church did not teach that religious freedom is a natural right of every person. Rather the Catholic Church held firmly to the view that the only people who have the right to religious freedom are Catholics and the Catholic Church itself. Other people and other religions and denominations do not have this right. There are many official and indeed papal statements, particularly from the nineteenth century, affirming this position. Gregory XVI in his letter *Mirari Vos* (1832) spoke of religious freedom as the 'most fetid fount of indifferentism' and showed himself opposed to any collaboration with those who sought political and religious freedom. Pius IX also repudiated the right to religious freedom in his 1864 encyclical letter accompanying the *Syllabus.* In addition, he condemned the propositions that every person is free to adhere to and profess that religion which, guided by the light of reason, he shall consider true, and also that it is false, that freedom of worship of the individual leads to the corruption of morals and minds and to indifferentism. Leo XIII took essentially the same position, though he acknowledged that there can be a legitimate and healthy civil and political freedom. These strong statements of the church's teaching office are, of course, very deeply conditioned by the circumstances of the time and by the hostile opinions and movements that were so widespread especially in nineteenth century Europe. Nevertheless, if we examine the church's teaching, as these popes and all other popes down to John XXIII firmly maintained and taught it, religious freedom is nowhere affirmed.

We may mention briefly some implications of this official teaching of the church as we have just outlined it. The Catholic Church and its members have the right to religious freedom precisely because the Catholic Church is the one true church and so has the full truth. Since truth alone has rights in society, only the Catholic Church has the right to religious freedom. i.e. to hold,

---

1. Todd D Whitmore, 'Religious liberty' in Richard P. McBrien, General Editor, *The HarperCollins Encyclopedia of Catholicism* (HarperCollins Publishers, New York, 1995), 1097.

teach and practise its faith. And since religious unity and peace are essential for the preservation of political unity and peace, it follows that the ruler or government should make the Catholic religion the official state religion and constitute the Catholic Church as the established church of the state. This is the way things should be, the right arrangement in any state or society. Implied in all this is the belief that other Christian churches and denominations and other religions are in error and are false. Now since error has no rights in society, neither should these religious bodies. Hence, they should be suppressed by the state and not allowed the right of religious freedom. Though this teaching of the Catholic Church could not be implemented in non-Catholic societies and states, the Catholic Church still adhered to it and saw to it that it was abided by in Catholic countries. Even there, however, it was sometimes not expedient to suppress all religious error and so some measure of tolerance was exercised in the interests of the overall peace of the community.[2]

b) The second stage in the evolution of the Catholic Church's teaching on religious freedom may be said to have emerged in the wake of and in response to Pius XI's strong statements in the *Syllabus of Errors* (1864). Influential here was the work of Bishop Felix Dupanloup of Orleans, France (d. 1873). In his commentary on the *Syllabus,* and in an effort to calm the storm it had raised, he developed the distinction between thesis and hypothesis in Catholic teaching in regard to church-state relations. Dupanloup, of course, accepted the teaching of the church denying the right of religious freedom to anyone except Catholics and the Catholic Church but he asserted that what the pope was doing in the *Syllabus* was stating the universal ideal (thesis) in the matter of church-state relations, namely, that the church should, ideally, be established and error suppressed. But circumstances might make this inexpedient or impossible and, hence, some other arrangement between church and state could be tolerated. This latter situation or set up Dupanloup referred to as the hypothesis. Such an explanation of church teaching made room for the different church-state arrangements in countries like the USA, Latin America, Britain, France, etc, and was much appreciated at the

2. Vincent Grogan & Laurence Ryan, *Religious Freedom in the teaching of the Second Vatican Council and in certain civil declarations* (Scepter Books, Dublin, 1967), 15-8.

time by church members, many bishops and even the Vatican itself. Dupanloup, one might say, provided a theory to explain and
support the practice of the church, while at the same time de-
fending its teaching as set out in the pope's *Syllabus*.[3]

This thesis-hypothesis theory or explanation remained the official position of the Catholic Church right up to Pope John XXIII
in the 1960s and even to Vatican II itself in 1965, despite some
minor advances made by the popes in the intervening years.[4]

Now, given this clear and firm teaching that was held over
such a lengthy period, one would be inclined to think that there
was little possibility of the Catholic Church coming to recognise
officially the right to religious freedom for everyone in society,
with its consequences for church-state relations. But much historical research and theological thinking was going on in the church
in the first half of the twentieth century, and through this the way
was being prepared for a development of doctrine that was to be
effected by the Vatican Council in 1965. So we come to the third
and present stage of church teaching on religious freedom.

Preparing for Vatican II

The chief architect of the movement towards the acceptance of
the right of religious freedom as belonging to all people by their
very dignity as human persons was an American Jesuit, John
Courtney Murray (d. 1967). In the decades preceding the Council
Murray, basing himself largely on the teaching of Leo XIII on social
and political matters, had been making a strong case for saying
that the thesis-hypothesis teaching was so polemically and historically conditioned that it could not be regarded as doctrinally
binding on the church for all time. Rather it was a teaching that
was right and binding in and for its own time. Now, given this
and also the significantly changed political and ecclesiastical circumstances of the mid-twentieth century, there was in Murray's
view a possibility that the church's teaching on religious freedom
could be developed so as to recognise and accept the right to religious freedom as belonging to all people in society. Basic to this
argument were several factors: the recognition that the right to
religious freedom could be separated from the rationalist pre-

---

3. Whitmore, 1097; Grogan & Ryan, 19.
4. See John Courtney Murray SJ, *The Problem of Religious Freedom*
(Geoffrey Chapman, London-Dublin, 1965), chapter II.

suppositions that tended to accompany its early nineteenth century expositions;[5] the realisation that the principle that 'error has no rights in society, only truth has' needed to be amended to recognise that it is people who have rights or not; and also the development in Western societies which brought the emergence of constitutional democracies in which the state was seen as distinct from society and so as having limited powers in and over society and its members, unlike in the past where the state was understood as all powerful, even in relation to religion in society. Influential also were the United Nations affirmation of the right to religious freedom in its 1948 Universal Declaration of Human Rights, the European Convention for the Protection of Human Rights (1952)[6] and also a similar affirmation of this right by the World Council of Churches in 1961. We may note also that the Irish Constitution of 1937, art. 44, enshrines a guarantee of religious freedom and thus made what Enda McDonagh calls a notable contribution in theory and in practice to the evolution of Catholic thinking on the matter.[7]

This was the context and situation in which John XXIII issued his encyclical *Pacem in Terris* in 1963. This document is, basically, a charter of human rights that govern relations between people at all levels of society and also between societies themselves. One of these rights that John teaches is the right to religious freedom. He says (PT 14) that every human being has the right to honour God according to the dictates of an upright conscience and therefore the right to worship God privately and publicly. Later (PT 60) the Pope, quoting Pius XII, asserts that the chief duty of every public authority is to safeguard the inviolable rights of the human person and to facilitate the fulfilment of his duties. Obviously, that twofold duty of the state extends to the right of the citizen to religious freedom and involves providing immunity and protection for citizens in the holding and practice of their religion.

This theological work of Murray, and this clear teaching of John XXIII, laid the groundwork for the Second Vatican Council's *Declaration on Religious Freedom,* which represents the

---

5. Grogan & Ryan, 17.
6. See Grogan & Ryan, 52-61; Enda McDonagh, *Invitation and Response: Essays in Christian Moral Theology* (Gill & Macmillan, Dublin, 1972) chapter 10, 'The Declaration on Religious Freedom', 181.
7. McDonagh, 181.

culmination of the evolution of the church's teaching on this topic.[8]

The teaching of Vatican II [9]

In *Dignitatis Humanae* (1965) the Council was quite conscious that it was developing the teaching of recent popes (n. 1) in its teaching on the free exercise of religion in society. It was moving from the position summarised above, that only Catholics have the right to religious freedom, to a resounding affirmation (n. 2) that the human person as a person has a right to religious freedom. This right arises from the person's dignity as a person, which is known through divine revelation and by reason (n. 2) and consists essentially in an immunity that constitutes a moral claim against all others and in particular the state. This immunity has two elements: i) a person is not to be forced to act in a manner contrary to his/her religious beliefs, and ii) a person is not to be restrained from acting in accordance with those beliefs. This applies to groups also and holds both in private and in public (n. 2). Later in the Declaration this fundamental right is widened to include moral matters, when it is said that a person enjoys these immunities also in regard to matters of conscience.[10]

In addition, this right should be made a civil right by the state, thus ensuring its protection from encroachments of any kind (n. 2). The limits of the right are stated too and arise from the just requirements of public order (n. 2).

It is clear even from this very brief summary of the Council's teaching that the earlier position on toleration of other denomin-

---

8. See Josef Fuchs SJ, *Christian Morality: The Word Becomes Flesh* (Gill & Macmillan, Dublin, 1987), chapter XI; Murray, *The Problem of Religious Freedom*, chapter II.

9. See Laurence Ryan in Grogan & Ryan, chapter 2; McDonagh, chapter 10; J. Bryan Hehir, 'Church and state' in *The HarperCollins Encylopedia of Catholicism*, 314-7; Patrick Hannon, *Church, State, Morality and Law* (Gill & Macmillan, Dublin, 1992), chapter 7.

10. See Hannon, 94, and also Patrick Hannon, 'The Conscience of the Voter and Law-maker', *Doctrine & Life* (Special Issue: Abortion, Law and Conscience), May /June 1992, 248-9. Hannon shows how the Council's teaching on religious freedom may be transposed to the area of morality. In matters of moral belief and practice, he says, people shouldn't be made to go against their consciences nor should they be prevented from acting according to conscience, subject to the requirements of the common good.

ations and religions is left behind. There is, therefore, no question of suppressing or restricting the religious views and practices of any person or group, provided they do not trespass beyond the limits just mentioned. No longer is the principle 'error has no rights' taught but rather what is taught is that persons do have rights and, in particular, in the matter of religion in society. It follows from this developed teaching that the state does not have any competence or role in matters religious in society beyond protecting the rights of religious persons and groups. So the state is to be neutral in matters of religion. In its eyes all religions are equal, to be protected as stated and not to be interfered with so long as the common good is not infringed.

We may elaborate a little more fully on some of the elements of this conciliar teaching on religious and moral freedom in society by taking a quick look at the following points which need some explanation.

Within due limits: The Council mentions that one's right to religious freedom is limited; it is to be exercised 'within due limits' (n. 2). If we enquire what these limits are, the Declaration spells them out as being the just requirements of public order (n. 2, 3, 4), i.e. the common good of all (n. 7). The common good here may be understood as consisting in the sum total of those conditions of social life which enable people to achieve a fuller measure of perfection with greater ease (n. 6). Basic to this common good are peace, justice and public morality (n. 7) and, we may add, the fullest possible recognition of the personal freedom of all citizens (n. 7) and the fullest possible promotion of their human rights.[11]

It is relatively easy to see why care for the common good is said to include public peace and justice. The concept of public morality causes more difficulty both in regard to what it means and what its content includes or extends to. So a word on this concept seems called for.

Public morality: It is important to be clear that public morality does not mean moral or immoral actions that are done in public or are publicly known. Nor is it to be equated with what the majority of people in a particular society regard as morally right and wrong. Similarly, private morality does not refer to acts done in private or to matters on which one is free to make a private moral judgment. The correct description of public morality is

11. Hannon, *Church, State, Morality and Law*, 95, and 'The Conscience of the Voter and Law-maker', 248-9.

that it concerns those items of morality that should be enforced by law, that are the law's business. Correspondingly, then, private morality refers to the areas and items of morality that are not the law's business and so should not be enforced by the law in society.[12]

Even though these definitions may be accepted as basically accurate, they are not the end of the difficulty about public morality. We are still left with the question, which moral issues are the law's business and which aren't?

In other words, we are not yet clear on the precise content of public (and private) morality. It is here that the real problem presents itself, since experts are not agreed on what moral issues are enforceable by law and what ones aren't and shouldn't be. So, there is uncertainty about which immoral practices may be proscribed by law and which shouldn't be and this is an uncertainty which has not been dispelled even among the experts. We don't need to go into the debate on this matter here,[13] except to note that two very widely held positions are as follows:

a) Since public morality is the shared ideas on good and evil in a particular society, any immoral activity is potentially proscribeable by law, because such immorality poses a threat to society and its public morality simply because it is immoral. What is in fact proscribed has to be worked out in each individual case by balancing individual freedom and the public interest in the most reasonable way possible. This requires allowing maximum individual freedom, respecting privacy, taking account of what society will tolerate, while realising also that the law is concerned with minimum not maximum standards of behaviour.

b) Behaviour should not be forbidden by law unless it is demonstrably injurious to others in society, or in certain circumstances people need to be protected from their own destructive impulses.

Though they each have their problems, these two positions on the role of law in relation to morality are reasonable and either of them may be held by anyone, Catholics included. The former is usually referred to as the conservative position, while the latter is designated as liberal.[14]

---

12. Hannon, *Church, State, Morality and Law,* 96-8.

13. See Hannon, 99-106.

14. Hannon, 'The Conscience of the Voter and the Law-maker', 250; *Hannon, Church, State, Morality and Law,* 110-1.

Neither of them will, however, yield a clear specific answer in relation to a particular socio-moral issue that is in debate, e.g. civil divorce, abortion legislation, though along with the teaching of the Council on religious freedom they already provide us with significant guidance in terms of values and a principle that point us in the right direction.

The World Council of Churches
A brief word on the teaching of this body (WCC) will be of interest and will suffice at this point. At three of its major conferences the WCC spoke on religious freedom. At Oxford in 1937, in the context of the newly emerged totalitarian states, the WCC, as it made a clear distinction between the state and society, proclaimed the right of the churches to freedom from state interference in their internal life and to protection of their rights by the political authority. At Amsterdam in 1948 the WCC, this time in the atmosphere of the Cold War, insisted on certain basic freedoms for the church in terms of human rights and these included the right to religious freedom. This latter right is founded on the nature and dignity of the person by virtue of that person's creation, redemption and calling. The third time the WCC addressed itself to the issue of religious freedom was at New Delhi in 1961. There it re-affirmed its earlier teaching and amplified it. In particular the conference insisted on the freedom of the act of faith and the distinctive Christian basis for the right to religious freedom. It stated also that the pursuit of religious freedom is directly related to the pursuit of other freedoms and of social justice.[15]

This teaching of the WCC has significant similarities with that of the Second Vatican Council but one cannot fail to notice that it was arrived at over twenty-five years before the Council!

The Irish Experience (1951-2000)
In this discussion of the situation in Ireland in the last fifty years, in connection with issues of social morality and religious freedom, our aim is to illustrate the practical influence of the Catholic Church's teaching on the positions taken by the Irish Catholic bishops on the various issues that arose. It will also become clear that the teaching of Vatican II has had a decisive impact on the approach taken by the Irish Catholic hierarchy after the Council

---

15. See P Bock, *In Search of a Responsible Society* (Philadelphia: The Westminster Press, 1974).

on issues like the availability of contraceptives, legalising abortion, civil divorce.

The Mother and Child Scheme (1950-1)
In mid-1950 the Health Minister of the Irish Government, Dr Noël Browne, put forward proposals for a health programme for pregnant women and mothers of young children, aiming to provide them with gynaecological care, education for motherhood and care for the physical health of their children under sixteen. It was to be free for all and optional and to be run by local doctors who would keep the necessary records. This package of measures is what came to be called the Mother and Child Scheme.

The Catholic bishops objected to this scheme on moral grounds, alleging that the state was over-stepping its authority and infringing the rights of parents, doctors, the church and private institutions. Such proposals were, they said, contrary to Catholic social teaching. In April 1951 the proposals were dropped and Dr Browne resigned.[16]

From our viewpoint here, the relevant and interesting points concern the bishops' role in this affair and how that role was understood by the bishops themselves and by the government ministers and politicians, nearly all of whom were Catholics. We may set out what seems to have been the general understanding as follows:

a) All agreed it was an issue of public morality, i.e. the welfare of Irish society and its members was involved.

b) All agreed it was the right and duty of parliament alone to make laws for Irish society.

c) All agreed that the hierarchy had the right and duty to pass a moral judgment on such an issue and – this is the vital point – that the hierarchy's judgment was decisive and final.

d) It seems true to say also that all were agreed that the Irish state was bound by Catholic moral and social teaching, at least to the extent that civil law should contain nothing contrary to that teaching and perhaps even to the extent that the state should enforce Catholic moral teaching on issues of public morality.

16. On this famous church-state clash see J. H. Whyte, *Church and State in Modern Ireland 1923-1979* (Second Edition) (Gill & Macmillan, Dublin, 1971 and 1980), chapters VII & VIII; John Horgan, *Noël Browne: Passionate Outsider* (Gill & Macmillan, Dublin 2000), chapters 4 & 5; John Cooney, *John Charles McQuaid, Ruler of Catholic Ireland* (O'Brien Press, Dublin, 1999), chapter 17.

It would seem from these last two points, c) and d), that the bishops and indeed the politicians too were operating from a theological position which held that, since the Catholic Church is the one true church and the great majority of the citizens of the Irish Republic are members of that church, therefore, Catholic moral teaching should at least not be contradicted by any civil law and perhaps such teaching should be enshrined in the law of the land. Such a position could only come out of and be supported by some version of the pre-Vatican II official teaching on church-state relations and so also on religious freedom. The expectation that the politicians will and should accept this view, and indeed their actual acceptance of it come, likewise, from such a pre-conciliar standpoint.

There can be little doubt that an incident or clash of church and state such as has been described – and in Ireland it is regarded as *the* famous instance of church-state conflict – could not happen in Ireland today, not merely because the state and its politicians have changed, but also and especially because the Catholic Church no longer sees its role or its powers in relation to the state and civil legislation as it did in 1951. Vatican II's *Declaration on Religious Freedom* has been the decisive factor here, as can be well illustrated by a brief look at how the Irish bishops taught and acted in relation to some issues of social morality that arose and were vigorously debated in the decades after the Second Vatican Council.

Legislating for the availability of contraceptives in Ireland (1973-9)
Laws enacted in 1929 and 1935 forbade in Ireland the importation, sale and advertising of artificial contraceptives. In 1973 it was proposed to change these laws so as to allow contraceptives to be made legally available in this country, though in a controlled manner. The Irish bishops issued statements on this proposal in 1973 and again in 1978. They make the point explicitly that those who see the issue in debate 'in terms of the state enforcing or not enforcing Catholic moral teaching are missing the point'. That is not the issue. There is here, of course, a question of public morality and that means that the welfare of Irish society and its members is at stake. This is the central concern in this whole matter and it is from this viewpoint and this alone that all are to look at the issue of permitting or not permitting the availability of contraceptives in Ireland. The bishops also make the

point that they, as the chief moral teachers of the great majority of the citizens and indeed as a group of concerned citizens, have a right to express their opinion on the question under discussion. But – and here especially we see the change from 1951 – it is the business of parliament to make laws and also to make the final decision on what laws to enact. What the bishops say is not, then, binding teaching but, simply their informed opinion on the issue in question from the viewpoint of the welfare of Irish society and its citizens. What the legislators are to weigh and consider as they approach the question of changing the law on the availability of contraceptives is one issue and one only: will the new law be for the good of Irish society and its members? But, the bishops note finally, that, whatever law is passed, it cannot and will not change the Catholic Church's teaching on the morality of contraception itself.

It will already be clear that this episcopal approach is inspired by Vatican II and its teaching on religious freedom. That teaching states, as we have already seen, that in moral as in religious matters in society all people, individuals and groups, Catholics included, are to be left free to act according to their own consciences and beliefs (*Declaration*, n. 3). Both the bishops and the politicians understood this clearly and each remained faithful to the principle involved throughout the controversy and the lawmaking. Thus, voters and law-makers felt free to make up their own minds when voting and/or legislating in regard to contraceptives and the issues that came up in subsequent years.

Other issues of public morality in Ireland (1980-2000)
The position that the Irish bishops took on the matter of the availability of contraceptives in Ireland in the 1970s continued to be their position when in subsequent decades other issues of social morality came into the public arena in the context of proposed new legislation or of a referendum to change the Constitution of our country. The two major issues of social morality that did emerge were abortion and civil divorce. In 1983 and again in 1991 we had referenda on whether abortion should be made legal in Ireland, and in 1986 and 1995 referenda on the availability of civil divorce in Ireland were held.

In 1983 the question of amending the Irish Constitution to recognise explicitly the right to life of the unborn was put before the people in a referendum and the amendment was passed. In

1991 the abortion issue was revisited in the wake of the X case, in which the Irish Supreme Court had ruled that abortion is permissible when there is a real and substantial risk to the life as distinct from the health of the mother, arising even from a threat of suicide. In that referendum the proposed amendment to the Constitution was rejected by a majority of roughly two-thirds and so the X case ruling remained and remains today the constitutional position on abortion in Ireland. In the same referendum the Irish electorate voted not to limit people's freedom to travel to get an abortion abroad or their freedom to get information relating to abortion services in another state.

In 1986 and again in 1995 there were referenda on whether civil divorce should be made available in Ireland. In 1986 the answer was 'no' but in 1995 the Irish people voted 'yes' by a very slim margin.

From all that has been said in the preceding pages it will be plain that the 1951 position adopted by the Irish bishops in relation to the Mother and Child Scheme, and that upheld in subsequent controversies on issues of social morality, are significantly different. The cause of the difference is, undoubtedly, Vatican II's teaching on religious freedom. Now we all see clearly, with the church itself, that the church has no direct or indirect temporal power, except only what influence it has or can have on the consciences of citizens who are its members. The state, we are clear, has no competence in religious matters and must have as its sole aim the welfare of society. As it does that, it is bound to protect the freedom of the various religions and churches to live according to their beliefs, but it itself is not bound by the teaching of any religion or church. Society is distinct from the state as are the churches and religions. Church and state have their own proper role in society and neither is to usurp that of the other. And in matters of religion and morality everyone is free, as *Dignitiatis Humanae* teaches, to follow his/her conscience within due limits.

Church teaching today on how to prepare to vote:
The 1995 Divorce Referendum
On 24 November 1995 a referendum was held in the Republic of Ireland. The purpose of it was to ask the people of the Republic if they would agree to a change in the Constitution of the Irish state in relation to the prohibition in the Constitution on all civil divorce. The Constitution of the Irish Republic was drawn up in

1937 and stated as follows: No law shall be enacted providing for
the grant of a dissolution of marriage. In 1986 a first referendum
had been held with the aim of having this provision of the
Constitution deleted and replaced by one allowing divorce when
a marriage had failed irreparably. In that referendum the people
voted by a majority of about two to one to retain the original provision. Now in 1995 the government re-introduced the issue,
judging that, according to recent opinion polls, the people would
this time vote in favour of a change in this provision of the
Constitution. On this occasion it was planned to replace the article of the Constitution forbidding a dissolution of marriage by
another which would permit divorce and remarriage when a
marriage had broken down irretrievably but only after a couple
had lived apart for a period of at least four out of the previous
five years.

   In the run up to this referendum (in which, as we noted
above, the 'yes' voters had a very narrow victory) the following
understanding (here slightly revised and extended) of the
church's teaching on how to prepare to cast one's vote in such a
referendum or election, was published in a church magazine[17]
with the intention of helping Catholic voters, particularly as they
got ready to make their choice on the question they were called
on to answer in the polling booth. It is an approach that is valid
and binding, as far as Catholics are concerned, in relation to any
election or referendum.

   Making civil divorce available to citizens or not is a constitutional, legal and political issue but it is also a matter of social
   morality. In addition, it is highly contentious as we all know
   from the experience of the 1986 referendum on the same
   issue. So, it may be of help, especially to Catholics, to set out
   clearly, at this point in time, what the church teaches in regard
   to how we should understand the question of civil divorce,
   what the issues involved are and how we should approach
   the problem of actually voting. We will not, however, discuss
   the most practical question of all, how one should cast one's
   vote in the referendum (yes or no). As always, that has to be
   left, for reasons that we will see, to each voter in the privacy
   of the polling booth.

17. *Intercom* (Catholic Communications Institute of Ireland, Dublin,
September 1995), 6-8.

All the issues are moral issues

Many people seem to take the view that the issue of whether civil divorce should or should not be available in the Republic of Ireland (it is already available in the North) is a purely constitutional, legal and political question. This is not the case, however. While it is true that civil divorce has constitutional, legal and political dimensions, it also has a moral dimension.

The moral dimension of civil divorce arises from the fact that the availability or non-availability of civil divorce concerns and influences the welfare of Irish citizens and of Irish society and can work helpfully or harmfully for us in Ireland. Hence, there is here an issue of right and wrong, i.e. an issue of morality and, ultimately, this is the most important aspect of civil divorce.

Voting is a political but also a moral act

In our democratic society we are blessed to have the freedom to vote in elections and referenda. This freedom is ours, because we are citizens of this country and, if we weren't citizens, we wouldn't have this freedom and right to vote in Ireland. We vote, then, as citizens and in doing so we perform a political act, in and for Irish society. But voting is also a moral action. It involves a free choice by the voter that affects the welfare of Irish society and its members for good or ill. Hence, voting has a moral dimension and in consequence can be right or wrong in moral (as in political and constitutional) terms. Thus it is possible to do the morally wrong thing when you vote (or fail to vote). It follows, then, that we are called as citizens to do all possible to make a careful and discerning choice when we vote (or do not vote), so as to ensure that the welfare of our society and its citizens is promoted. It follows too that we have not merely a right to vote but a duty to do so, since we have a duty to promote the welfare of our society in every way we as citizens can. Not voting can, then, be a failure in one's duties as a citizen and can be a form of immorality.

We may note here that, since one votes as a citizen and because one is a citizen, it is not directly relevant what church or religion, if any, one belongs to. One does not vote as, say, a Catholic who happens to be a citizen of Ireland. Rather, it is the other way round. One votes as a citizen who happens to be a Catholic or Anglican or whatever. Hence, there can't be such a thing as a Catholic vote or a Presbyterian vote as such.

There are only Irish votes and voters who, coming from different religious traditions or none are, in voting, exercising their right and doing their duty as citizens of Ireland.

Getting the question to be voted on right
It follows from what has been said above that when a Catholic (or other) voter comes to consider how to vote in the divorce (or any) referendum (or election), he/she should have only one question in mind. This question is simply: which vote on my part (yes or no) will best promote the welfare of Irish society in this matter of civil divorce (or whatever)? It may well be that the Catholic Church has no explicit teaching on this or a similar precise question or point but, in any case, such teaching of our (or any) church is beside the point in the referendum. The teaching of the Catholic (or any) Church is not the issue in the forthcoming referendum and, hence, is not affected by the outcome of that poll. Rather, what is in question is the welfare of Irish society and its citizens and only that.

The Catholic Church teaches that civil divorce (and that includes remarriage) is immoral. In the referendum, however, the voter is faced with a different, even if related, question, when she or he enters the polling booth. This question is as follows: will the availability or non-availability of civil divorce best promote the welfare of Irish society, the common good of Ireland?

It may well be that the Catholic voter is influenced in approaching and answering this question by her church's position on the moral issue of divorce itself. This is understandable and right. But that teaching on divorce does not, in and by itself, answer the question the voter is faced with, nor does it automatically mean or imply that the Catholic voter must vote 'no' when going to the polls in the referendum before us.

We can see, then, that in this matter the distinction between voting as a citizen who happens to be a Catholic and voting as a Catholic who happens to be a citizen is crucial. We vote as citizens of the Irish Republic and it is because we do so that we have the freedom to vote yes or no, as we judge correct. And the question to be kept in mind when voting concerns only one thing, the welfare or common good of Irish society.

A Catholic should vote according to conscience
The central principle of the church's teaching on this question

is contained in Vatican II's *Declaration on Religious Freedom* (1965). In this document the church teaches that every human being has the right to religious freedom in society. This means that every person in society is entitled to hold and practise whatever religion (or no religion) that he or she chooses. Hence, no one may be forced to act in a manner contrary to one's religious beliefs or be prevented from acting in accordance with them, but within due limits. It is implied here in this teaching, as all accept, that this principle extends also to one's moral beliefs and, in consequence, every society and state is morally bound to give its citizens this same freedom in relation to moral beliefs.

It follows from this that a Catholic, when considered as a citizen of the Irish Republic or wherever, has this right to religious and moral freedom. Hence, when the Catholic acts as a citizen in society, as distinct from as a Catholic within the church, then he or she has the right to freedom in relation to his or her moral beliefs and, consequently, may vote as he or she judges fit. In the upcoming referendum on civil divorce, therefore, the Catholic (or any) citizen is free to vote as he or she decides in conscience. And official church teaching affirms this freedom to say yes or no, when one comes to cast one's vote.

It should be made quite clear in this context that this teaching on religious and moral freedom in society applies to the Catholic citizen only when he or she acts as a citizen in Irish or some other society. In other words, this right to religious freedom is a right in and against civil society only. It is not a right in and against the church or its teaching authority or its teaching. Hence, a Catholic may not invoke this right as a Catholic to disagree with some church teaching, e.g. contraception, the real presence of Christ in the eucharist, infallibility. As a Catholic one is bound to accept these teachings and any possible disagreement with them may not be based on the right to religious freedom.

The Irish bishops affirm the right to religious freedom
Given what has just been explained about the teaching of Vatican II on religious freedom, it is to be expected that the teaching of the Irish Catholic bishops on that topic since the Council will coincide with the conciliar declaration. This is

what we find in fact when we examine the Irish hierarchy's
statements on matters that were put to referendum in Ireland
since 1965 or on other issues of social morality, e.g. the availability of contraceptives in Ireland in the 1970s, the right to
life of the unborn in 1983 and civil divorce in 1986. Thus in
1978 the Irish bishops said that those who insist on seeing the
issue (the availability of contraceptives in Ireland) purely in
terms of the state enforcing or not enforcing Catholic moral
teaching are missing the point. In 1983 the bishops said they
recognised the right of each person to vote according to conscience; and so on at other times.

It is true that some over-zealous Catholics, laity and clergy,
apparently failed to notice or ignored these statements of
principle by the bishops and, hence, at times claimed that our
bishops were obliging us Catholics to vote in a particular
way. This is, however, mistaken. If the bishops did this, they
would be contradicting the church's official teaching as proclaimed at Vatican II. One can, then, be certain that the bishops of Ireland have not taken such a course, though it is true,
that at some times they were less clear and unequivocal in
their assertion of the right of Irish Catholics to freedom in
matters of social morality than at others.

The Irish bishops also express their own opinion
Another point needs to be made here. While respecting the
right of Irish Catholics to religious and moral freedom in society, the Irish hierarchy have not in the past hesitated to state
their own considered opinion about the issue of social morality
they were addressing. So, e.g. in 1983 they stated their considered opinion that the proposed constitutional amendment
guaranteeing the right to life of the unborn was a good thing.
In 1986 they expressed the view that a no vote on the divorce
issue would be the right thing for Ireland.

It is essential to note in relation to these statements of the
Irish bishops, however, that they were only the opinion of the
hierarchy and not binding teachings. Hence, a Catholic was
free to consider them carefully and then, if he or she so decided,
vote contrary to them. This is what many Catholics seem to
have done and they were quite within their rights in doing so
and also quite in line with the church's official teaching on
religious and moral freedom in society.

There is no reason to believe that the bishops of Ireland will not follow this same pattern in the forthcoming referendum on civil divorce and in other referenda and elections in the future, namely, assert the right of all to religious and moral freedom in society and also state their own considered opinion on the issue of civil divorce (or whatever).

We may, then, summarise the Irish bishops' consistent approach to socio-moral issues or issues of public morality in recent years as follows.[18]

1) They distinguish between the substantive morality of the issue in question (contraception, abortion, divorce) and the legal aspects of the issue.

2) They set out the church's teaching on the substantive or moral issue but also state that the legal, political and constitutional aspects of the issue are matters for the citizens and lawmakers to decide on, according to their conscientious judgment.

3) They give their own view on the legal, political or economic aspects of the matter using such arguments as they judge to be weighty and even decisive.

The Catholic citizen's main task: Inform your conscience

The main task of every citizen and, hence, of the Catholic who is a citizen is, then, to study the issues that are to be voted on in the coming referendum, try to understand them and what is at stake as fully as possible and so come to an intelligent, informed and balanced judgment and decision on how to vote. In more theological terms the citizen is called to inform his or her conscience in relation to the whole matter of civil divorce in Ireland. That means making a sincere effort, according to one's capacities and circumstances, to find the truth. Then one is obliged to cast one's vote in accordance with the truth as one has come to see it. Finding the truth in this case is not at all easy, since there are positive and negative aspects to both the yes and the no options. It would, however, be a failure in citizenship not to vote at all or to vote blindly or in an ill-informed manner. It would also be a moral failure to approach this or any referendum in such an irresponsible way. No good

18. See Hannon, *Church, State, Morality and Law*, 140-4 at p 140; Patrick Hannon, 'Church-State Relations: Post 1992', *The Furrow*, November 1993, 587-595 at p 593.

226 CHRISTIAN LIVING TODAY

citizen, and certainly no good Catholic citizen should, knowingly, be guilty of such a failure now or at any time.[19]

Further Reading
Bock, P., *In Search of a Responsible Society* (Philadelphia: The Westminster Press, 1974);
Cooney, John, *John Charles McQuaid, Ruler of Catholic Ireland* (O'Brien Press, Dublin, 1999), chapter 17;
Curran Charles, E., *American Catholic Social Ethics* (University of Notre Dame Press, Notre Dame, 1982), chapter 5, especially pp 192-213;
Fuchs, Josef, *Christian Morality: The Word Becomes Flesh* (Gill & Macmillan, Dublin, 1987), chapter XI;
Grogan, Vincent, & Ryan, Laurence, *Religious Freedom in the teaching of the Second Vatican Council and in certain civil declarations* (Scepter Books, Dublin, 1967);
Hannon, Patrick, *Church, State, Morality and Law* (Gill & Macmillan, Dublin, 1992), chapters 7-9;
Hannon, Patrick, 'Church-State Relations: Post 1992', *The Furrow*, November 1993, 587-595;
Hannon, Patrick, 'The Conscience of the Voter and Law-maker', *Doctrine and Life*, (Special Issue: Abortion, Law and Conscience), May/June, 1992, 244-252;
Hehir, J. Bryan, 'Church and State', McBrien, Richard P., General Editor, *The HarperCollins Encyclopedia of Catholicism* (HarperCollins Publishers, New York, 1995), 314-7;
Horgan, John, *Noël Browne: Passionate Outsider* (Gill & Macmillan, Dublin, 2000), chapters 4 & 5;
McDonagh, Enda, *Invitation and Response: Essays in Christian Moral Theology* (Gill & Macmillan, Dublin, 1972), chapter 10;
Murray, John Courtney SJ, *The Problem of Religious Freedom* (Geoffrey Chapman, London-Dublin, 1965);
Vatican Council II, *Declaration on Religious Liberty* in Flannery, Austin, O.P., *Vatican Council II: The Conciliar and Post-Conciliar Documents* (Dominican Publications, Dublin, 1975), 799-812;
Whitmore, Todd D., 'Religious liberty', McBrien, Richard P., General Editor, *The HarperCollins Encyclopedia of Catholicism* (HarperCollins Publishers, New York, 1995), 1097-8;
Whyte, John H., *Church and State in Modern Ireland* 1923-1979 (Second Edition) (Gill & Macmillan, Dublin, 1980), chapter 7.

---

19. In forming one's conscience as one prepares to cast one's vote, some practical guidelines are suggested by the experts. For these see Hannon, *Church, State, Morality and Law*, 111-3, and Hannon, 'The Conscience of the Voter and Law-maker', 250-2. In relation to the politician or lawmaker see Hannon, *Church, State, Morality and Law*, 116-124.

CHAPTER 11

Christian Spirituality Today

One of the areas of the Christian life that has undergone significant renewal in the wake of the Second Vatican Council (1962-5)
is spirituality. This fact is clear on the practical level in the great
growth of interest in doing retreats of various kinds, in the
spread of the charismatic movement, in the proliferation of
prayer and Bible study groups, in the ever-growing call for spiritual direction, in the upsurge of the study of the spiritual life, past
and present, in the renewed interest in going on pilgrimage, in
intensified social justice activity and in the massive number of
books and magazines on spiritual matters that have been appear-
ing in recent years. Here surely is a growth area in the Christian
community in general and in the Catholic community in particular. This is a phenomenon worthy of some reflection and analysis,
especially when we hear so much about shrinking congregations,
declining church membership, loss of religious faith and the
growth of agnosticism and atheism. In this chapter, then, we will
focus on some of the main developments and trends in relation to
Christian spirituality in post-conciliar times, especially those in
the Catholic community. We will be attempting to gather the
fruits of the current phase of renewal and outline them in summary fashion, so as to present at least a partial answer to the
question, what are they saying about Christian spirituality
today?

Spiritual hunger and the interest in spirituality today
One often hears it stated nowadays that modern people, especially
in the Western world, are experiencing a deep spiritual hunger,
which is not satisfied by the abundance of material things west-
erners now possess and enjoy. It might even seem that the more
we grow rich in this world's goods, the greater our hunger and
need for a spirituality that makes sense of human existence in our
day and satisfies our deep need for meaning and direction in life.

It is of great interest to note also that the ways people are endeav-
ouring to satisfy this spiritual hunger are very diverse, with the
result that there is a vast pluralism of spiritualities on offer at the
present time. This is enriching and stimulating but it also gives
rise to confusion and uncertainty as people seek to work out for
themselves a satisfying spirituality. Many seem to have great difficulty doing so, as the very existence and pervasiveness of the
spiritual hunger just referred to indicates. This fact is also made
clear by the prevalence in Western society of such deeply personal,
yet also social, problems as depression, alcoholism, substance
abuse, violence and suicide. Even among Christians these problems are common and this spiritual hunger seems to gnaw at
their souls just as destructively as in the case of non-Christians.
No doubt the churches as communities and institutions provide
an inspiring and meaningful spiritual vision for many among
their members, but it seems clear that there are many others who
do not find the teaching and ministry of the churches very nourishing or helpful to them in meeting their deep spiritual needs.
This is one of the main reasons for the drift from the churches in
Western countries in recent times.

Thus, while the renewed interest in spirituality in our day is a
positive and welcome reality, it also presents the churches with a
challenge that so far they haven't been meeting with any very
obvious success. It remains for the churches, despite a great deal
of renewal, to discern more clearly and set about satisfying more
fully the spiritual hunger that makes life so difficult for so many
in our society at present.

Contemporary spiritual trends
It will be of interest to mention briefly some of the spiritualities
or spiritual trends that have become prominent in recent times in
our world, many of which seem quite positive, while others are
of doubtful or little value.[1]

One of the most notable trends or movements today is the
spirituality that is usually referred to as the New Age Movement.
New Age is an umbrella term covering very diverse and at times
conflicting ideas, activities and practices drawn from numerous
sources: East and West, religious and philosophical, the human
and physical sciences, and at times coinciding with the ideas and

---

1. See Michael Downey, *Understanding Christian Spirituality* (henceforth
UCS) (Paulist Press, New York, 1997), 6-13.

interests of the peace, ecology, feminist, human potential and natural health movements. This New Age movement believes basically that a new age is at hand in which humanity will experience a radical transformation of consciousness and awareness and this will dramatically improve human living. Adherents tend to pick and choose from this New Age spirituality. While many of the New Age beliefs and practices are not in accord with Christian teaching, some are acceptable and can be helpful. So an informed and critical attitude is here called for.[2]

In an effort to assuage their spiritual hunger, many today turn to psychology and not a few seem to consider it the new religion. Since spirituality is concerned in the first place with the experience of the sacred, rather than with religious beliefs and obligations, people find psychology helpful in the struggle for spiritual development, as it facilitates us in experiencing ourselves at a deeper emotional level and, properly used, is conducive to personal growth and maturation. Some see all this as the swamping of spirituality by psychology and as giving way to self-absorption rather than as authentic spirituality. Whatever about such a charge, few would contend that psychology alone can satisfy our deep hunger for a spirituality that gives depth and meaning to human life. But equally, few would deny its important contribution in the arena of the spiritual.[3]

There has been a notable turn to the East in recent decades in search of spiritual enlightenment and wisdom. Many find significant illumination in the Eastern spiritual traditions, especially in regard to meditation and various disciplines of mind and body as well as rich insights into human living, the world itself and the sacred.[4]

Another trend in Western life today that is linked to spiritual-

2. See Richard Woods OP, 'New Age Spirituality', in Michael Downey, Editor, *New Dictionary of Catholic Spirituality* (henceforth NDCS) (Michael Glazier Book, The Liturgical Press, Collegeville, Minnesota, USA, 1993), 704; Jack Finnegan, 'The New Age Movement – a New Religion?' *The Furrow,* June 1992, 351-9; Kathy Walsh, 'The Age of Aquarius', *The Tablet,* 10 May 1995, 629-630; Downey, *UCS,* 7-8; Donal Dorr, *Divine Energy: God Beyond Us, Within Us, Among Us* (Gill & Macmillan, Dublin, 1996), 119-131.
3. Downey, *UCS,* 8-9; H. John McDargh, 'Relationship and Contribution of Psychology to Spirituality', *NDCS,* 792-800.
4. Downey, *USC,* 9; William Cenkner OP, 'Eastern (Asian) Spirituality', *NDCS,* 309-318.

ity is the very extensive and popular self-help movement. This includes the many 12-step and other programmes and books dealing with such diverse things as building self-confidence, coping with stress, healing the emotional wounds and traumas of our early lives and help in dealing with bereavement, major losses, divorce, addictions, etc. Again there is value here as many can attest but a balance must be struck lest more be claimed than is justified and the spiritual be confused with the emotional and the therapeutic.[5]

Important also among the many currents of spirituality in the contemporary world is the emergence of feminist spirituality and, even more recently, masculine spirituality. The former has been and is very influential in ensuring that women's experience, so long neglected, is brought to bear in the area of the spiritual, Christian or otherwise, and that the insights it yields are made use of to provide us with a more integral and balanced spirituality.[6]

Mention may be made also of the ecological movement which has promoted a new interest in caring for the earth as an element of contemporary spirituality.[7]

Closely related to this in important ways is Celtic Spirituality, which of late has become the focus of considerable scholarly and popular interest and has several valuable insights and emphases for the contemporary Christian.[8]

Religion and Spirituality
In the contemporary world religion is denigrated and even dismissed by not a few writers and people engaged in what you might call the spiritual search, while spirituality is seen as essential for a meaningful and fulfilled life. This is a surprising stance and, from our Catholic viewpoint, one that is novel and regrettable, even if one can understand the point of it and at times feel a certain sympathy with those who see things in this way.

5. Downey, *UCS,* 10.
6, Downey, *UCS,* 11; Sandra M. Schneiders IHM, 'Feminist Spirituality', *NDCS,* 394-406; Richard Rohr OFM, 'Masculine Spirituality, Men's Spirituality', *NDCS,* 645-7.
7. Downey, *UCS ,* 9-10.
8. See Diarmuid Ó Laoghaire SJ, ' Celtic Spirituality', *NDCS,* 134-8; Philip Sheldrake, 'Celtic Spirituality', in Richard P. McBrien, General Editor, *HarperCollins Encyclopedia of Catholicism* (henceforth HCEC) (HarperCollins Publishers, New York, 1994), 292.

The key to understanding this negative attitude to religion resides in the fact that those who espouse it usually see religion in the narrow sense of institutional religion. Indeed they seem to take the view that religion is to be equated with some religious institution rather than with faith in God, community worship, the spiritual life, etc. On the other hand, these writers and searchers see spirituality as a very individual, personal and indeed private matter, which one works out and commits oneself to in the course of one's spiritual quest for a meaningful experience of life. Since institutional religion is judged by many today as not satisfying their deep spiritual hunger, we find that a large number of people are abandoning it, leaving the churches and turning to spirituality in some shape or form in an effort to meet their spiritual need. There is no doubt that these people are genuine spiritual searchers and it has to be admitted that the churches as institutionalised religious bodies often fail to provide a vibrant, life-giving spiritual vision and experience of life for their members. Still, the sharp distinction between religion and spirituality as here understood is not one that can be accepted as accurately drawn. In particular, the individualism of this manner of perceiving spirituality neglects the community dimension of human life and of the spiritual quest, while equating religion with its institutional aspect. Hence, it is too narrow and thus impoverishes both religion and spirituality. We must, therefore, maintain the importance of the communal aspect of both religion and spirituality, refuse to allow religion to be reduced to a one-dimensional reality, and insist that spirituality needs to be seen as essentially communal if it is truly to nourish the spirit and prove meaningful and life-enhancing. In short, religion and spirituality are not opposed to each other but are rather two elements or dimensions of the one reality, namely, the spiritual search for the sacred and for the deeper meaning of life, carried out and lived out in community. This holds true even though religion tends to be understood as pointing to the external, objective beliefs and structures of that community or religious body, while spirituality is generally seen as being concerned with its more personal elements.[9]

---

9. Downey, *UCS*, 20-5, 13; Brian O'Leary SJ, 'Developments in Christian Spirituality since Vatican II', *Religious Life Review,* Dublin, July 1999, 216. See also Donal Dorr, *Divine Energy,* 116-9.

What is Christian Spirituality?

The word 'spirituality' is an abstract one related to the words 'spirit' and 'spiritual'. These latter refer, in Pauline terms, to the person who is under the influence of God's Spirit and they are the words that were most commonly used throughout Christian history. But the word 'spirituality' itself is a relatively new arrival on the scene and has only become popular and widely used in the last hundred years or so, frequently replacing terms such as 'devotion', 'piety', 'interior life', 'spiritual life', etc.[10]

So popular has this new word become, in fact, that it is now widely used by people who are not Christian or even religious. This widening use of the word prompts the question, what is this spirituality they are all talking about? What is being referred to when such a vast spread of people of all religions and none invoke it? Simply, what is spirituality?

Everyone agrees that it is very difficult indeed to give an adequate description of spirituality as such. It is a most slippery and vague word that seems to elude precise description or definition, though numerous attempts of varying adequacy have been made to do so. Here we will confine ourselves to a brief effort to describe what spirituality is and then move on to our main concern, Christian spirituality and its various elements and dimensions.

Spirituality

As Gregory Baum says,[11] spirituality signifies inwardness, dedication and vision. It refers to things that involve the human spirit: what that spirit is committed to, how it sees human living, what it considers to be the goal of human existence and the basic values to be pursued in attaining that goal, how the final destiny of the human spirit is to be attained, how that spirit expresses itself in our daily life, etc. Spirituality is not, then, narrowly focused on things like techniques of meditation, forms of prayer or self-denial or explicitly religious language or experience. Rather it encompasses one's entire life in all its diversity and so extends to and involves our relationships, work, love, suffering, creativity and so on.[12]

---

10. Walter H. Principe CSB, 'Spirituality, Christian', *NDCS*, 931. Downey, *UCS*, 60.
11. Gregory Baum, 'Management in God', *The Furrow*, May 2000, 267.
12. Elizabeth Dreyer, 'Christian Spirituality', *HCEC*, 1217.

To unify and give meaning to all these elements of one's life, one's spirituality provides one with a vision of life and the ideals, values and priorities that give focus and inspiration to one's daily living. Central to spirituality is the striving to integrate one's personality, character and lifestyle into a unified and mature whole as one seeks to become the best person one can become, chiefly through living in love and freedom.

Authors are usually at pains to emphasise that spirituality is primarily concerned with human experience rather than theories or doctrines or philosophies of life. One's spirituality is, then, about why and how one lives and acts, about the depth dimension of one's human existence. It concerns your moral (and religious) outlook, the attitudes and values that shape and motivate you and from and by which you act in relation to other people, to society, to the created world and, for the religious person, to God.

We can say that one's spirituality is what gives meaning to one's life, what motivates one at the deepest level and gives one direction in one's relating and working, one's valuing and prioritising, in one's choosing and acting. So without some kind of spirituality your life would be meaningless; you would have nothing to aim at or commit yourself to, to motivate or inspire you, to fight for or against.

Clearly, then, everyone has and, to continue living humanly, must have a spirituality of some sort. Spirituality is thus a constitutive dimension of human nature and experience.[13]

It would seem obvious, given this, that there will inevitably be a vast plurality of spiritualities as people and groups work out the spirituality by which they choose to live.[14]

To sum up, we may quote two contemporary efforts to describe or define spirituality as such, whether religious or not. One writer says that spirituality in the broadest sense refers to the experience of consciously striving to integrate one's life in terms, not of isolation and self-absorption, but of self-transcendence towards the ultimate value one perceives.[15]

A second author views spirituality as a way of consciously striving to integrate one's life through self-transcending knowledge, freedom and love in light of the highest values perceived and pursued.[16]

13. Downey, *UCS*, 14.
14. See Sandra M. Schneiders as quoted in Downey, *UCS*, 15.
15. Schneiders as quoted in Downey, *UCS*, 15.
16. Downey, *UCS*, 15.

We may note here too that scholars speak of spirituality in a second sense or at another level. This is spirituality understood as the scholarly or academic study of spiritual experience, or of in-depth experience or of spirituality as lived out in daily life, whether these are religious or not. In this sense, spirituality has been described as the field of study which attempts to investigate and understand more fully in an interdisciplinary way the spiritual experience as such, i.e. as spiritual and as experience.[17]

Spirituality in this second meaning has been receiving very extensive attention in recent times and, as we will see, much development has taken place.

Christian Spirituality
The foregoing reflections provide significant illumination for our approach to and understanding of Christian spirituality. What is needed is a Christian religious interpretation of spirituality that takes account, in an adequate manner, of all the dimensions and aspects of that spirituality and of the Christian gospel. Now, since, as we have already noted, spirituality focuses, first of all, on experience, it will be appropriate as our starting point to turn our attention here to the experience of the sacred which is available to Christians.

If we reflect on our Christian experience, i.e. our experience of human living as believers in the God of Jesus Christ, then we have to say that it remains human experience. But in and through that experience, especially its deeper and more heartfelt elements, God is present and active, gracing, calling and moving us to be more truly ourselves as Christian believers and to live more fully in accordance with the Christian vision of life in both its religious and moral dimensions.

We must remember that God is not present and active in our lives in the same way as human beings and created realities are, nor is God experienced as they are. The reason is, of course, that God as the Absolute Mystery infinitely surpasses human creaturely existence and experience, while at the same time God touches and is active within that existence and experience. In more philosophical terms, God is transcendent in relation to human existence and created reality, while also being immanent within all creation, including especially us humans. As a result of this we discern or sense God's presence, grace and call only in

17. Schneiders as quoted in Principe, *NDCS*, 938.

and through created realities. We co-experience God as we experience these earthly beings in our daily life. So, God remains mysterious and elusive to us as Christian believers but also real, present and active within our lives and experience.[18]

Now this experience is, as it were, the raw material and the foundation of our Christian spirituality. By reflection on that experience each of us Christians, and the Christian Church too over the centuries and today, works out the Christian spirituality from and by which we and it will live as Christians. That spirituality will be focused around and inspired by our belief in the God of Jesus Christ, who is Father, Son and Holy Spirit, and the religious and moral ideals and values which Jesus taught and which we as his disciples make our own, and by which we shape our characters and lives. Of course none of us does this from scratch, as it were. The community of disciples that we call the Christian Church has been doing reflection on and theologising about Christian spiritual experience for up to twenty centuries. So it has a rich understanding of that experience, and we Christians are all shaped by that from our earliest days. We can and should draw continually on this body of spiritual reflection to enrich our own understanding of and commitment to Christian spiritual living.

In the light of these reflections we may now provide a summary description of Christian spirituality before we go on to focus on some of its more specific aspects and elements.

We may describe Christian spirituality as the way of life of the Christian, based on and inspired by his/her understanding of and commitment to the Christian vision of life, with its religious and moral ideals and values, centred on the God of Jesus Christ, Father, Son and Holy Spirit and lived out in the community of the church. More precisely, it might be said that one's personal Christian spirituality consists of those elements of the Christian vision of life which actually inspire and motivate one and, hence, shape one's lifestyle and make it what it is.[19]

---

18. Dorr, *Spirituality and Justice* (Gill & Macmillan, Dublin 1984), 21-2; See Dermot A. Lane, *The Experience of God* (Veritas, Dublin, 1981), chapter 1.

19. See Dreyer, *HCEC*, 1216; Downey, *UCS*, 32-49; Michael Downey, 'Christian Spirituality', *The Modern Catholic Encyclopedia* (henceforth *TMCE*) (A Michael Glazier Book, The Liturgical Press, Collegeville, Minnesota, USA,1994), 166-7; Principe, NDCS, 932; Dorr, *Spirituality and Justice*, 19-21; William Cosgrave, 'Christian Spirituality Today' *The Furrow*, September 1995, 502.

The descriptions of Christian spirituality by two contemporary authors will help to clarify and fill out this way of stating the issue. One[20] states that Christian spirituality is the daily, communal, lived expression of one's ultimate beliefs, characterised by openness to the self-transcending love of God, self, neighbour and world through Jesus Christ and in the power of the Spirit. The second author[21] characterises Christian spirituality as a way of living for God in Christ through the presence and power of the Holy Spirit.

There are of course, many different types of Christian spirituality, differentiated by their diverse emphases on particular elements of the Christian vision and way of life. Examples are: Jesuit spirituality, Dominican spirituality, liberation spirituality, monastic spirituality, feminist spirituality, etc. These are all valid and good spiritualities and make their appeal to different people, though at times they too may need renewal due to the tendency of things human to become dated and to neglect particular elements of the overall Christian vision of human existence and living.

The contemporary need for renewal
It is clear to all that the Second Vatican Council both initiated significant renewal in Catholic spirituality and served as a catalyst for continuing renewal and development in subsequent years. Few will deny that this renewal was badly needed and long overdue. We may mention briefly the main areas in question here.

In the centuries and decades prior to the Council, spirituality and the literature on it tended to be very clerical and monastic, not merely in the sense that it was nearly exclusively priests and religious who wrote about the spiritual life, but they did so largely *for* priests and religious, male and female. In addition, this spirituality for priests and religious was seen as superior to that of the laity, a fact often summarised in the statement that priests and religious were called to and actually lived the way of life of the evangelical counsels, while the laity were called to and lived only the way of life of the commandments. Lay spirituality was thus often seen as peripheral and inferior to the primary spiritual business of the church.[22]

---

20. Dreyer, *HCEC*, 1216.
21. Downey, *UCS*, 43.
22. Dreyer, 1216.

Pre-Vatican II spirituality often seemed to be very negative in regard to significant aspects of human life. Examples are the human body and its emotions or passions, as they were usually called, sexuality, women, human society and the material world and involvement in them, development of the human person and one's potential, talents and skills. In these matters there was not infrequently a measure of dualism that fostered a split between soul and body, with the emphasis on saving the soul while restraining the body and its wayward passions and tendencies. Hence, the strong stress on self-denial, self-restraint, separation from the world and even from other people. In this context a degree of other-worldliness was also to be found, which gave the impression that it was the next life that really mattered, while this life was less important and perhaps dangerous to one's spiritual life. Obedience tended to be seen as the dominant virtue in the spiritual life, with little being said about personal responsibility, taking personal initiatives, growth as a person and a Christian or being creative in the area of spirituality and Christian living. There was the additional weakness that the spiritual life in Catholic circles tended to be viewed in the rather narrow sense of prayer and mortification, with relatively little reference to daily moral living and, least of all, to the call to action for justice in society.

The fruits of the contemporary renewal
One of the most significant teachings of Vatican II in relation to spirituality is that in the *Constitution on the Church,* chapter five, concerning the universal call to holiness (nn. 39-42). Everyone is called to holiness, says the document (n. 39); one and the same holiness is cultivated by all (n. 41); all of Christ's followers are invited and bound to pursue holiness and the perfect fulfilment of their proper state (n. 42). The implications of this are very important, especially for lay people. No longer are they confined to pursuing the way of the commandments. Now their vocation is clearly seen to be to the fulness of life in Christ, the same goal as everyone else in the church, a goal that can be attained in any state or walk of life. The basis of this call to holiness is baptism, not ordination or religious profession. Because one is baptised into Christ and his church, one is called to the fulness of holiness. From this conciliar teaching there has resulted in recent decades a much greater emphasis on lay spirituality, numerous lay peo-

ple devote themselves assiduously to the spiritual life and many grassroot movements for spiritual renewal have emerged in the church community.[23]

Another very necessary and welcome emphasis in recent writing on spirituality may be referred to as its holistic dimension. In the past, as already noted, there was a tendency to oppose the soul to the body, so that the spiritual life seemed to be about saving souls rather than people. Today major progress has been made in laying aside this dualism and in developing a spirituality of and for the whole person and his/her whole life in all its aspects. Contemporary psychology has been especially valuable here, providing much help in the construction of what is often referred to nowadays as an acceptable theological anthropology, i.e. an understanding of the human person that does justice to our entire humanity and also to our relationship with God.

The human person is a unity with many dimensions – material, spiritual, emotional, social, sexual, developmental, cosmic. All are God's creation, all are good and we are called by our very humanity itself to respect, appreciate and care for each and all of them as for the whole person. The Christian vocation is to develop our humanity and enhance it, so that each one becomes the best person she/he can become, realising all our potentialites and making full use of our talents. Essential and foundational here is a proper love of oneself. Not merely is this not selfishness but it is the essential prerequisite for loving others and God. So, today we hear a lot – and rightly – about self-development, self-fulfilment and working to become mature persons. This growth at the personal and emotional levels will involve and require increased self-knowledge and self-awareness, improved self-esteem and self-confidence as well as emotional and sexual maturing and much growing and learning in what many today refer to as relationships skills. All this is basic for our Christian spirituality. Personal growth is essential for and is a major part of spiritual growth. Undeveloped and immature people are likely to be seri-

---

23. See Joann Wolski Conn, 'Spirituality', in Joseph A. Komonchak, Mary Collins & Dermot A. Lane, Editors, *The New Dictionary of Theology* (Gill & Macmillan, Dublin, 1987), 980; Downey, *UCS*, 75-8; Eileen C Burke-Sheridan, 'Lay Spirituality', in Peter. E. Fink SJ, Editor, *The New Dictionary of Sacramental Worship* (Gill & Macmillan, Dublin, 1990), 673-680; Michael Downey, 'Holiness', *TMCE*, 384-7; Brian O'Leary SJ, *Religious Life Review*, July 1999, 213-4.

ously disadvantaged when it comes to spiritual, including moral, maturity. As Downey says,[24] today there is a strong conviction that human development and spiritual development are interrelated. And while personal wholeness is not simply equivalent to holiness, there is a close link between them, so that when the former is compromised significantly, the latter is unlikely to grow as it should.[25]

Of central concern in a holistic spirituality is the matter of our relationships with other people. No man or woman is an island; we are by nature relational or social beings. Only in relationship can we live and grow to the fulness of our potential and become good mature human beings and Christians filled with faith, love and hope. We need other people to become the persons and Christians we can be. Christian spirituality must, then, be relational and communal, recognising and fostering human and Christian relationships and community as the context for our spiritual living and growing. This relational perspective must be broadened out to recognise and take account of the fact that we live and must live in society. Our Christian spirituality will, then, be essentially social as well as personal and this is God's plan for us. This makes it clear that those who live and work in society or, in traditional terms, in the world, can become holy in and through that living and working and so they can reach the perfect fulfilment of their proper state, as Vatican II teaches.

This does not rule out the monastic vocation and way of life, or that of the hermit, as forms of Christian spirituality in which holiness and Christian fulfilment are possible. These will be exceptional vocations for a small minority of Christians, but such a 'flight from the world' does not prevent one from finding God and developing a deep and saving relationship with God in faith, love and hope. Rather it can facilitate and enrich it. It may be added, though, as Downey also reminds us, that the idea of holiness pertaining to those set apart in monasteries, etc. may properly be understood to be grounded in a particular understanding of God who dwells in light inaccessible, in solitary simplicity, un moved by the events of human history.[26]

---

24. *UCS*, 100.
25. See Dreyer, *HCEC*, 1218; Downey, *UCS*, 100-104; McDargh, *NDCS*, 792-800; O'Leary, 217-8; Tony Baggot,'Getting the Spiritual Life Together', *The Furrow*, November 1991, 629-635.
26. Downey, *TMCE*, 386.

Today, however, there is a strong emphasis on the fact that Christian spirituality is and must be essentially trinitarian as God is. A recently renewed theology of the Trinity facilitates this development and has important implications for how we view the spiritual life. To understand the God of Jesus Christ as a Trinity of Father, Son and Holy Spirit is to say that God is profoundly relational; God is a communion of equal Persons, interdependent and diverse.[27]

In this context Christian living is our response to Jesus, the Incarnate Word of God, who reveals the face of the invisible God, and this is done in and assisted by the Holy Spirit. So a Christian spirituality rooted in this mystery of the triune God emphasises community rather than individuality. It stresses that holiness, the goal of the spiritual life, is attained through the perfection of one's relationships with others rather than through an ever more pure gaze of the mind's eye on some eternal truth 'out there' or in one's interior life. Such a trinitarian spirituality naturally connects with the Christian moral life, which is essentially concerned with these same relationships with other people. These relationships are gifts to us but they call also for appropriate responses in Spirit-filled love. It is in and through these responses that our communion with others and so with the triune God grows and reaches perfection.[28]

The social dimension of Christian spirituality
In the past, Christian spirituality, in its Catholic form at least, tended to be individualistic. Contemporary theology and spirituality have recovered the necessary emphasis on the social dimension of the Christian life and, so, of Christian spirituality and in particular on social justice as an essential requirement of the Christian gospel. This emphasis is rooted in a renewed understanding of the human person as essentially a relational and social being and also in the trinitarian spirituality we have been discussing.[29]

Significant here also, as we have seen in chapter 9, has been the influence of liberation theology.

Today, therefore, Christian spirituality in the Catholic Church

---

27. Downey, *UCS*, 44-5; Catherine Mowry LaCugna & Michael Downey, 'Trinitarian Spirituality', *NDCS*, 969.
28. Downey, *UCS*, 45; LaCugna & Downey, *NDCS*, 969-970
29. Downey, *UCS* , 96-7; LaCugna & Downey, *NDCS*, 979.

is a spirituality of social justice. It calls us Christians as individuals and as church to be concerned about society and its moral health and to see the creation of a just social order as an essential demand of the gospel to which we are committed. Action for justice is thus understood as a constitutive dimension of the Christian gospel and the fruit of an authentically lived Christian spirituality.[30]

This is well captured in the phrase 'an option for the poor' that has been so central to the theology of liberation and also in recent years to the church's social teaching. In this context justice is to be understood primarily as being concerned with how society is organised, how wealth, power, privileges, rights and responsibilities are distributed at every level, local, nation and global. Justice in society means, then, working to build a society that is intrinsically just, and in which the structures, particularly, are just.[31]

To come to understand one's spirituality as involving this social justice dimension, and to commit oneself to it, there may well be need for a kind of moral conversion that is social and political in nature and that is basically the same as the option for the poor already discussed.[32]

It is of interest to notice at this point that even in the secular business community there is nowadays a growing focus on spirituality. Even the World Bank is concerned about it! Some promote what has been called a spirituality of personal transformation, in which people are helped to become more loving people in regard to their colleagues and neighbours and where they are impelled to lead a more simple life as they practise self-restraint. Prayer and meditation are often elements of this spiritual outlook.[33]

This is undoubtedly a valuable form of spirituality but it is criticised for taking little or no account of the social dimension of the lives of the business people who adopt it. In response to this a spirituality of good management has been developed.[34]

---

30. Dreyer, *HCEC,* 1220.
31. Donal Dorr, *Spirituality and Justice* (Gill & Macmillan, Dublin, 1984), 14-15.
32. See Dorr, *Spirituality and Justice,* 16-17 & Chapter 5 'Option for the Poor'; O'Leary, 218-220.
33. Baum, 'Management in God', *The Furrow,* May 2000, 267-8.
34. Baum, 274-6.

This focuses on the responsibilities of an enterprise for its employees and their families, for its customers and suppliers and for society as a whole and does so in the context of the Christian belief in God. Good and all as this spiritual view of things is, critics still find it lacking in the social justice area. It takes very little account of the total economic system in which business operates and so suffers from a serious blind spot in relation to global issues of social justice, like the impact of international market forces on regional or national economic development, the relentless demands of competitiveness and their effects on developing countries and their economies. The results of these forces are such that the world's economic life has really become a war where only the biggest players win.[35]

So, what is needed is a spirituality of economic life that has a global vision and which is characterised by qualities or attitudes such as a universal solidarity, service of the world, a prejudice or option in favour of the poor, and an inclination towards self-restraint. All this is required to ensure that social justice is done for everyone and not just the rich and powerful of this world.[36]

Other significant dimensions of Christian Spirituality
Catholic spirituality places great emphasis on the fact that we live our spiritual lives in the community of disciples called the church and that this church context is very important for our Christian living. Ours is an ecclesial spirituality: it is learned in the church, it is lived in the church, and living it plays its part in building up the church as a community of faith, love and hope. Basic for each church member will be the living out of her/his vocation as well and as fully as possible. This will involve a real openness to the wisdom and teaching of the church, past and present. A dedicated participation in the church's liturgical and pastoral life, alongside a rich life of personal prayer, are also central to the spiritual life of the Catholic Christian. Doing all one can in and for the Christian community of which one happens to be a member is also a clear indication of one's commitment to one's Christian spirituality and its ecclesial dimension.[37]

---

35. Baum, 269-271.
36. Baum, 274-8; also Donal Dorr, 'Spirituality and Business', *The Furrow*, July/August 2000, 421-6.
37. Downey, *UCS*, 81-4; Cosgrave, 504; See S. Shaun Madigan CSJ, 'Spirituality, Liturgical', *NDSW*, 1224-1231.

There is a strong movement today, outside and inside the Christian churches including the Catholic Church, to retrieve and give its proper weight and place to the experience of women and to women themselves. This has led to the emergence of feminist spiritualities of many varieties. The Christian insights and values that are stressed in these spiritualities seem set to have a significant impact on Christian and Catholic teaching and spirituality. Examples are: an emphasis on personal relationships, a concern for inclusiveness and connectedness, a focus on process and synthesis, giving due weight to the affective as well as to the intellectual, being oriented towards nature and taking the body and sexuality seriously, putting emphasis on the concrete as well as the abstract. In the past these elements were often marginalised; now they stand nearer the centre.[38]

There is a widespread conviction that the Christian tradition has been diminished by patriarchal bias and male domination in the church. Christian feminist spiritualities are making a valuable contribution towards reversing these distortions and mistakes and forging an understanding of Christian spirituality that is more adequate and more truly Christian.[39]

Not unconnected with the emerging feminist spiritualities is the powerful focus in many quarters, Christian and non-Christian, on ecological consciousness and the call to preserve and enhance God's earth, of which we humans are the stewards, not the masters. Our spirituality must, then, have a 'worldy' or environmental dimension in which we do all we can to appreciate the wonders and yet the fragility of God's creation and seek to move away from the destructive patterns of activity that humans have engaged in for so long, e.g. global warming, acid rain, the destruction of rain forests, the pollution of air and water systems. So the spiritual life of the Christian in the twenty-first century requires of us that we be intimately involved with caring for the earth, both because it is God's creation and God's gift to us humans, and because our welfare and future as a race depend very much on the wellbeing and the flourishing of planet earth and the indispensable ecosystem it provides for us.[40]

38. Dreyer, *HCEC*, 1220.
39. Downey, *UCS*, 93-4; Wolski Conn, *TNDT*, 982-3; O'Leary, 220-1.
40. John O'Donnell CSsR, 'In Search of Christian Spirituality Today' in Raphael Gallagher CSsR & Brendan McConvery CSsR, Editors, *History and Conscience: Studies in honour of Sean O'Riordan CSsR* (Gill &

Action and contemplation in the Christian spiritual life
In quite a lot of spiritual writing and reflection in the past, there was a clear distinction between action and contemplation in the spiritual life but also a clear subordination of the former to the latter. The contemplative life of monks and religious was understood as superior to and more holy than the active life of their married and single brothers and sisters 'in the world'. Mary was seen as having chosen the better part over Martha. Today there is a re-assessment of this two-tier spirituality, a re-assessment that springs largely from a better appreciation of the Christian life 'in the world', the lay vocation, in which the great majority of Christians live out their lives in response to God's call. Living and working in human society, whether married or not, is not to be seen as a distraction from God and one's Christian vocation, nor as in large part a source of temptation and moral and spiritual danger. This was the view taken often in the past, a view based, it would seem, on an unacceptable dualism which tended to oppose relationship to God to human relationships and to involvement in secular occupations.

Now in the light of Vatican II's teaching on the universal call to holiness and its more positive view of human secular occupations and activities, active involvement 'in the world' is seen as the very core of one's Christian spiritual life. It is in and through such involvement that one finds, responds to and loves God. And that holds for marriage and the single life also. So, for the 'ordinary' Christian the only way to live out the Christian spiritual life is to commit oneself as fully as possible to one's chosen vocation in the world: work, family, education, leisure, friendship, illness, failure, disappointment, etc. All these are at the heart of the journey to full Christian holiness. At the same time the Christian needs to and can cultivate a rich life of personal prayer and reflection, while also being an active member of the Christian Church in her/his local parish. In a real sense, then, the active and contemplative are two sides of the same coin, two aspects of the one Christian spiritual life, that can and should be fitted together to make a harmonious whole. The contemplative/prayer dimension of the spiritual life is not at all opposed to or cut off from its active dimension. Rather it too can be experi-

Macmillan, Dublin, 1989), 266-8; John T. Carmody, 'Ecological Consciousness', *NDCS,* 330-3; Dreyer, *HCEC,* 1219-1220; O'Leary, 221; Downey, *UCS,* 97-8, 135-6.

enced as profoundly relational and as engaged with and committed to the world.[41]

The moral life and the spiritual life of the Christian
Here too there has often been a dichotomy and even an opposition between these two dimensions or areas of the Christian life.
Dualism has often been at the root of this mistake, too, as somehow love of God seemed opposed to love of human beings and of
the created world. Some took it that the spiritual life was about
prayer, devotions, fasting and other forms of self-denial, while
moral living had to do with human relationships, virtue and sin,
right and wrong. Today we can move beyond such a split to understand that here too we are talking about two dimensions of
the one reality, two sides of the same coin, that of the Christian
spiritual life. As we have been trying to make clear in the preceding pages, the spiritual life of the Christian includes both our
moral life and our life of prayer; both are elements of that spiritual
life. In fact we see these two elements converging when we focus
on the basic reality of the Christian life, namely, the kind of persons we are called to become and the sort of lives we ought as
Christians to lead.[42]

To put it another way, we love God in and through loving
other people, oneself and the whole community and caring for
the earth. If we don't love them, and especially if we refuse to
love them, then we don't love God and in fact we sin against
God. So, central to the spiritual life of the Christian is the moral
life. Hence, we can and should say that the moral life and the
spiritual life come together in the good Christian life and that
good life is a life of friendship with God.[43]

The role of prayer in the Christian spiritual life
Most people seem to have the experience that prayer is difficult,
not just because they find it hard to get a suitable time, place and
method for it, or to get into the right mood or frame of mind to
pray, but also and more particularly because prayer seems to be
an activity that is very one-sided. It can feel like making a phone
call and getting no response from the other end, or talking to one-

41. Dreyer, *HCEC*, 1218.
42. Richard M. Gula, *The Good Life: Where Morality and Spirituality con-
verge* (Paulist Press, New York, 1999), 5.
43. Gula, 3, 6.

self when one had expected a response from the other. In other words, God seems to be silent most of the time, making no response to the one who is praying. God even seems to be absent more than present.[44] Real experiences of God in prayer seem to be rather rare. All this makes it rather difficult to continue with one's prayer as a regular part of one's spiritual life or even as a meaningful spiritual experience. Even when people have had some sort of experience of God or the divine in prayer (or indeed elsewhere), it remains very difficult to describe what that experience involved and was and how the person discerned that he/she was being touched, as it were, by God.

At the same time, however, the Christian tradition sees prayer as absolutely essential for a Christian spiritual life, since without it one's explicit relationship with God, i.e. the religious dimension of one's life as a Christian believer, will probably fade away and disappear. So, despite the difficulties and in a sense because of them, some reflection on prayer and its role in and contribution to our spiritual lives seems necessary and important at this point.

Understanding prayer in the broad sense as the thoughts, words and activities that are directed explicitly to God both personally and communally, we can say that prayer fulfils four functions in the life of the Christian.[45]

a) *Remembering:* Since God is the Absolute Mystery and is present to us in the ordinary run of things only in and through ourselves, other people and creation itself, there is need to remind ourselves constantly of God's presence and graciousness to us. This is what prayer does. So, by praying we remember God's love and respond to it and so we are helped in keeping our religious faith alive and strong. This is paralleled in human relationships where the friends or partners involved need to remember each other and keep in contact, if their relationship is to remain strong and perhaps even grow.

44. See the hymn for Morning Prayer for the Memorial of Ss Joachim and Anne, 26 July, in The Divine Office:

    Lord God, we give you thanks for all your saints
    Who sought the trackless footprints of your feet,
    Who took into their own a hand unseen,
    And heard a voice whose silence was complete.

45. Cosgrave, 506-8; LaCugna & Downey, *NDCS*, 973-5; Michael Downey, *Altogether Gift: A Trinitarian Spirituality* (Dominican Publications, Dublin, 2000), 119-129.

b) *Spending time together:* As in relationships between human beings, so in our relationship with God it is essential to spend time with God in explicit awareness. This is what we do in prayer. Such togetherness is usually enjoyable and enriching at the human level and so it can be, at least sometimes, in our spiritual lives. However, the mysterious and elusive manner of God's presence to us makes spending time with God in prayer difficult and demanding for very many Christians. In faith, though, it is time well spent, even if to the outsider and the non-believer it doesn't seem that way.

c) *Communicating:* A relationship is as good or as bad as the communication within it. This is true at the level of human persons in relationship and it holds true also in regard to our relationship with God. Prayer is our way and means of communicating explicitly and directly with God, Father, Son and Holy Spirit. Virtuous action and good moral living are, of course, real but implicit forms of communication with and love of God and are none the less important for that. But to sustain and nourish our relationship with God we need the explicit communication which prayer provides, just as we need explicit and direct communication to keep our human relationships rich and strong.

d) *Signifying the deepest meaning of the Christian life:* The activity we call prayer is a sign or symbol of the fact that all our relationships, activities and commitments find their ultimate meaning and goal in the love and worship of the God of Jesus Christ. Our prayer carries the meaning that at its deepest level the Christian life is about worshipping God and responding to God's love as that is experienced in our relationships with ourselves, others, society, the material world and the church. By praying we say that for us Christians our whole life is about doing God's will and loving God above all things.

Asceticism in the Christian spiritual life

When we think of asceticism, we frequently call to mind the very severe forms of self-denial of some of the early Christians and especially the monks of the early centuries. They submitted themselves, and in particular their bodies with their unruly passions, to rigorous practices of penance and mortification. The harsh penances given in confession in its first centuries seem to resemble the ascetical practices in question here. This heavy emphasis on the ascetical dimension of the Christian life continued for many centuries and even down to the time of the Second Vatican Council (1962-5). So much was this aspect of the Christian life stressed that one could be pardoned for thinking that Christian living was basically ascetical or penitential in character. This created the impression among many that what was intended as good news and a life of joy and peace appeared to be, and was in danger of becoming, an endurance test and a joyless journey to the kingdom of a strict and demanding God.

St Paul first introduced the word 'ascetic' into Christianity, using it to refer to the self-sacrifice, discipline and self-control involved in living as a dedicated and single-minded Christian in a pagan and hostile world. Jesus refers to the same idea in talking about taking up one's cross and losing one's life in order to save it. This New Testament basis understands asceticism in a broad sense and uses it to refer to what might be called the asceticism of daily living. This will be our first and primary concern in what follows. We will also discuss briefly asceticism in the narrow sense of ascetical practices.

The asceticism of daily living

It is important to note, first of all, that the Christian life as preached by Jesus and the church is primarily a life of love of our neighbours and of God. The Christian way of living is our response to God's love for us in Jesus and is truly good news, bringing fulfilment, happiness and peace and ultimately eternal life in its fulness. Now experience as well as Christian teaching indicates that this life of love necessarily implies and involves a very significant asceticism which may be called the asceticism of daily living. This has often been given inadequate attention or even largely overlooked in an over-concern with ascetical practices, especially those that involve mortification of the flesh, including especially the sexual abstinence that goes with virginity and celibacy.[46]

This asceticism of daily living is a built-in feature of the Christian life that makes its demands every day and even every hour as one tries to live as a Christian should. It involves and requires effort, struggle, self-denial, sacrifices and self-discipline. One could say that this ascetical dimension of the Christian life is the reverse side of the coin of Christian love. Some examples will enable us to understand more fully what is in question here.

---

46. Downey, *Altogether Gift*, 110-1.

To respond wholeheartedly to the many demands of our relationships, our work and our prayer life, will require us to forego,
not merely selfish and evil pursuits, but also many good and
wholesome things. It will call for a great deal of dedication and
self-sacrifice as we face difficulties and obstacles and put in the
effort needed to make truly loving responses in all areas of our
lives. A parent, for instance, finds she/he has many significant
duties to fulfil. These make demands in terms of time and energy,
of care and attention and involve limitations and expenses often of
major proportions. A farmer has to cope with the uncertainties of
the weather and of the markets as well as putting in the effort to
reap the crops, look after the cattle, etc, as he/she seeks to make a
livelihood from the land. The poor have terrible daily struggles
for mere subsistence; a student must make the sacrifices required
to do his/her study and complete his/her education, while
probably having to cope also with not a little anxiety. All of us
need to care properly for our health; a priest is called on to make
the sacrifices involved in being celibate as well as those needed to
ensure that his ministry is dedicated, caring and fruitful.[47]

It will be important to mention another aspect of this asceticism of daily living that to some extent overlaps with what we
have been saying but is also in very significant ways a separate
dimension of it. We may perhaps refer to it as the asceticism involved in becoming a good and loving person. It has five elements that may be presented as follows:

a) The Christian has to engage in the usually lifelong struggle
to overcome or uproot his/her sinfulness and give up all the sinful habits, attitudes, values, priorities and activities which may
still be part of his/her life. This is very difficult and demanding
and will require growth in self-awareness, in sensitivity of conscience and in conversion of heart in perhaps many areas of one's
life.

b) The Christian has also to make a dedicated effort to grow in
virtue all her/his days. This is more than giving up sinfulness
and involves positive growth especially in the virtues he/she
most lacks, e.g. patience, meekness (maturity in managing anger
and aggression), truthfulness, empathy, individual, social and
ecological justice, chastity, etc.

c) To facilitate the above two major obligations for the
Christian, it may well be necessary that one set about healing the

47. Downey, *Altogether Gift*, 111-2; Cosgrave, 221-2.

emotional wounds inflicted in one's early life and which are frequently at the root of one's sinful habits and attitudes. Examples
are: low self-esteem, emotional insecurity, poor self-image, feelings of inferiority or superiority or jealousy, etc. Not many people
are even aware of these roots of their sinful attitudes and habits,
and even fewer make significant efforts to engage in the emotional therapy needed to arrive at the emotional maturity that is essential, if moral maturity is to be reached in the areas in question
here. (See chapter three above).

d) Everyone has to cope with a fair share of what might be
designated, in the popular phrase, as the snags of life. Here we
are referring to things like illness or injury, old age, failure, loss of
one's job and/or wealth or property or one's reputation, death in
the family or other tragedy, loneliness, stress, worry, marriage
breakdown, divorce, alcoholism, substance abuse, scandal, etc.
These can tax the best of us and some get more than their fair
share of them. To cope courageously and in an adult way with
even one of these crosses, not to speak of more than one, is seldom easy and can at times involve an asceticism of virtually
heroic proportions. Experience teaches us that here is a major element in the asceticism with which daily living sooner or later
confronts us. Responding well to it is part of what being a strong
human being and a mature Christian involves.

e) Jesus calls us to love our enemies. We all know how hard
that can be. To be kind, patient and even helpful towards those
who get on our nerves, whom we have fallen out with, who hate
the sight of us, etc, is no mean achievement. Few do it well consistently. Yet it is what we Christians are expected to do as an
essential element of our Christian spirituality. And to turn our
enemies into friends, or even people we are on friendly terms
with, can demand almost saint-like goodness, which few if any of
us possess. Clearly here a very demanding asceticism shows itself. It is without doubt very much an asceticism of daily living
and one we are called as Christians to undertake, if we are to love
others in the manner in which Jesus did.

All this makes it abundantly clear that the Christian cannot
avoid taking up the cross every day, if he/she is to follow Jesus in
being a truly loving and caring person and, so, to live out her/his
Christian spirituality as the Christian should.

What has been said here about the asceticism of daily living
justifies us in saying that the Christian life and its spirituality is

both a gift and a task or, more precisely, a gift involving a task. It is a gift or blessing to be called to live as a follower of Christ, but it is a task or challenge also, as has just been seen. As such it requires single-mindedness, courage and readiness to give oneself without counting the cost.

We may note too that being a very ascetical, disciplined and detached person is, of course, a very good thing. It would be more in line with our present line of thinking, however, if one sought, first, to become a loving person, i.e. an understanding, compassionate, wholehearted, yet strong, person. Then one would be well placed to undertake and cope with the asceticism of daily living, which is the other side of the coin of Christian love. This asceticism must, then, take precedence over any other forms of asceticism one may voluntarily take on. To these we now turn.

Ascetical practices voluntarily undertaken
Here we are talking about asceticism in the narrow sense mentioned earlier and are referring to such practices as fasting, almsgiving, the spiritual and corporal works of mercy, giving up alcohol, cigarettes, chocolate or sweets, going on a penitential pilgrimage like Lough Derg or Croagh Patrick, or taking on something difficult like getting up earlier, taking a long walk every day, giving more time to prayer or meditation, doing more work, etc. These practices are usually thought of as penitential or as forms of mortification or self-denial and they have long been practised in the Catholic tradition and highly esteemed as valuable in the struggle against sin and for virtue.

It seems true to say that it is very hard to measure the good effects of any of these ascetical practices on the person who undertakes them. At times it may be difficult to discern any noticable improvement, despite the use of some of these practices for a significant time. The real test of the value of these practices is: are they helping the person to get over one or other of his/her moral faults or weaknesses and/or to cope better with the demands of the asceticism of daily living? If over a good period of time one cannot discern real progress and growth, then the question has to be asked: is the particular practice in use suitable for the end in view? or is the person assuming that, because it is difficult, therefore, it is good for him/her? If, for example, one engages in fasting in an effort to help one control one's aggression or tendency to be domineering, one has to fear that the person may be missing the point, perhaps because he/she does not understand the root cause of this aggression or bossiness. Or if one prays more, without taking any other steps, to inculcate moderation in the use of alcohol or in relation to one's attachment to material things, one may suspect that little improvement will be forthcoming, because the means taken are not, alone, enough for the task in hand.

The increased psychological knowledge of recent times has made the point here clearer, and this is reinforced by our experience, that some very ascetical people continue to have significant faults and weaknesses that seem largely unaffected by the ascetical practices in which they engage.

The practical conclusion from all this is that voluntarily assumed ascetical practices, despite their long-attested value, which no one would want to dispute, may not at times be very helpful in fostering the asceticism of daily living. To make real progress in this latter area and to grow as a loving person, it may well be necessary to take on some ascetical practice or difficult therapy which is directly contrary to or focuses on the root of the particular fault or weakness one is struggling with, rather than being content with what seems to be viewed by some as a kind of cure-all ascetical practice, in the possibly vain hope of uprooting some specific fault or promoting growth in some virtue.

Further Reading
Baggot, Tony, 'Getting the Spiritual Life Together', *The Furrow*, November 1991, 628-635;

Dorr, Donal, *Spirituality and Justice* (Gill & Macmillan, Dublin, 1984);

Dreyer, Elizabeth, 'Christian Spirituality', in Richard P. McBrien, General Editor, *The HarperCollins Encyclopedia of Catholicism* (HarperCollins Publishers, New York, 1995), 1216-1220;

Downey, Michael, *Altogether Gift: A Trinitarian Spirituality* (Dominican Publications, Dublin, 2000);

Downey, Michael, *Understanding Christian Spirituality* (Paulist Press, New York, 1997);

Finnegan, Jack,'The New Age Movement: A New Religion?', *The Furrow,* June 1992,

LaCugna, Catherine & Downey, Michael, 'Trinitarian Spirituality' in Michael Downey, Editor, *The New Catholic Dictionary of Spirituality* (The Liturgical Press, Collegeville, Minnesota, USA, 1993), 968-982;

Principe, Walter H., 'Spirituality, Christian', in Michael Downey, Editor, *The New Catholic Dictionary of Spirituality* (The Liturgical Press, Collegeville, Minnesota, USA, 1993), 931-8.

Index